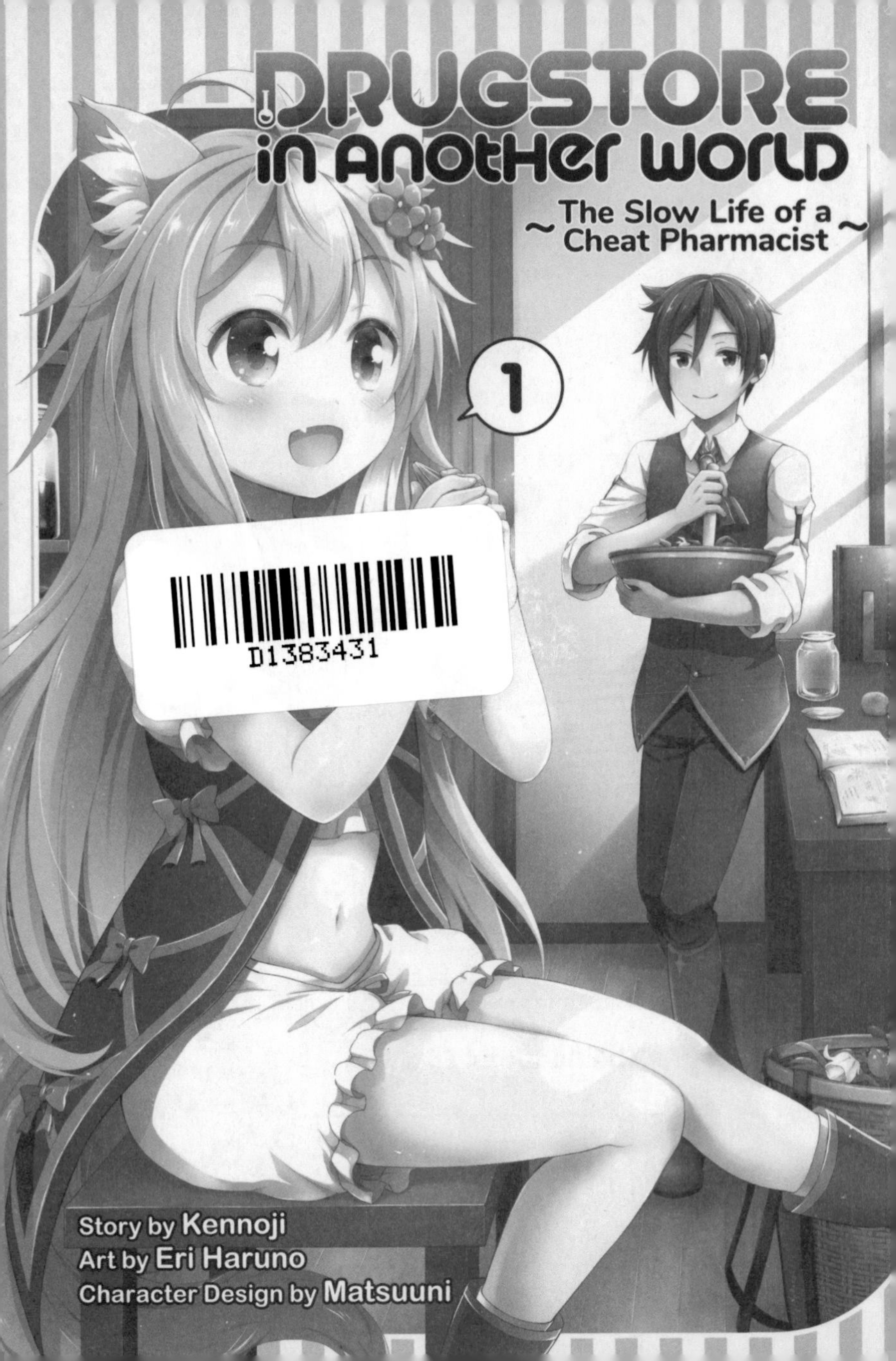
DRUGSTORE in ANOTHER WORLD
~The Slow Life of a Cheat Pharmacist~
1
Story by Kennoji
Art by Eri Haruno
Character Design by Matsuuni

CONTENTS

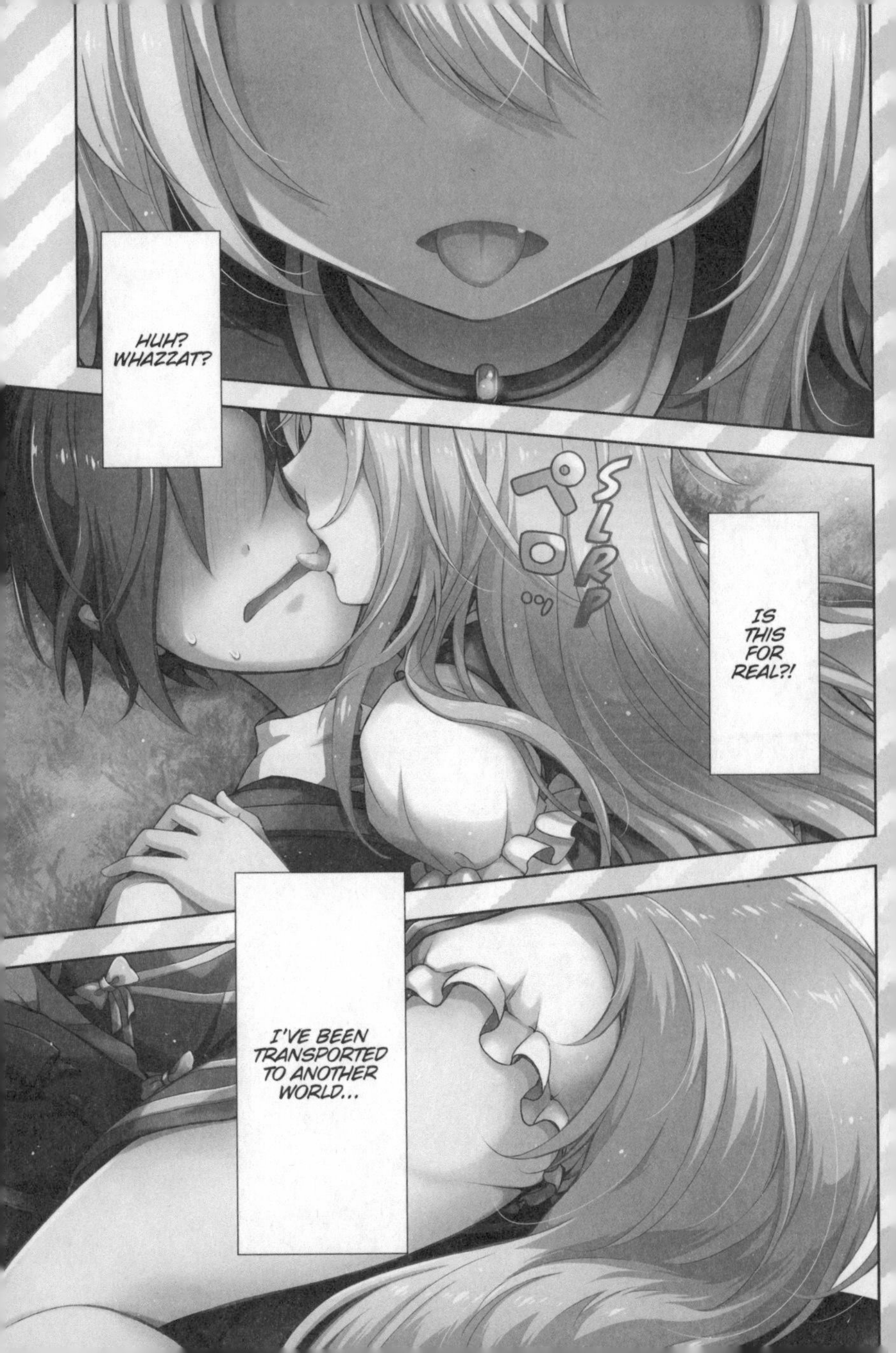
HUH? WHAZZAT?
ペロ
SLRP
IS THIS FOR REAL?!
I'VE BEEN TRANSPORTED TO ANOTHER WORLD...

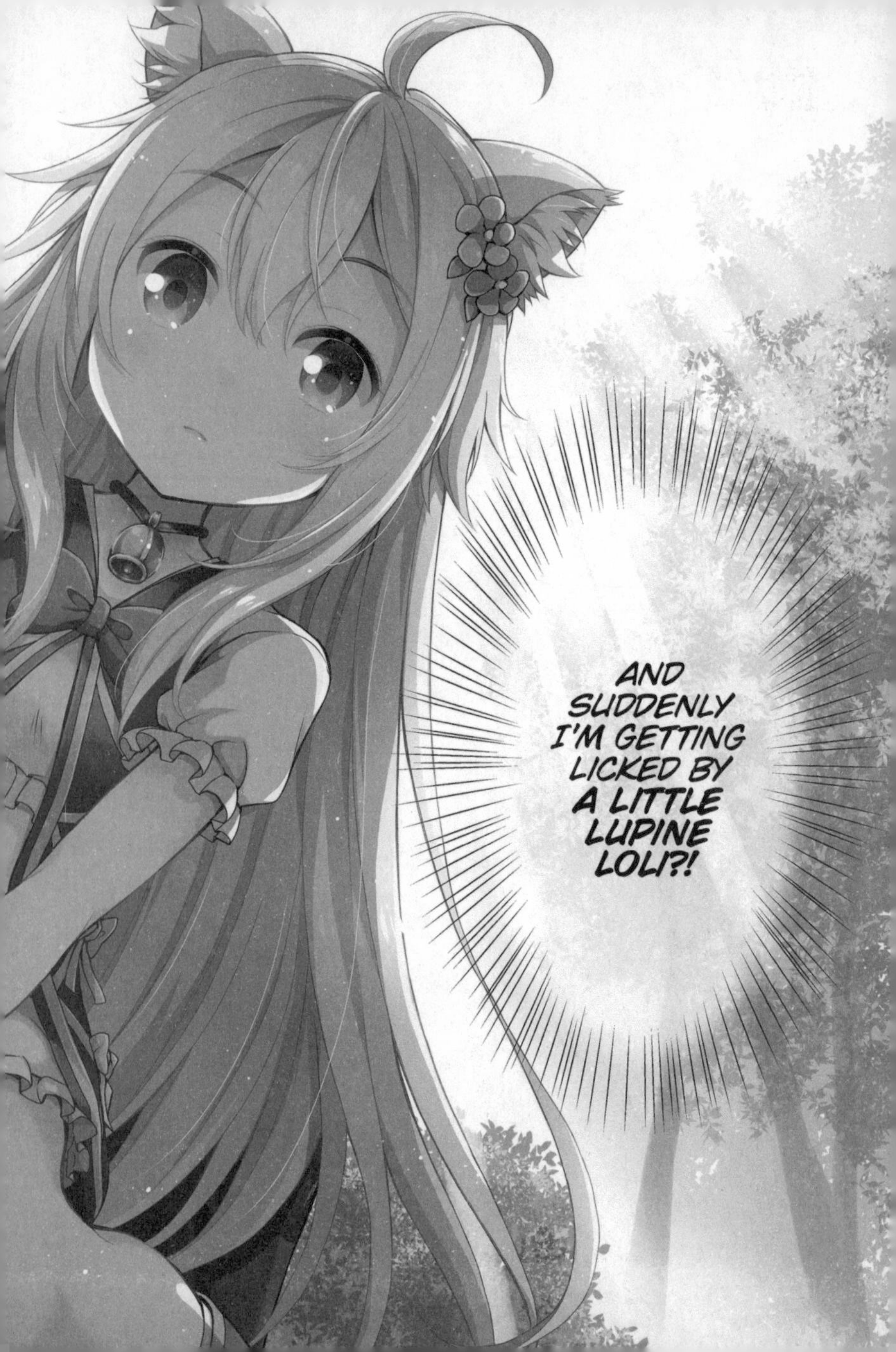
AND SUDDENLY I'M GETTING LICKED BY A LITTLE LUPINE LOLI?!

VIAL 1 Noela

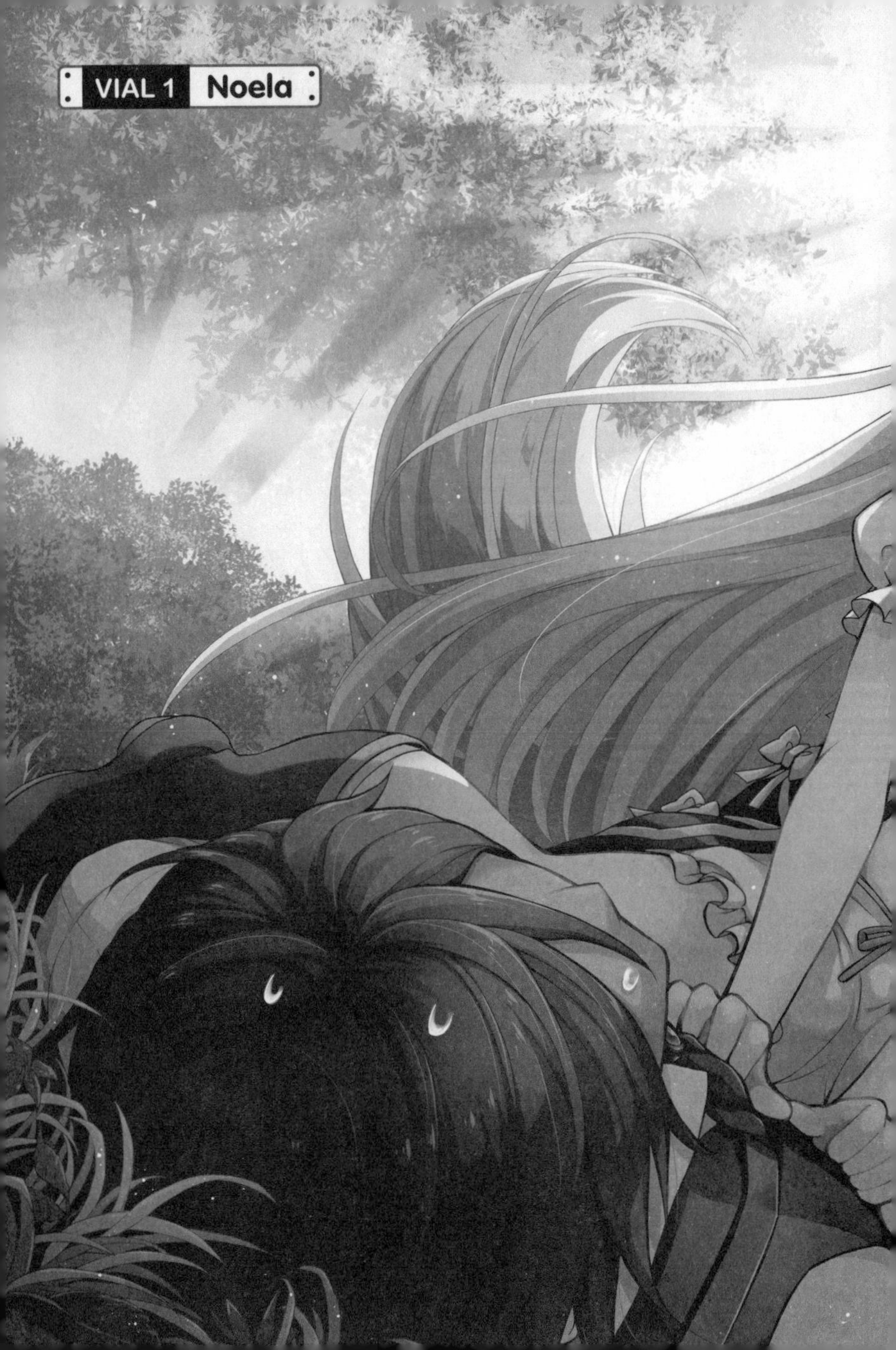

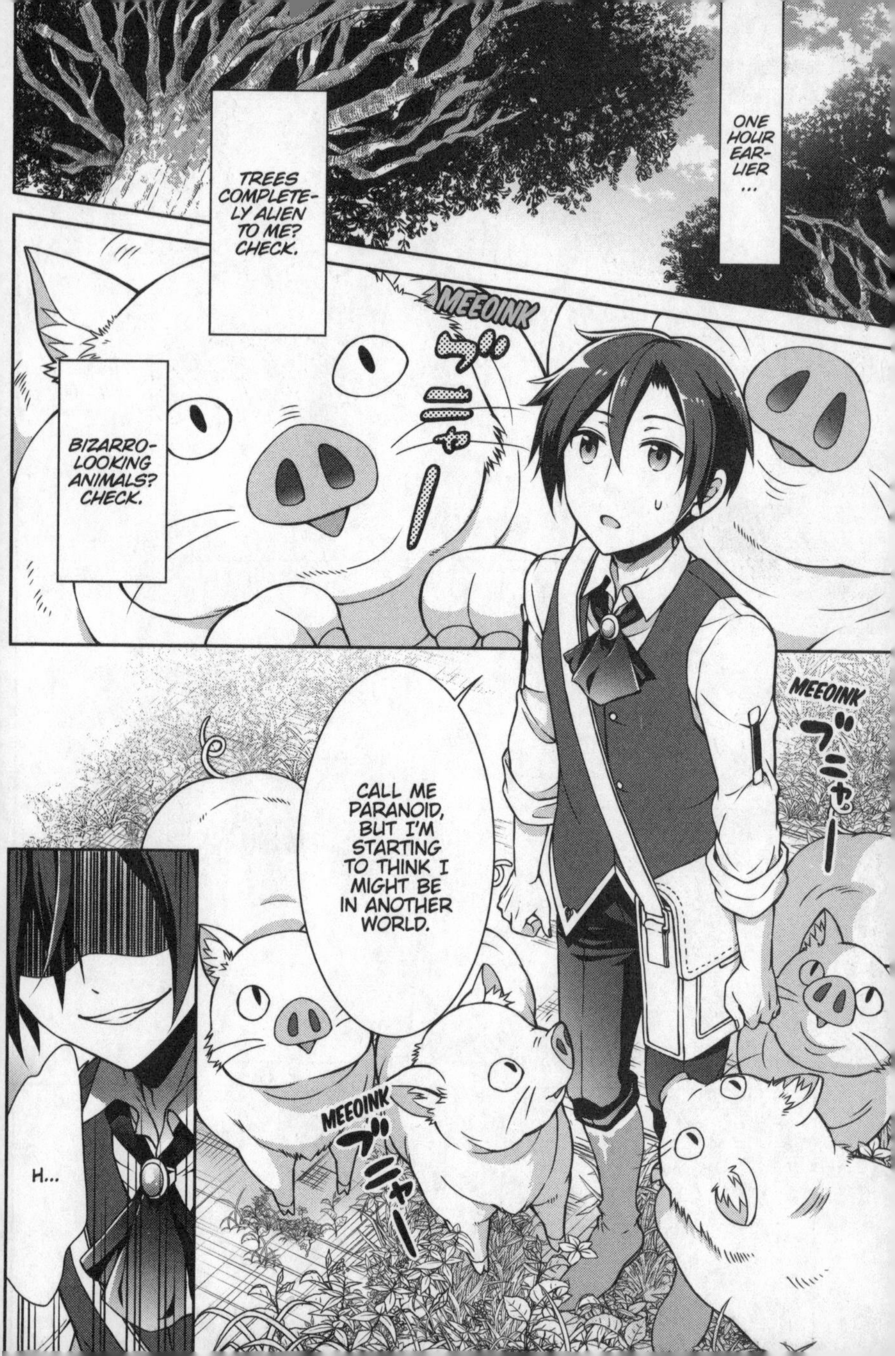
ONE HOUR EAR-LIER ...
TREES COMPLETE-LY ALIEN TO ME? CHECK.
MEEOINK
ブニャー
BIZARRO-LOOKING ANIMALS? CHECK.
MEEOINK
ブニャー
CALL ME PARANOID, BUT I'M STARTING TO THINK I MIGHT BE IN ANOTHER WORLD.
MEEOINK
ブニャー
H...

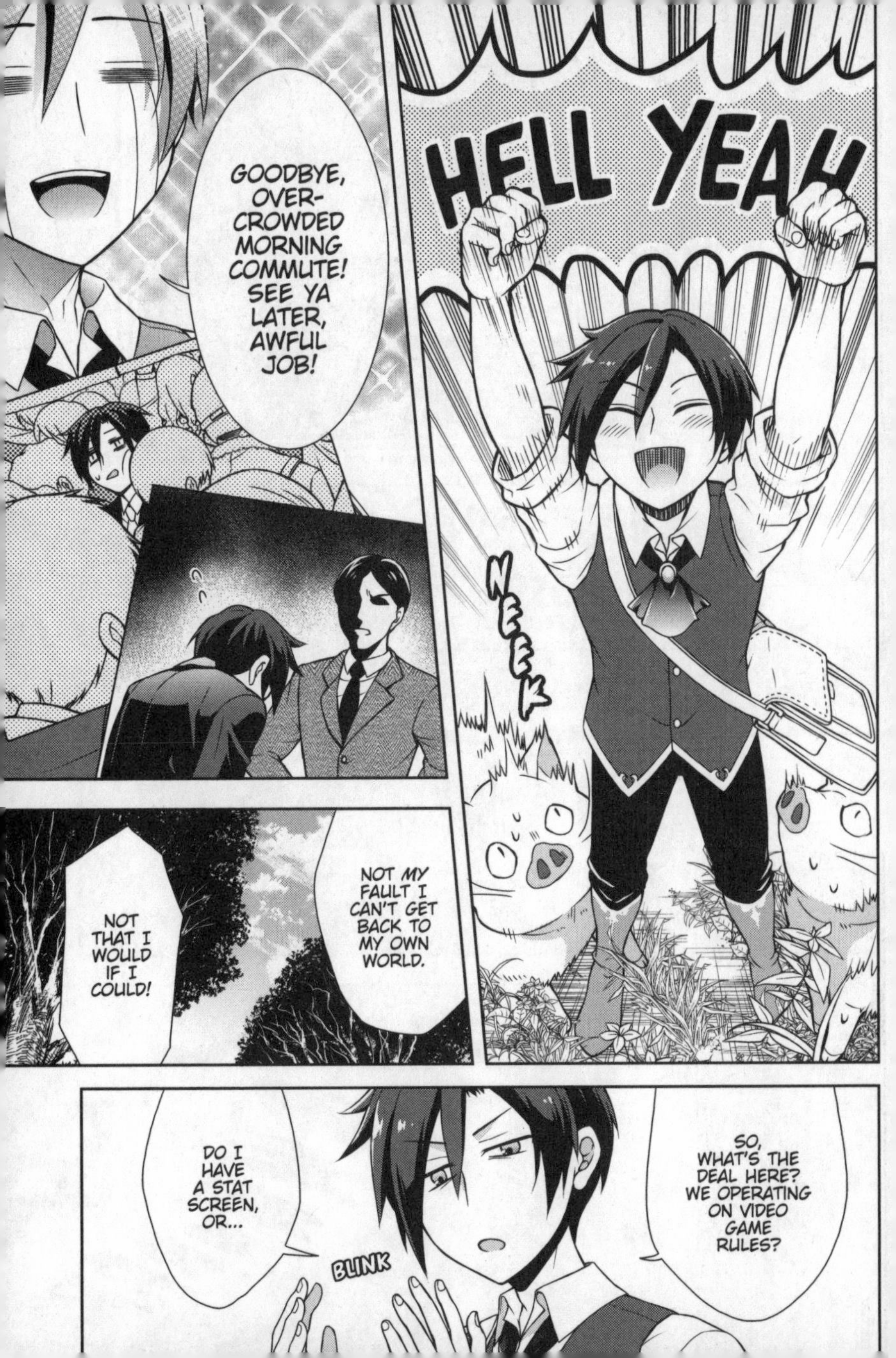
HELL YEAH
NEEEEK
GOODBYE, OVER-CROWDED MORNING COMMUTE! SEE YA LATER, AWFUL JOB!
NOT MY FAULT I CAN'T GET BACK TO MY OWN WORLD.
NOT THAT I WOULD IF I COULD!
SO, WHAT'S THE DEAL HERE? WE OPERATING ON VIDEO GAME RULES?
BLINK
DO I HAVE A STAT SCREEN, OR...

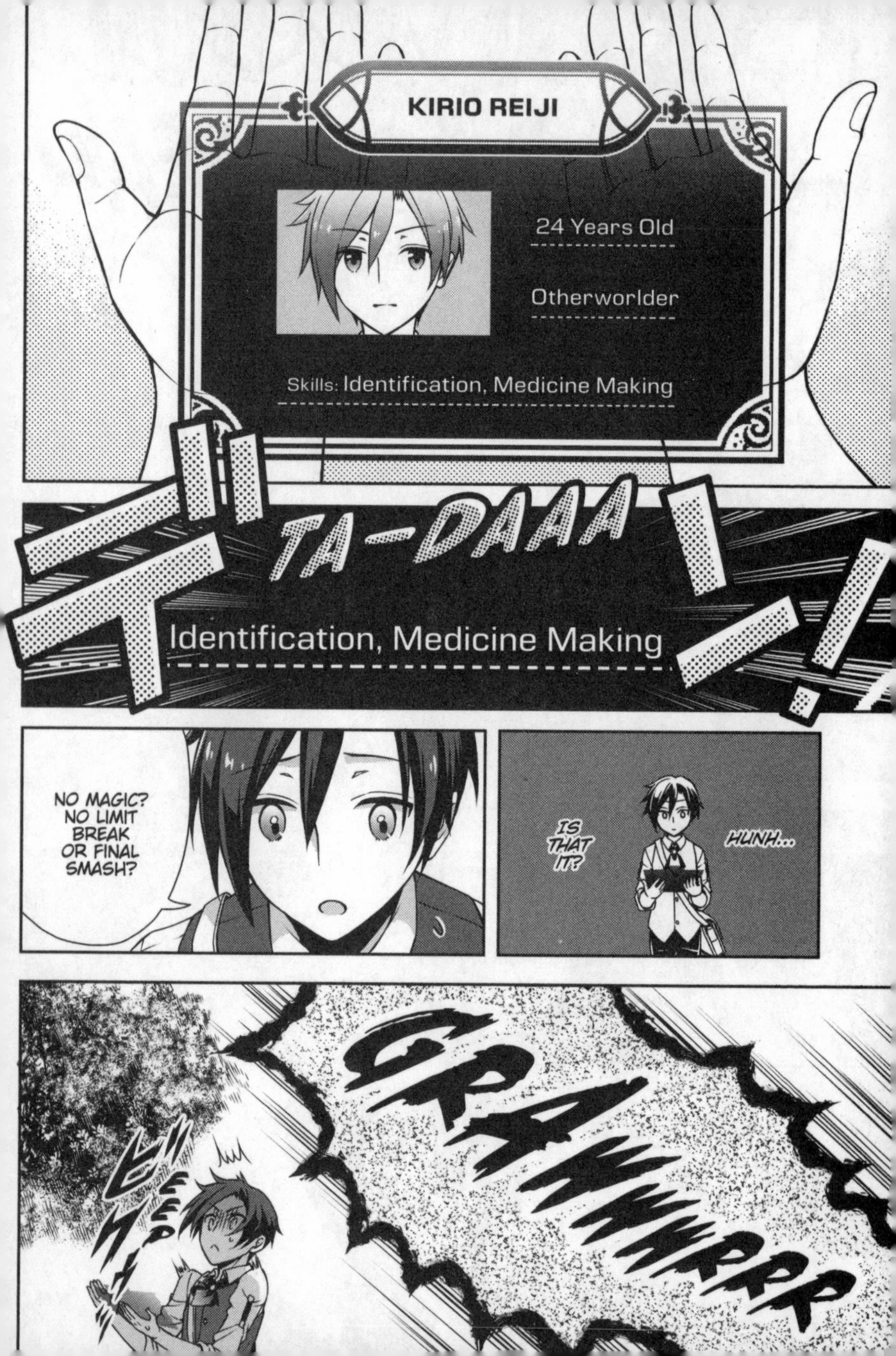
KIRIO REIJI
24 Years Old
Otherworlder
Skills: Identification, Medicine Making
TA-DAAA
Identification, Medicine Making
HUNH...
IS THAT IT?
NO MAGIC? NO LIMIT BREAK OR FINAL SMASH?
GRAHHHRRR
EEEP

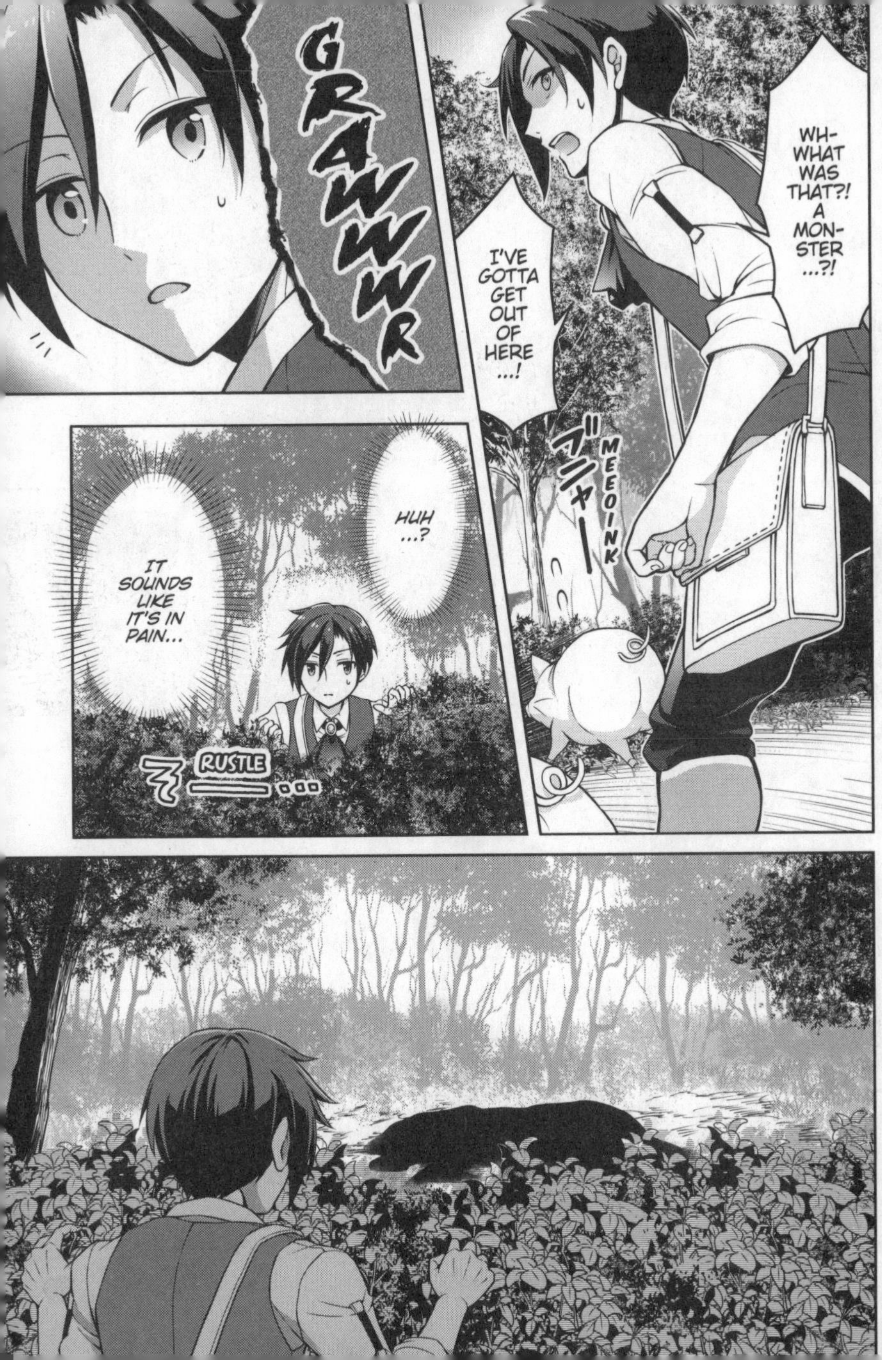

WH-WHAT WAS THAT?! A MONSTER...?!
I'VE GOTTA GET OUT OF HERE...!
ブニャー
MEEOINK
GRAWWWR
HUH...?
IT SOUNDS LIKE IT'S IN PAIN...
RUSTLE

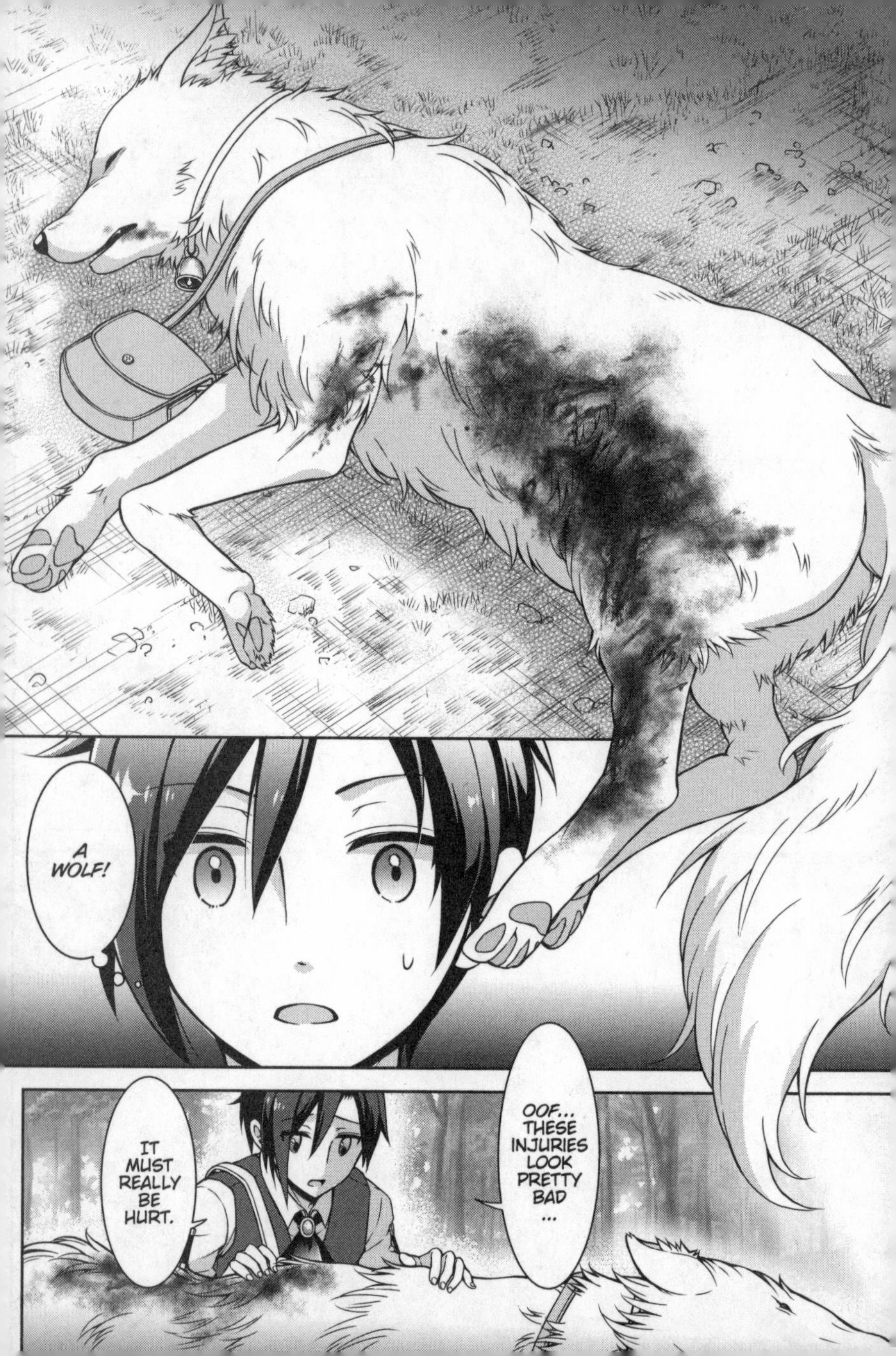
A WOLF!
OOF... THESE INJURIES LOOK PRETTY BAD ...
IT MUST REALLY BE HURT.

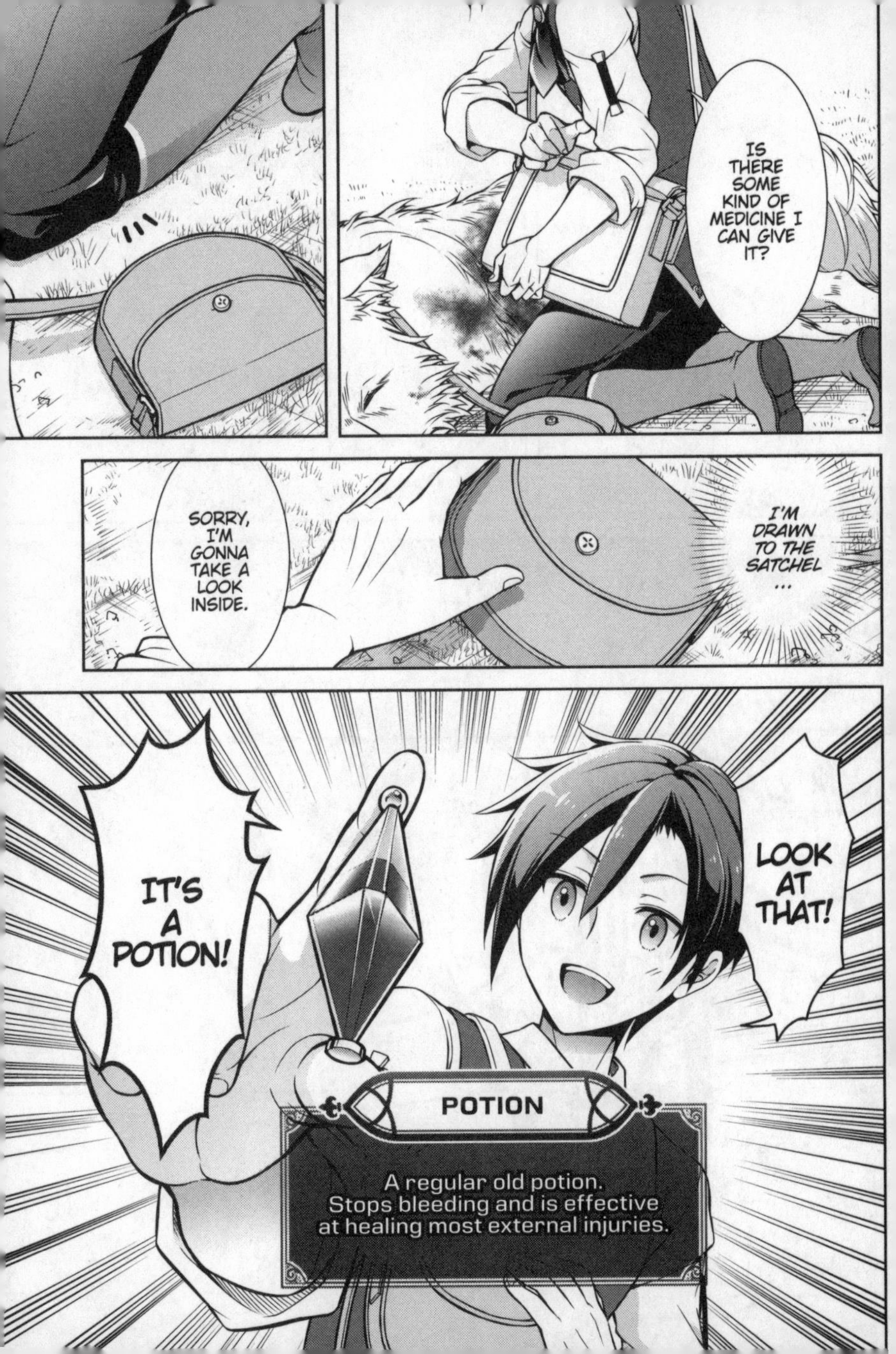
IS THERE SOME KIND OF MEDICINE I CAN GIVE IT?
I'M DRAWN TO THE SATCHEL ...
SORRY, I'M GONNA TAKE A LOOK INSIDE.
LOOK AT THAT!
IT'S A POTION!
POTION
A regular old potion. Stops bleeding and is effective at healing most external injuries.

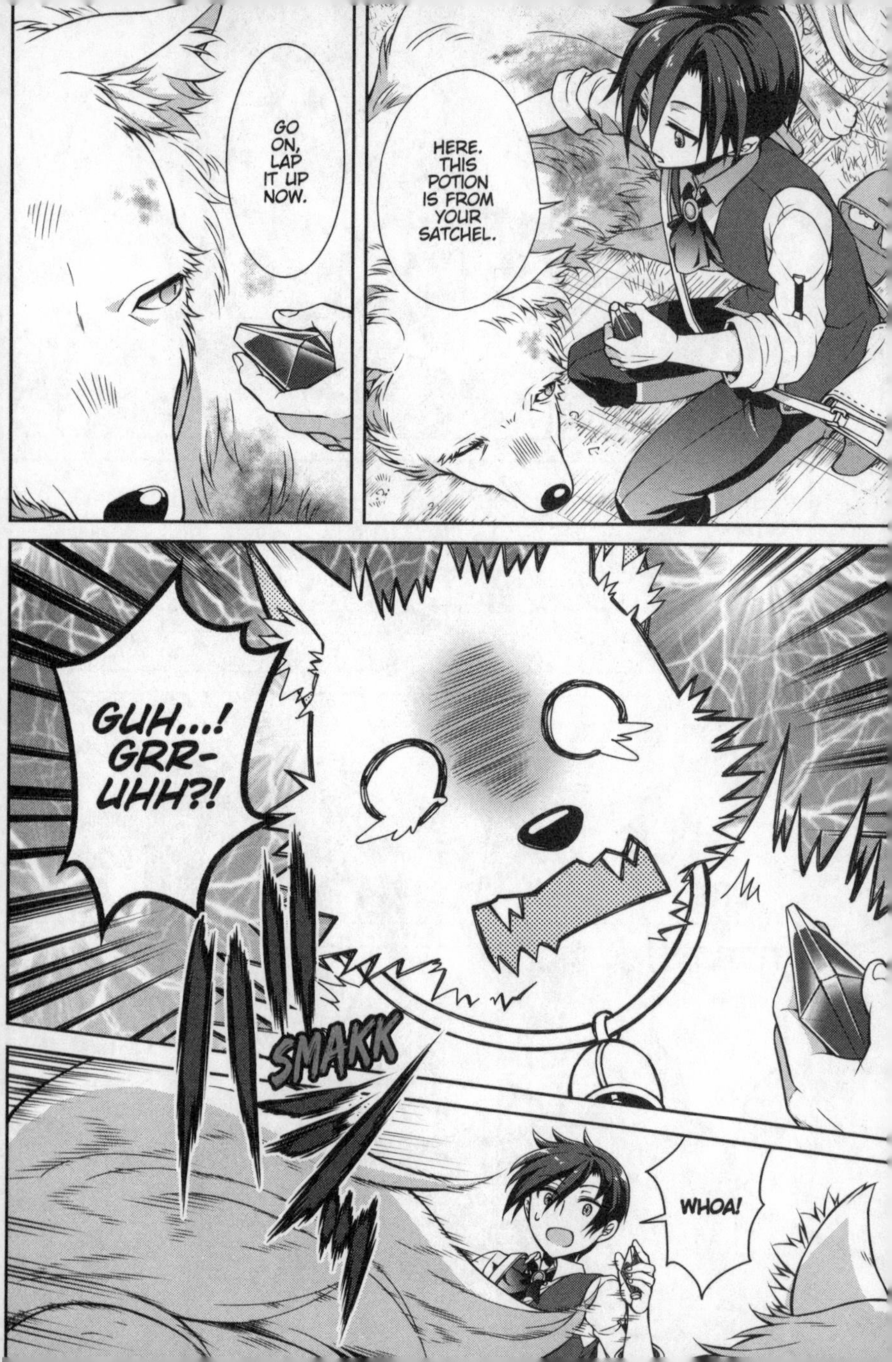
HERE. THIS POTION IS FROM YOUR SATCHEL.
GO ON, LAP IT UP NOW.
GUH...! GRR-UHH?!
SMAKK
WHOA!

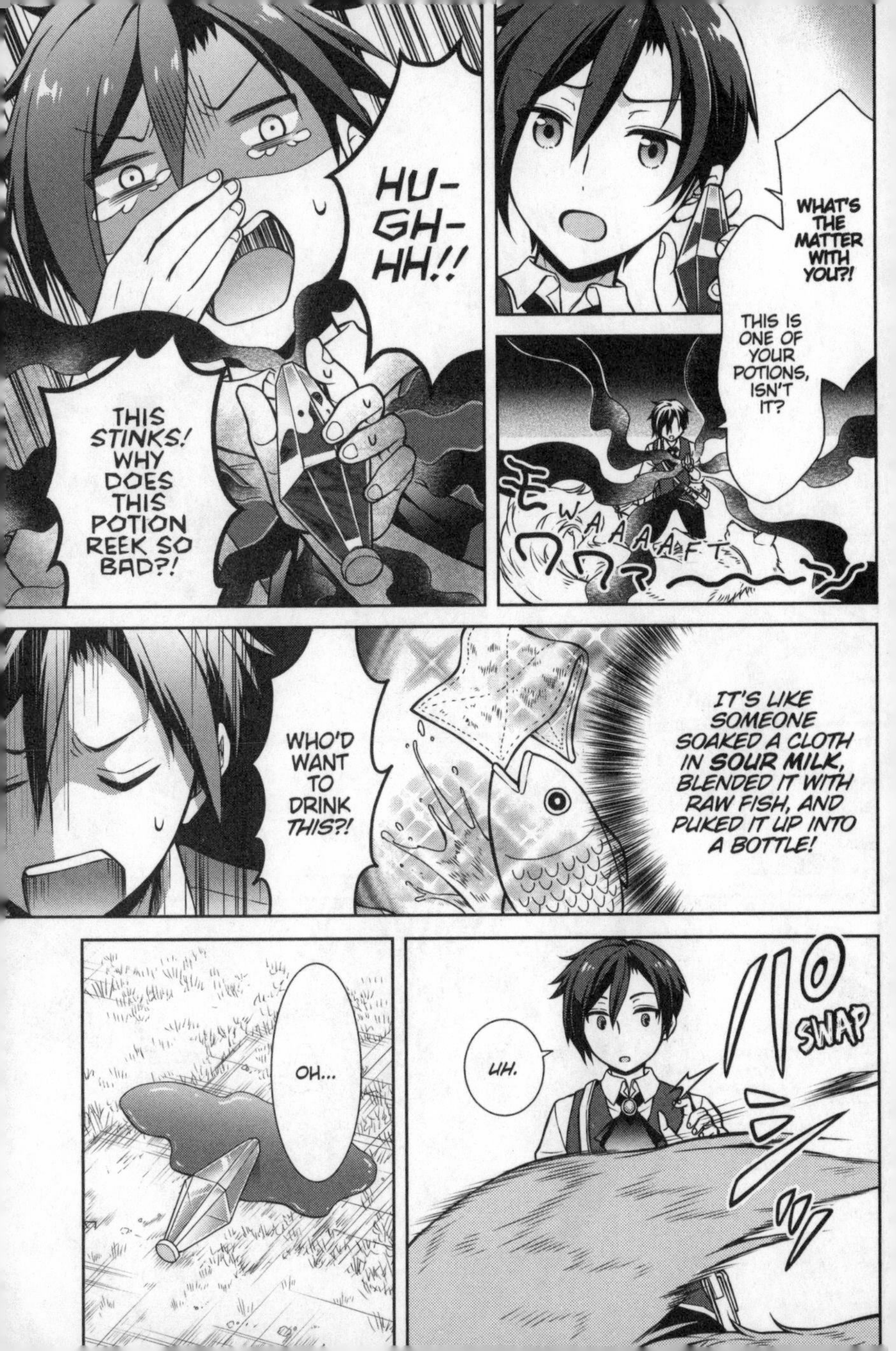
WHAT'S THE MATTER WITH YOU?!
THIS IS ONE OF YOUR POTIONS, ISN'T IT?
WAAAAAFT
HU-GH-HH!!
THIS STINKS! WHY DOES THIS POTION REEK SO BAD?!
IT'S LIKE SOMEONE SOAKED A CLOTH IN SOUR MILK, BLENDED IT WITH RAW FISH, AND PUKED IT UP INTO A BOTTLE!
WHO'D WANT TO DRINK THIS?!
SWAP
UH.
OH...

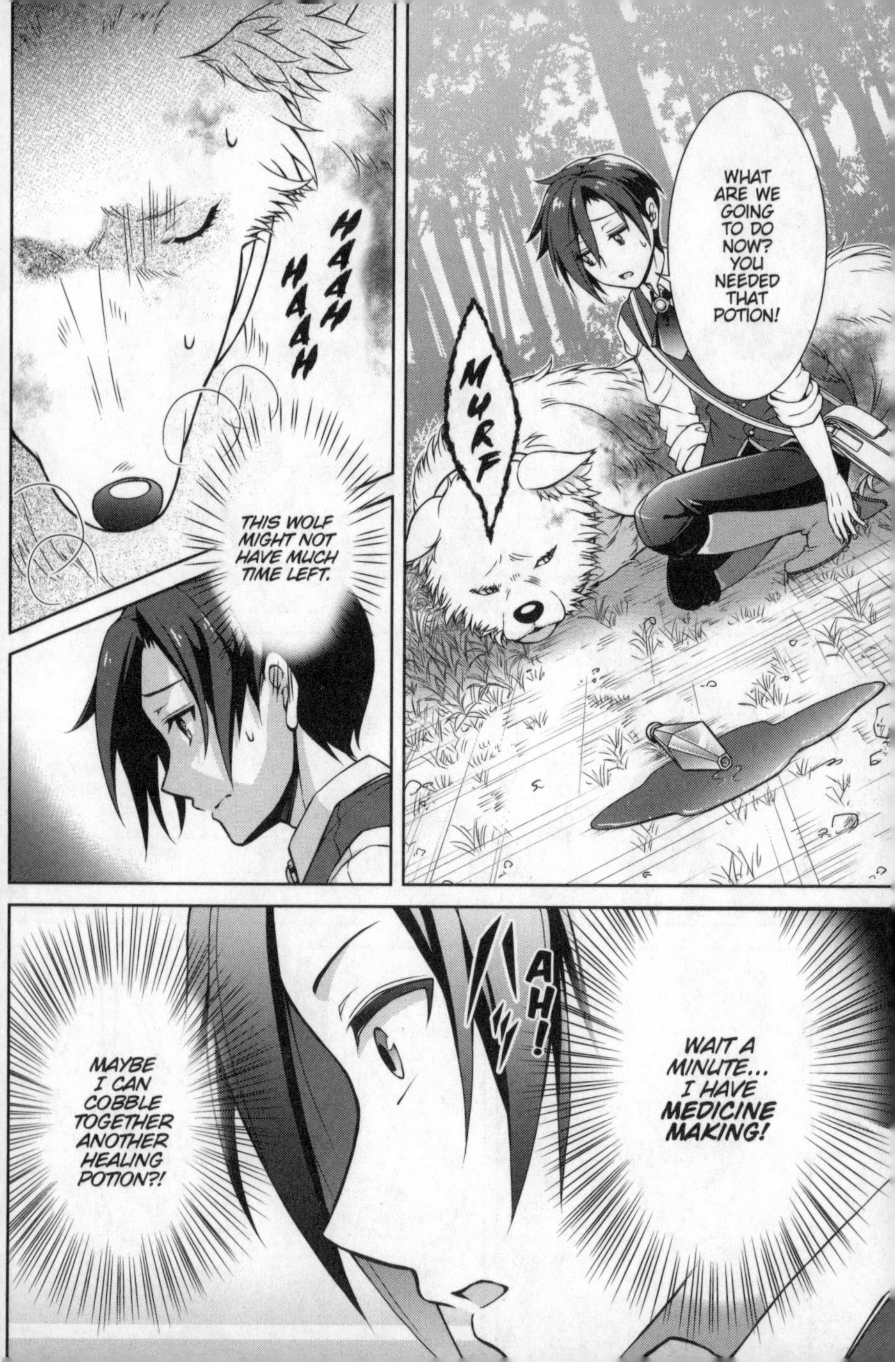
WHAT ARE WE GOING TO DO NOW? YOU NEEDED THAT POTION!
MURF
HAAAH HAAAH
THIS WOLF MIGHT NOT HAVE MUCH TIME LEFT.
AH!
WAIT A MINUTE... I HAVE MEDICINE MAKING!
MAYBE I CAN COBBLE TOGETHER ANOTHER HEALING POTION?!

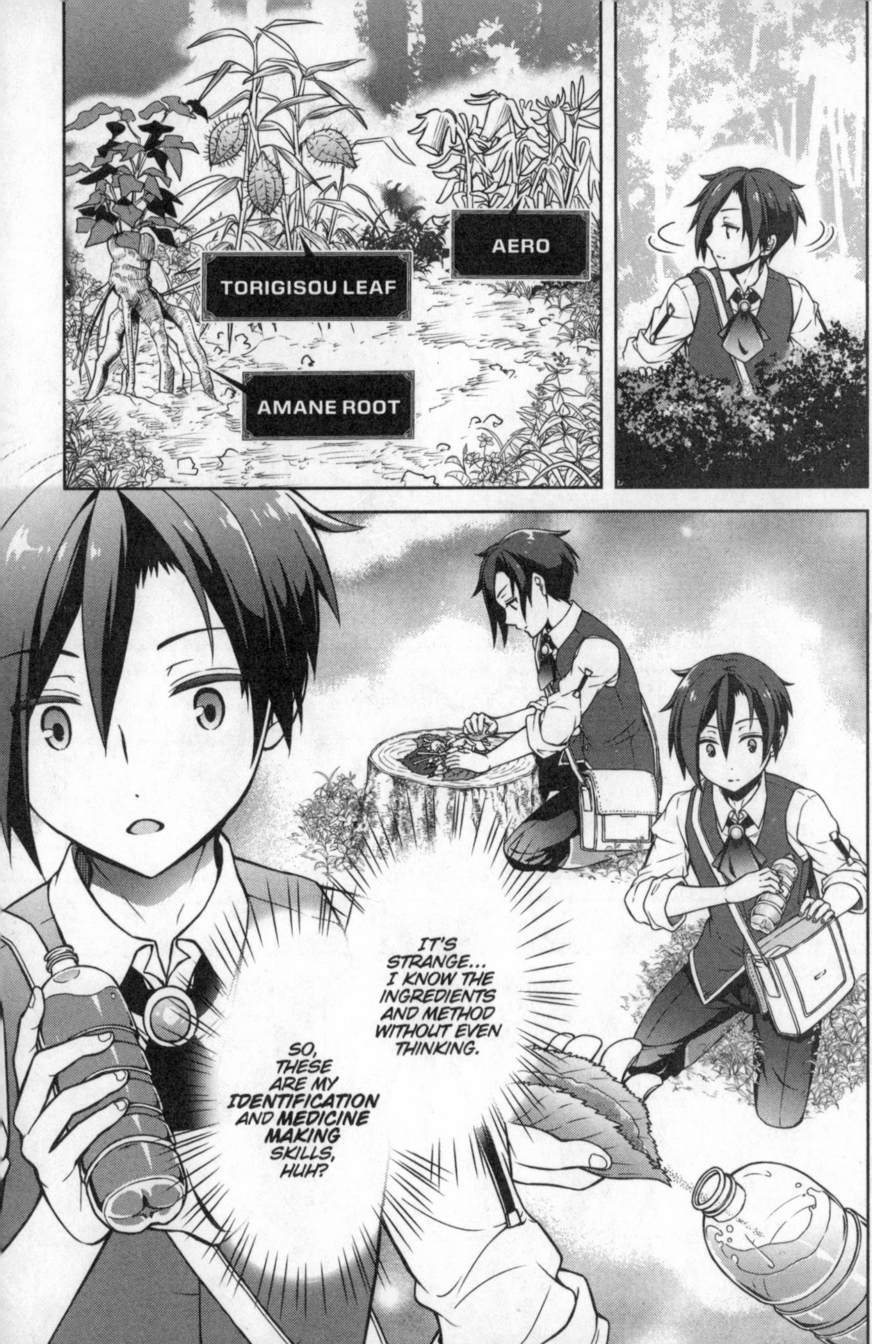
AERO
TORIGISOU LEAF
AMANE ROOT
IT'S STRANGE... I KNOW THE INGREDIENTS AND METHOD WITHOUT EVEN THINKING.
SO, THESE ARE MY IDENTIFICATION AND MEDICINE MAKING SKILLS, HUH?

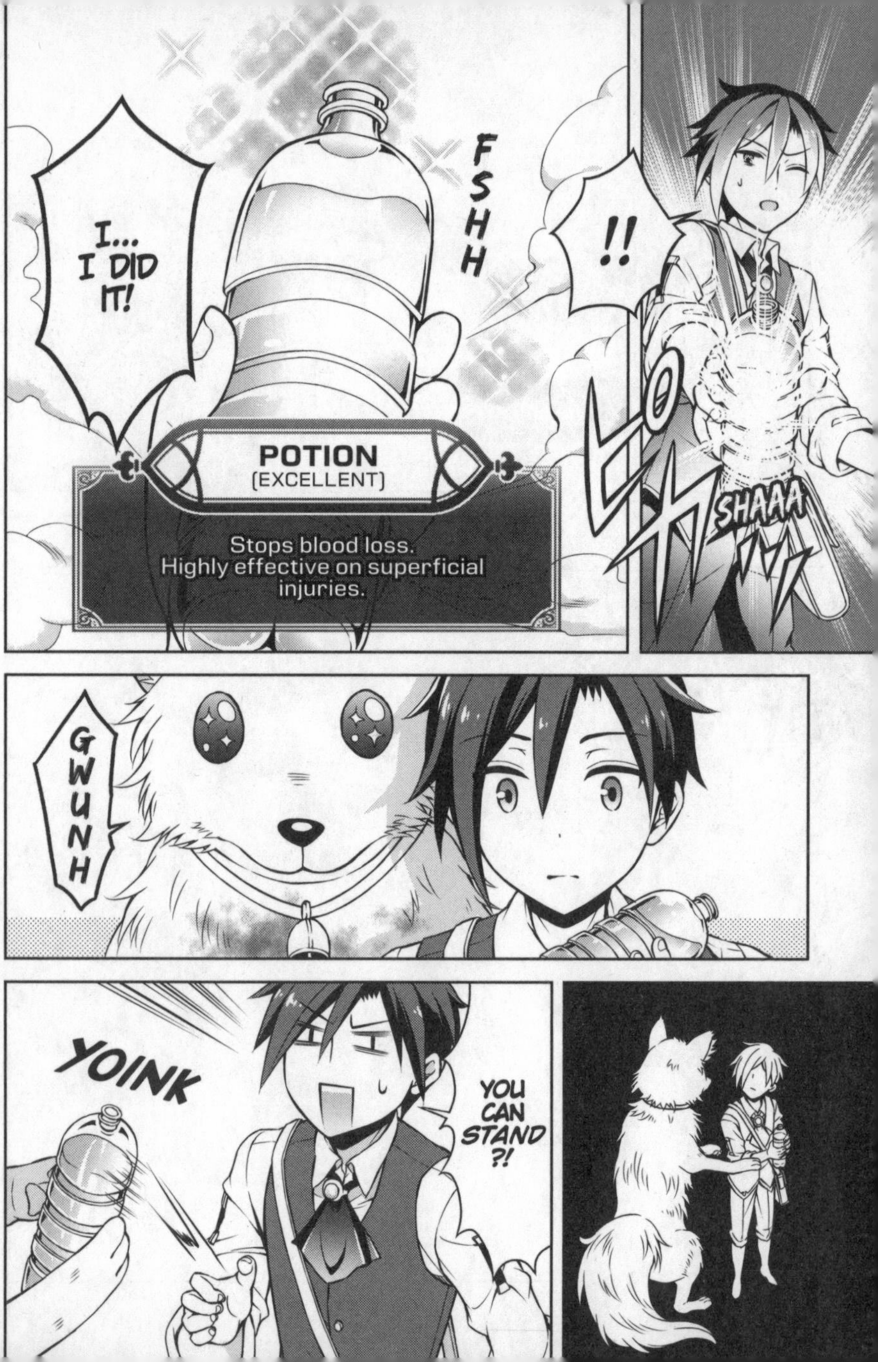
!!
SHAAA
I... I DID IT!
FSHH
POTION
(EXCELLENT)
Stops blood loss.
Highly effective on superficial injuries.
GWUNH
YOINK
YOU CAN STAND?!

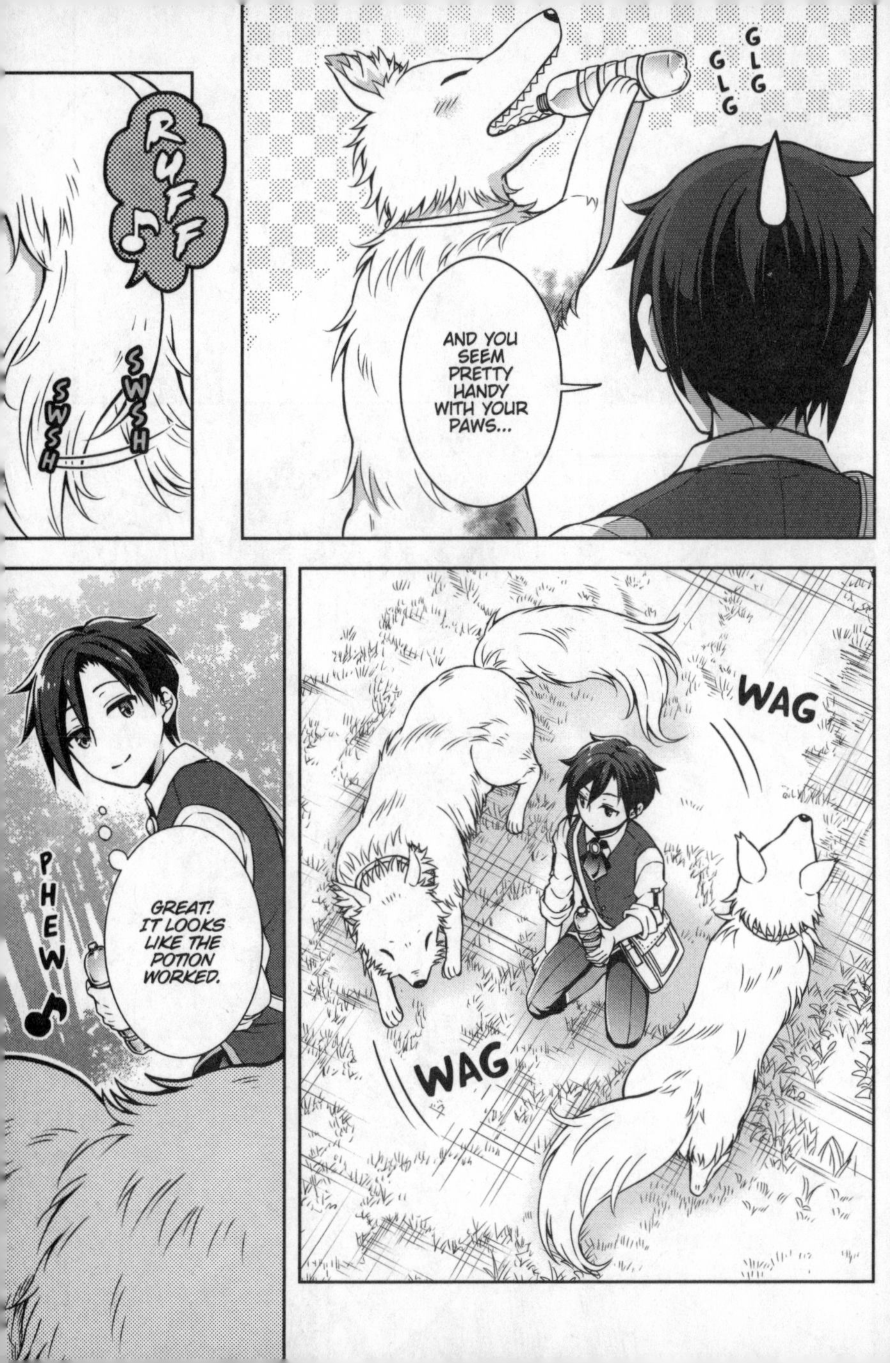
GLG GLG
AND YOU SEEM PRETTY HANDY WITH YOUR PAWS...
RUFF ♪
SWSH
SWSH
WAG
WAG
PHEW ♪
GREAT! IT LOOKS LIKE THE POTION WORKED.

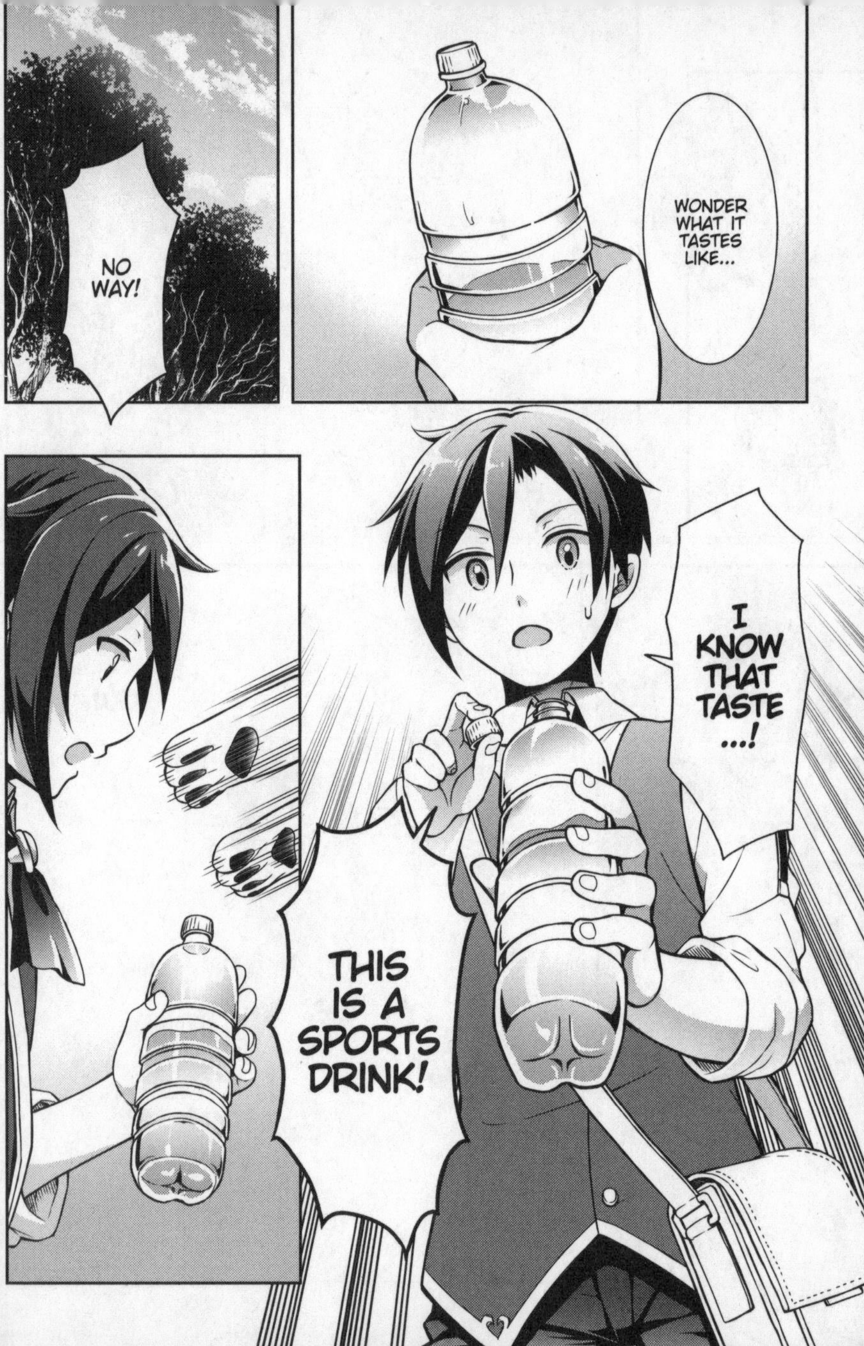
WONDER WHAT IT TASTES LIKE...
NO WAY!
I KNOW THAT TASTE ...!
THIS IS A SPORTS DRINK!

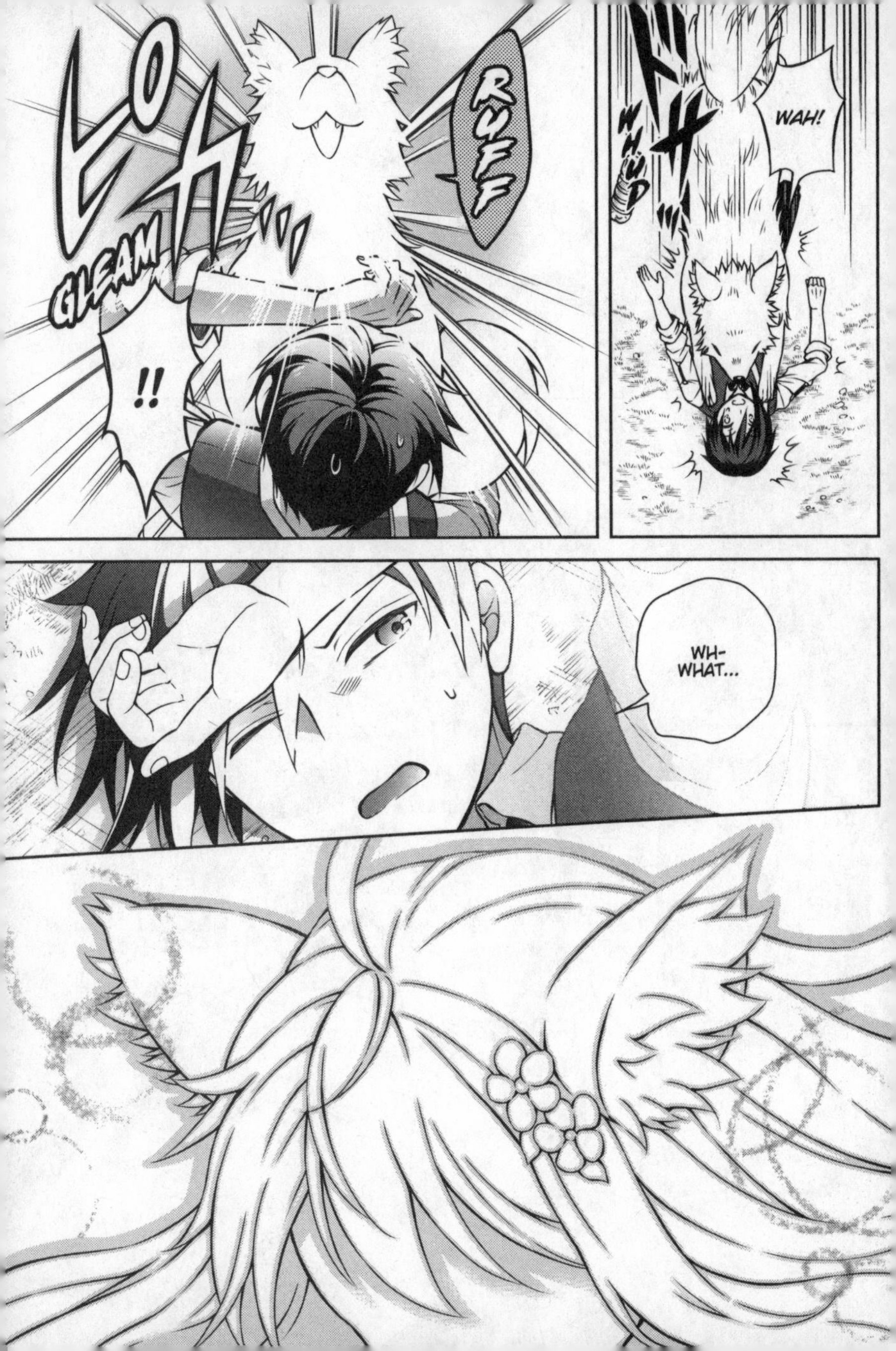
WAH!
WHUD
RUFF
GLEAM
!!
WH-WHAT...

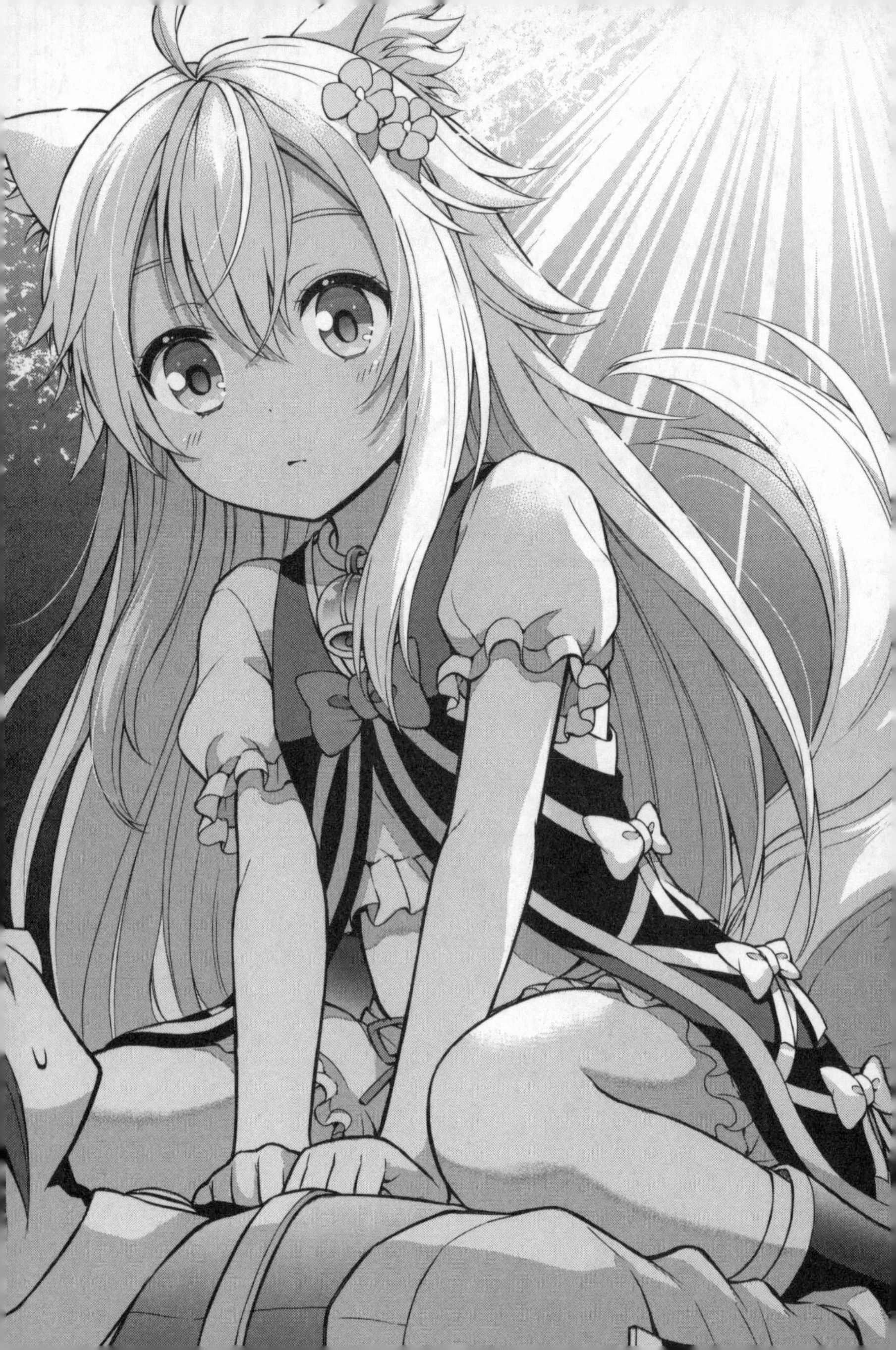

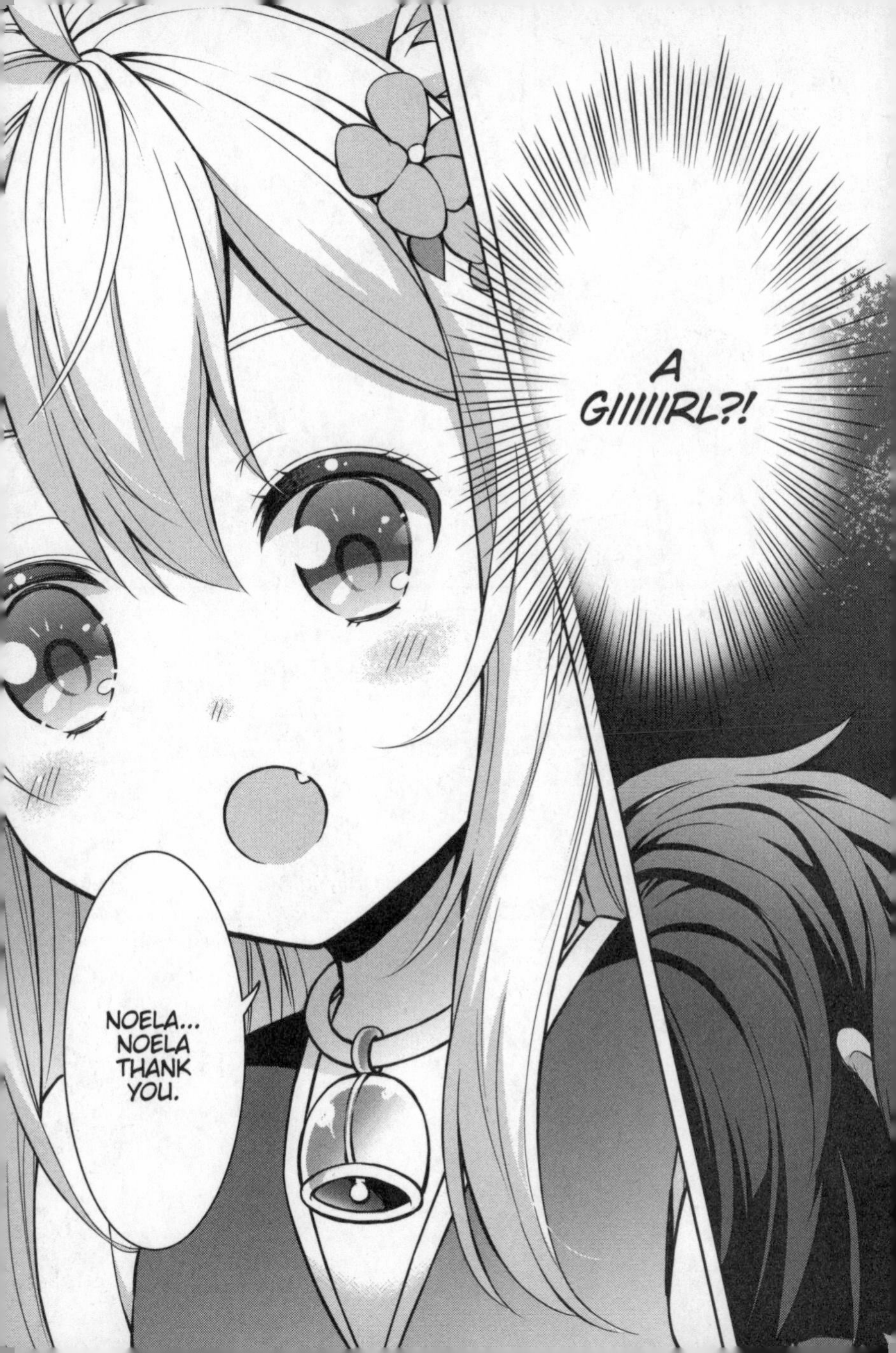
A GIIIIIRL?!
NOELA... NOELA THANK YOU.

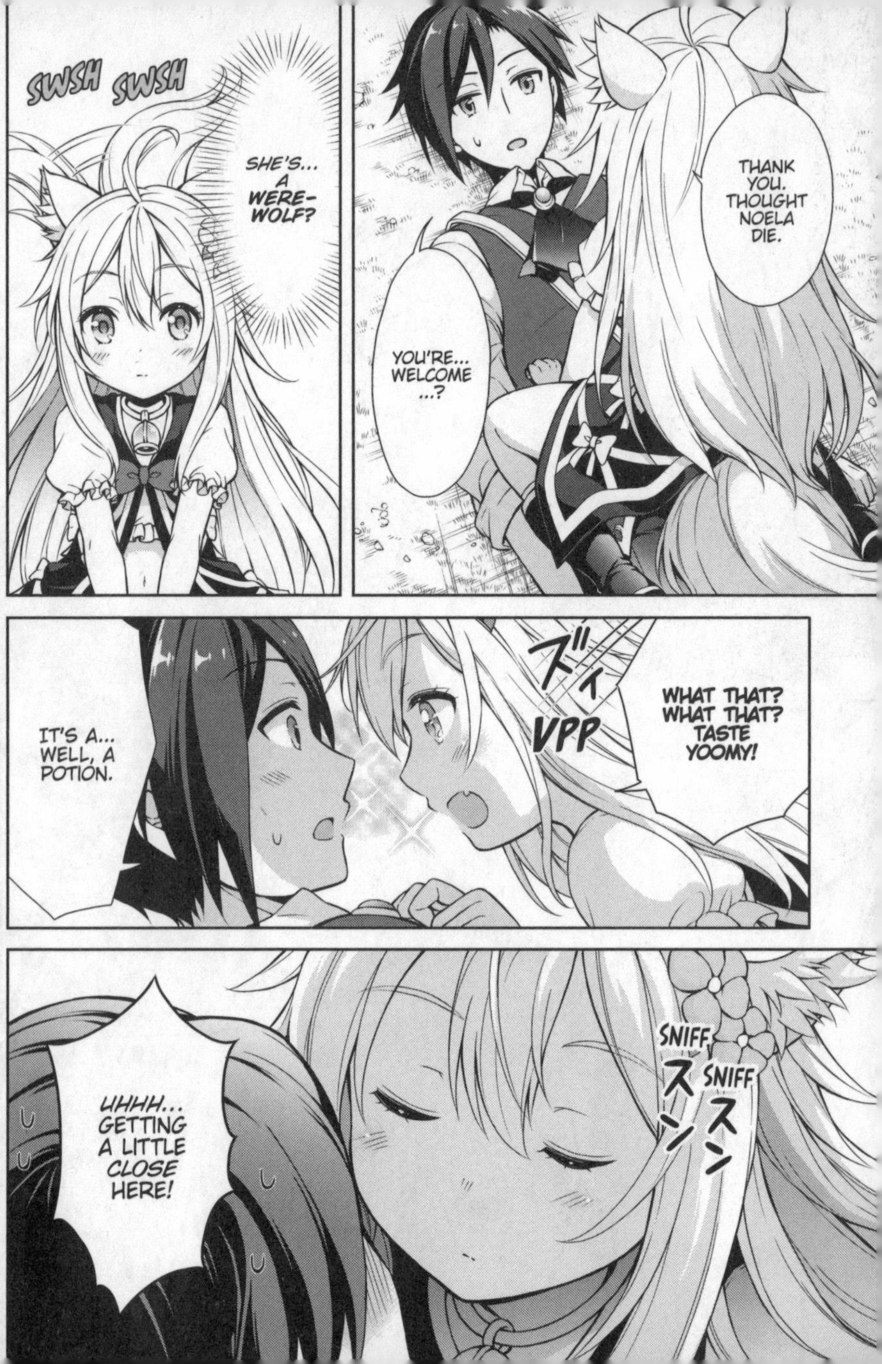
THANK YOU. THOUGHT NOELA DIE.
YOU'RE... WELCOME ...?
SWSH SWSH
SHE'S... A WERE-WOLF?
ズィ
VPP
WHAT THAT? WHAT THAT? TASTE YOOMY!
IT'S A... WELL, A POTION.
SNIFF
スン
SNIFF
スン
UHHH... GETTING A LITTLE CLOSE HERE!

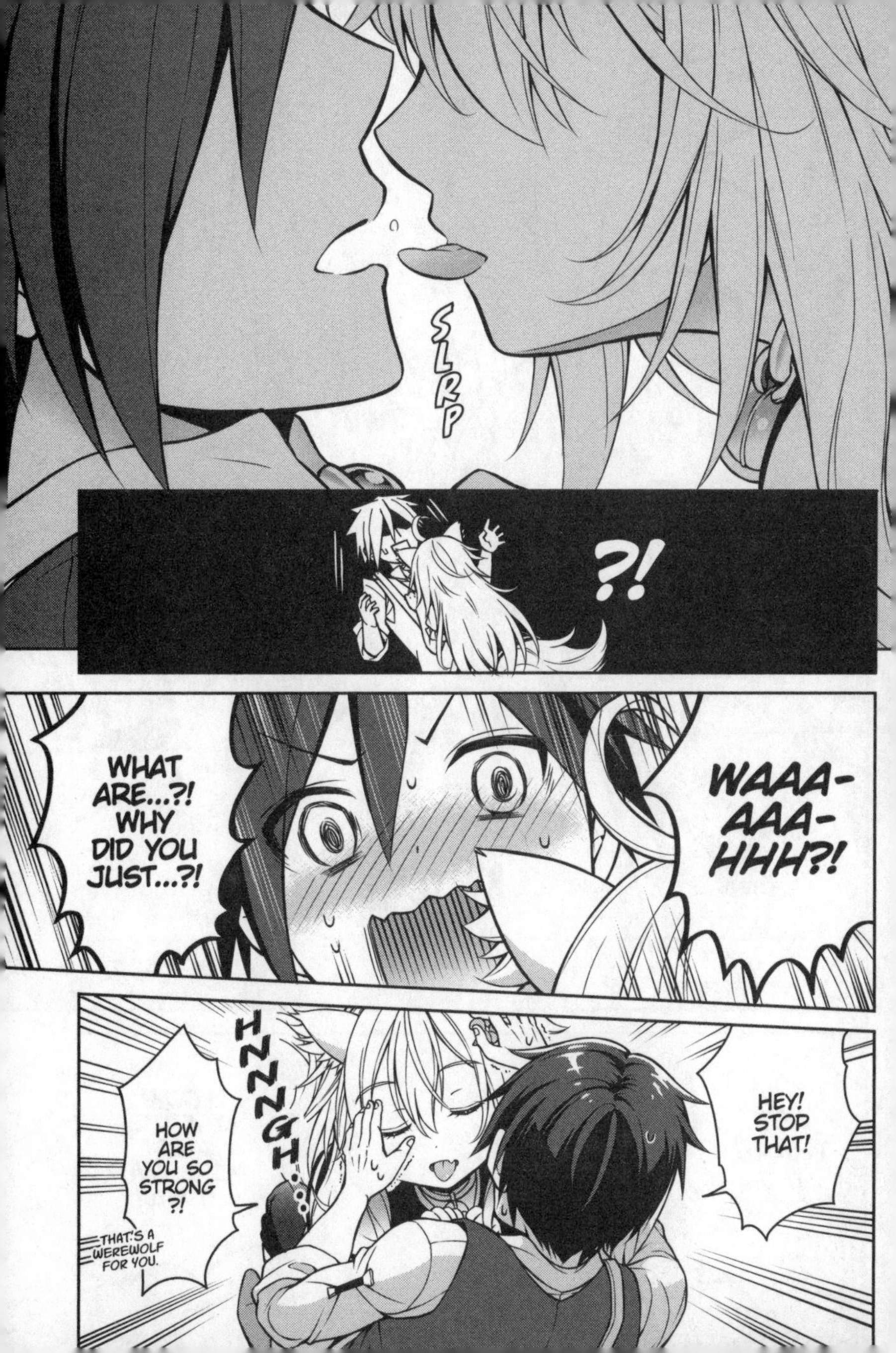
SLRP
?!
WAAAAAAHHH?!
WHAT ARE...?! WHY DID YOU JUST...?!
HEY! STOP THAT!
HNNNGH...
HOW ARE YOU SO STRONG?!
THAT'S A WEREWOLF FOR YOU.

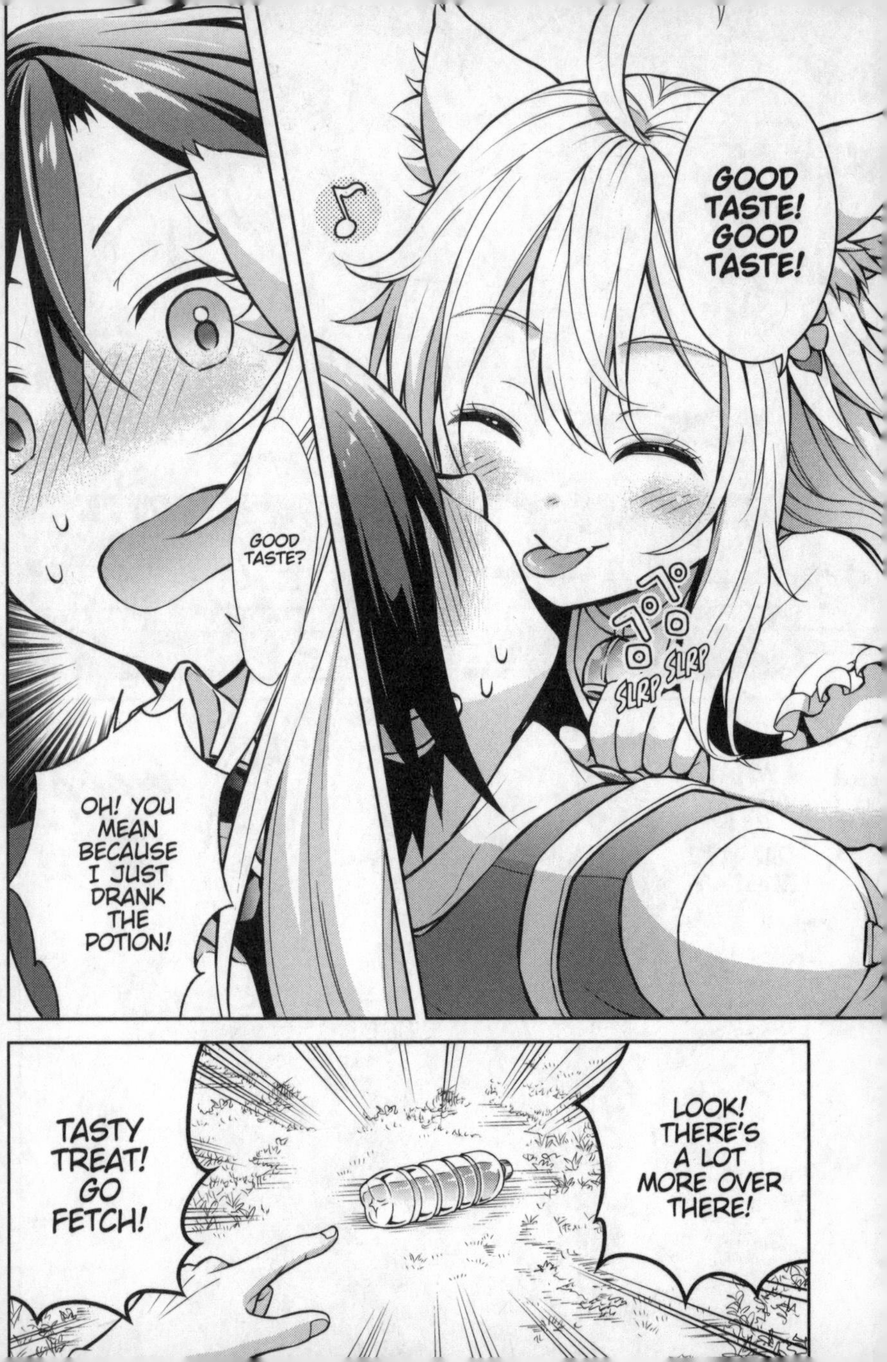

GOOD TASTE! GOOD TASTE!
SLRP SLRP
GOOD TASTE?
OH! YOU MEAN BECAUSE I JUST DRANK THE POTION!
LOOK! THERE'S A LOT MORE OVER THERE!
TASTY TREAT! GO FETCH!

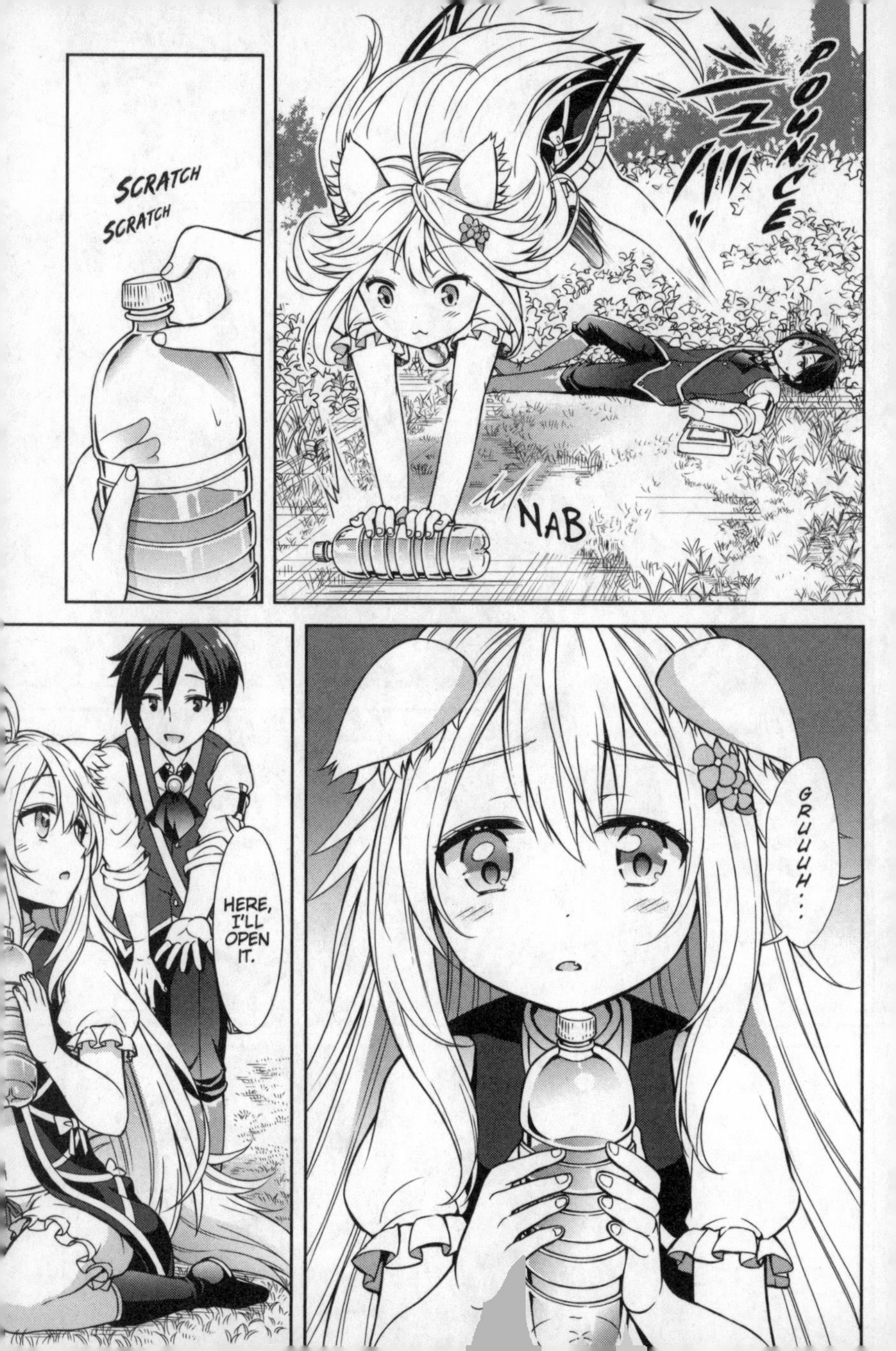
POUNCE
NAB
SCRATCH
SCRATCH
GRUUH...
HERE, I'LL OPEN IT.

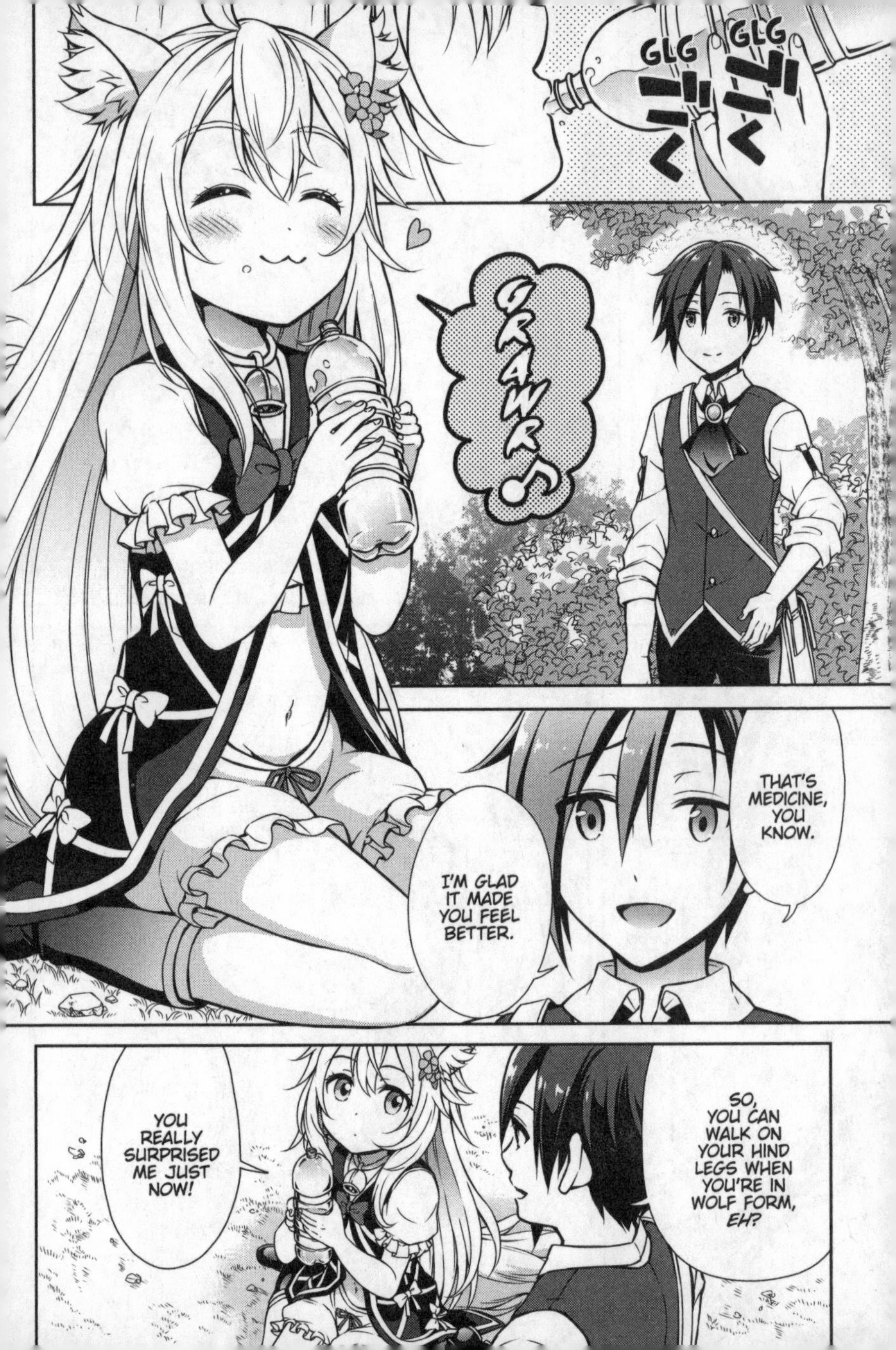
GLG GLG
ごくごく
GRAWR♪
THAT'S MEDICINE, YOU KNOW.
I'M GLAD IT MADE YOU FEEL BETTER.
SO, YOU CAN WALK ON YOUR HIND LEGS WHEN YOU'RE IN WOLF FORM, EH?
YOU REALLY SURPRISED ME JUST NOW!

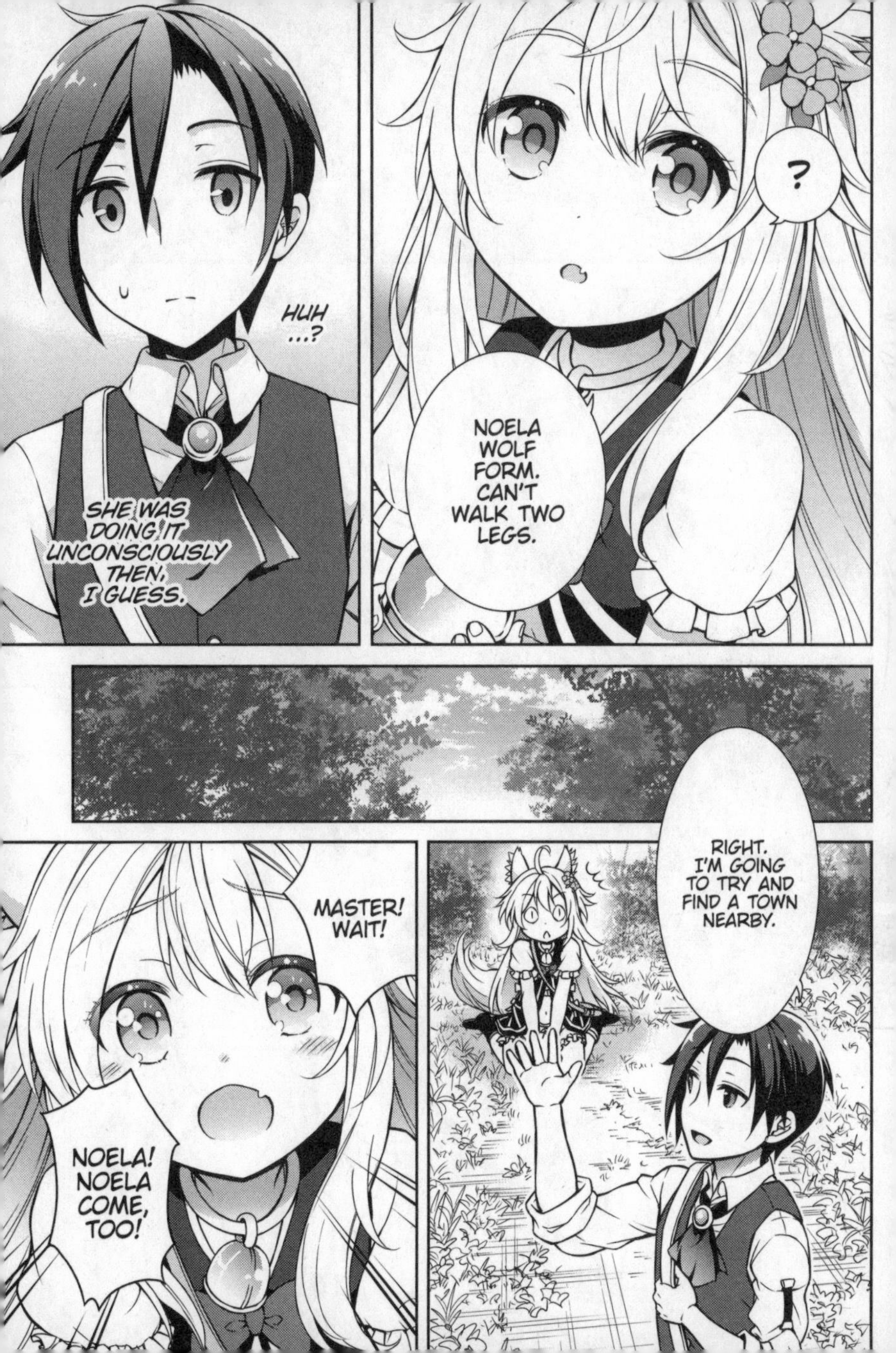
?
NOELA WOLF FORM. CAN'T WALK TWO LEGS.
HUH ...?
SHE WAS DOING IT UNCONSCIOUSLY THEN, I GUESS.
RIGHT. I'M GOING TO TRY AND FIND A TOWN NEARBY.
MASTER! WAIT!
NOELA! NOELA COME, TOO!

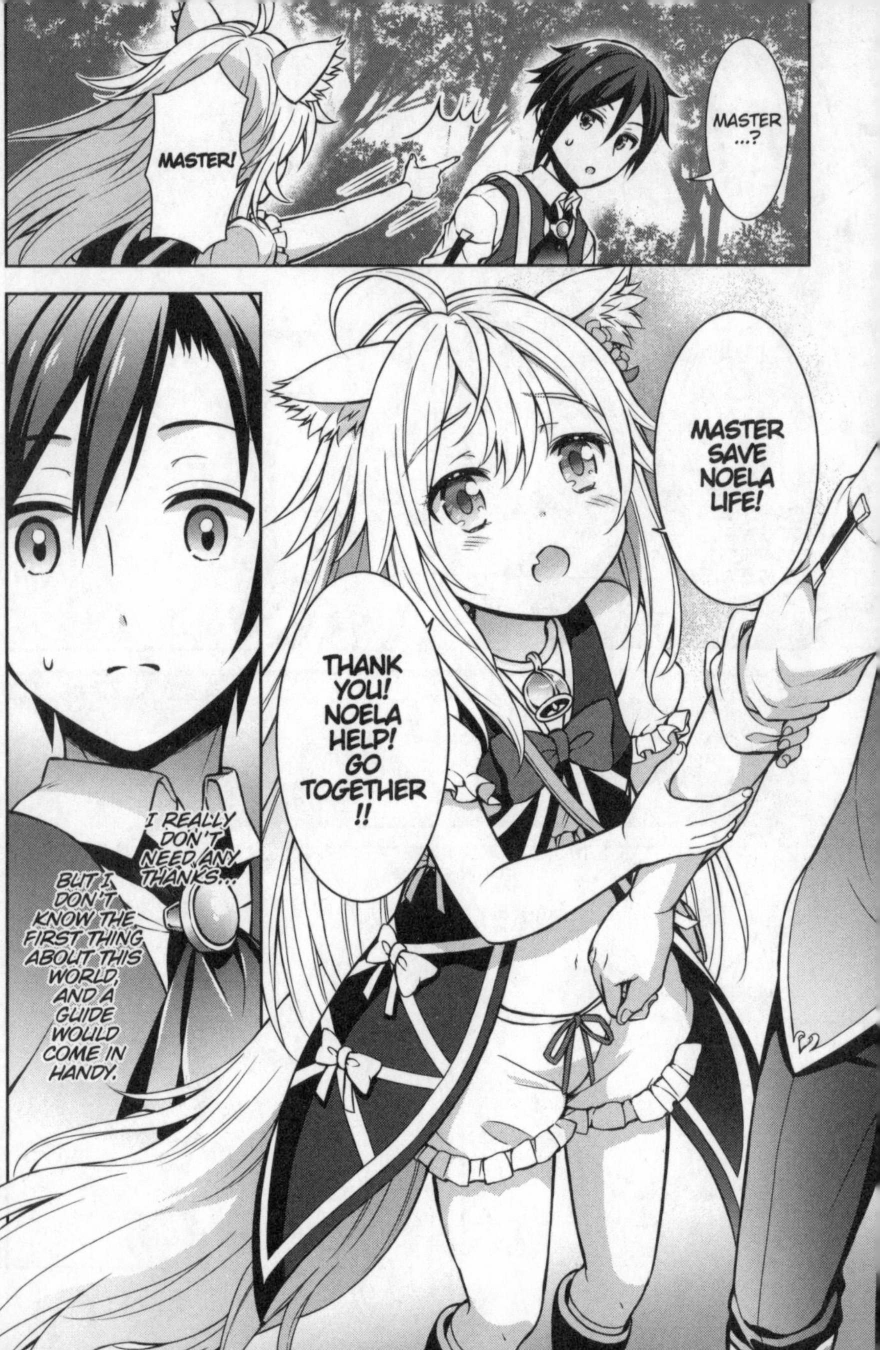
MASTER ...?
MASTER!
MASTER SAVE NOELA LIFE!
THANK YOU! NOELA HELP! GO TOGETHER !!
I REALLY DON'T NEED ANY THANKS...
BUT I DON'T KNOW THE FIRST THING ABOUT THIS WORLD, AND A GUIDE WOULD COME IN HANDY.

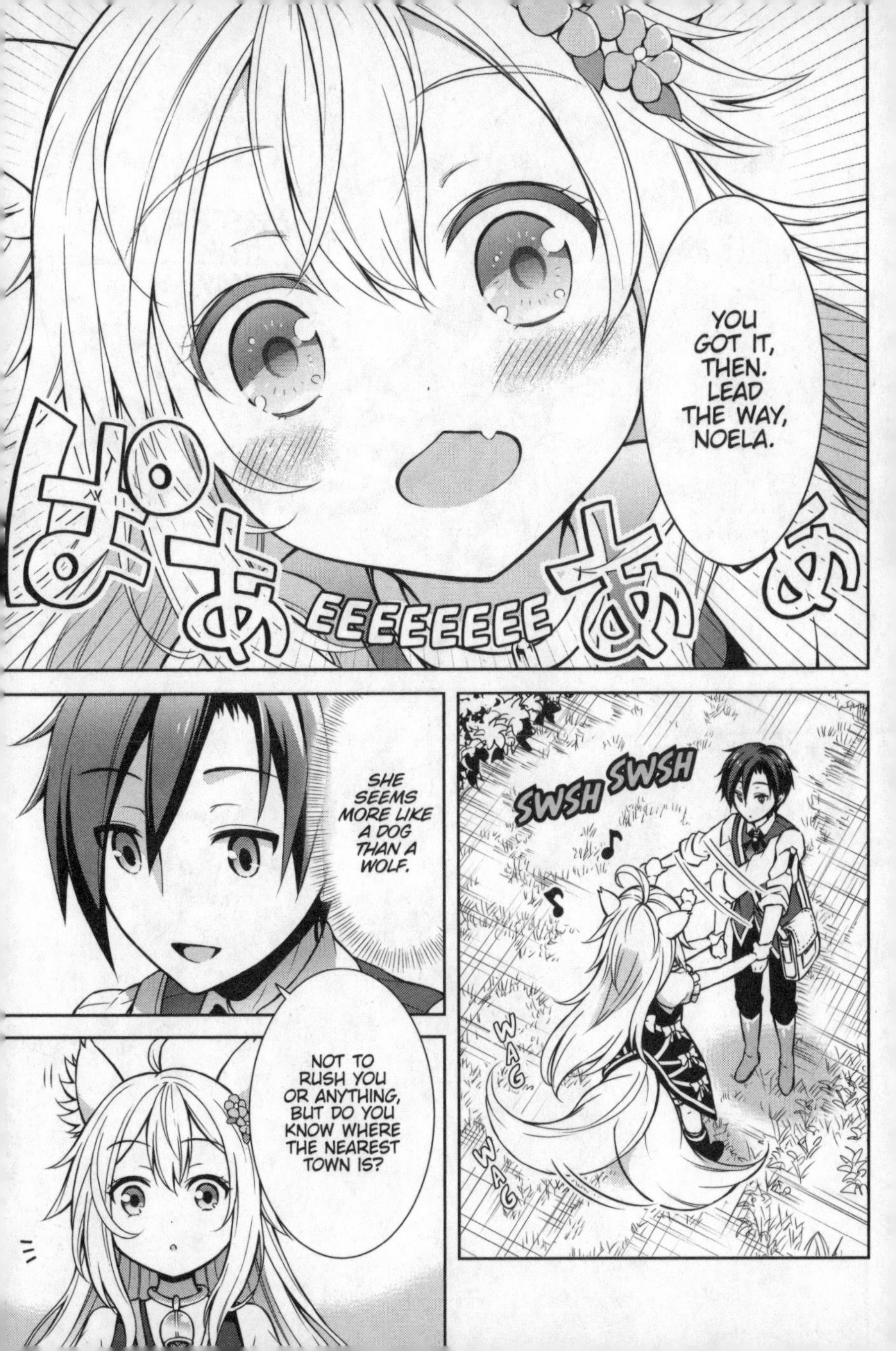
YOU GOT IT, THEN. LEAD THE WAY, NOELA.
ぱあEEEEEEEEああ
SWSH SWSH
♪
♪
WAG WAG
SHE SEEMS MORE LIKE A DOG THAN A WOLF.
NOT TO RUSH YOU OR ANYTHING, BUT DO YOU KNOW WHERE THE NEAREST TOWN IS?

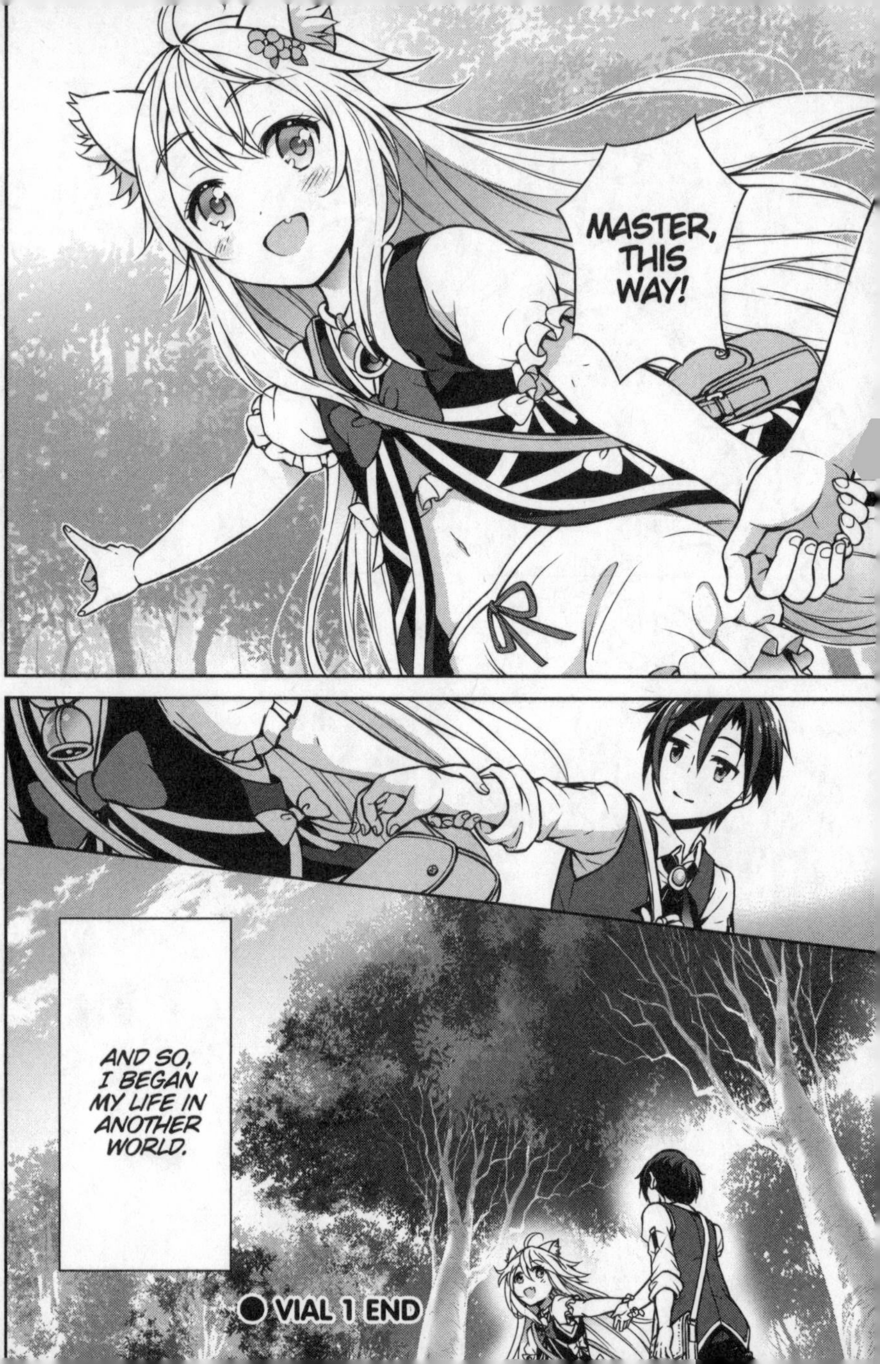
MASTER, THIS WAY!
AND SO, I BEGAN MY LIFE IN ANOTHER WORLD.
VIAL 1 END

DRUGSTORE in AnOTHer WORLD

~ The Slow Life of a ~ Cheat Pharmacist

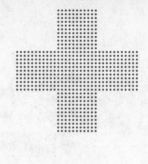

DRUGSTORE
iN ANOTHER WORLD
~ The Slow Life of a ~
Cheat Pharmacist ~

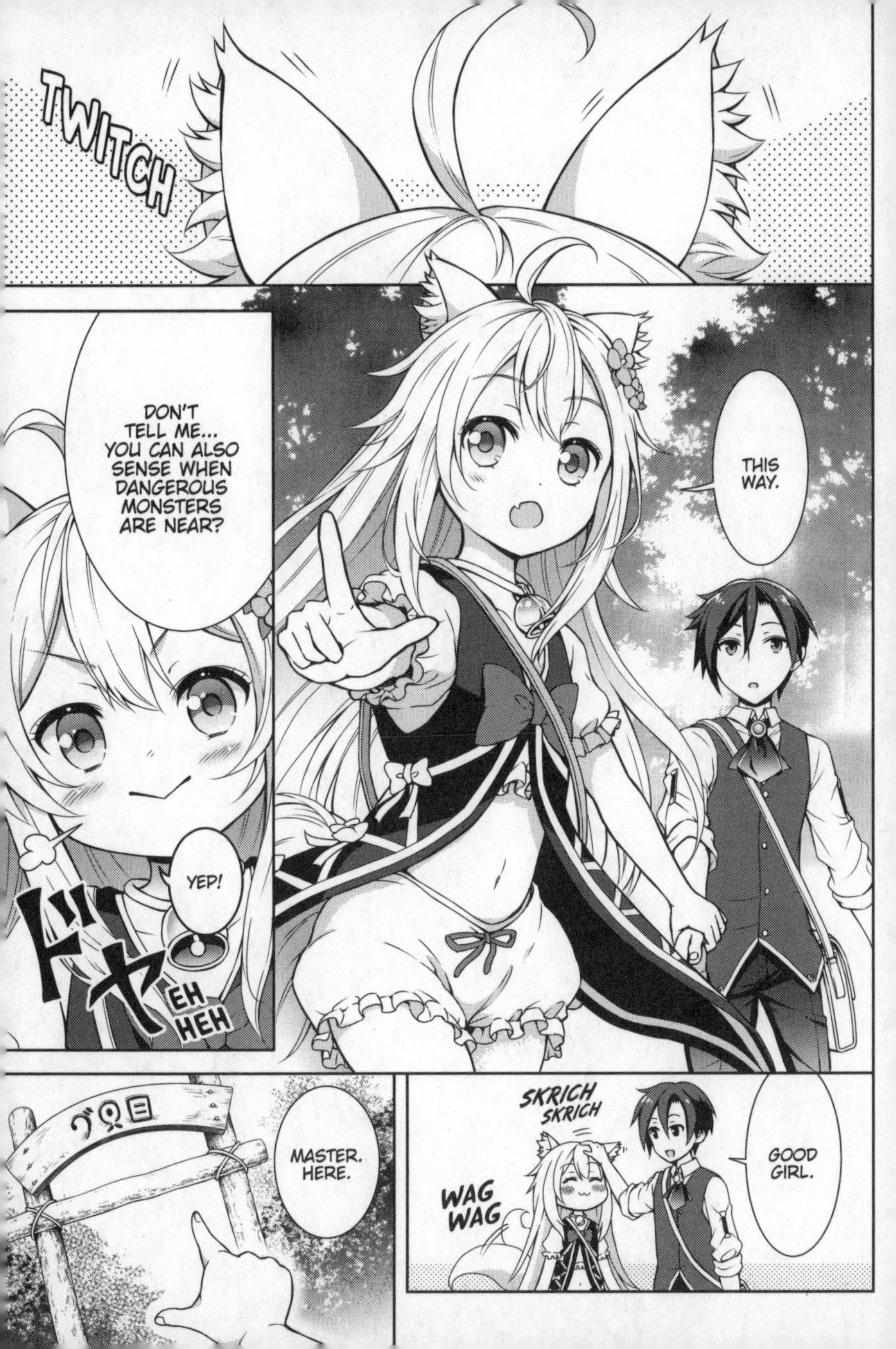
TWITCH
THIS WAY.
DON'T TELL ME... YOU CAN ALSO SENSE WHEN DANGEROUS MONSTERS ARE NEAR?
YEP!
ドヤ
EH HEH
GOOD GIRL.
SKRICH SKRICH
WAG WAG
MASTER. HERE.

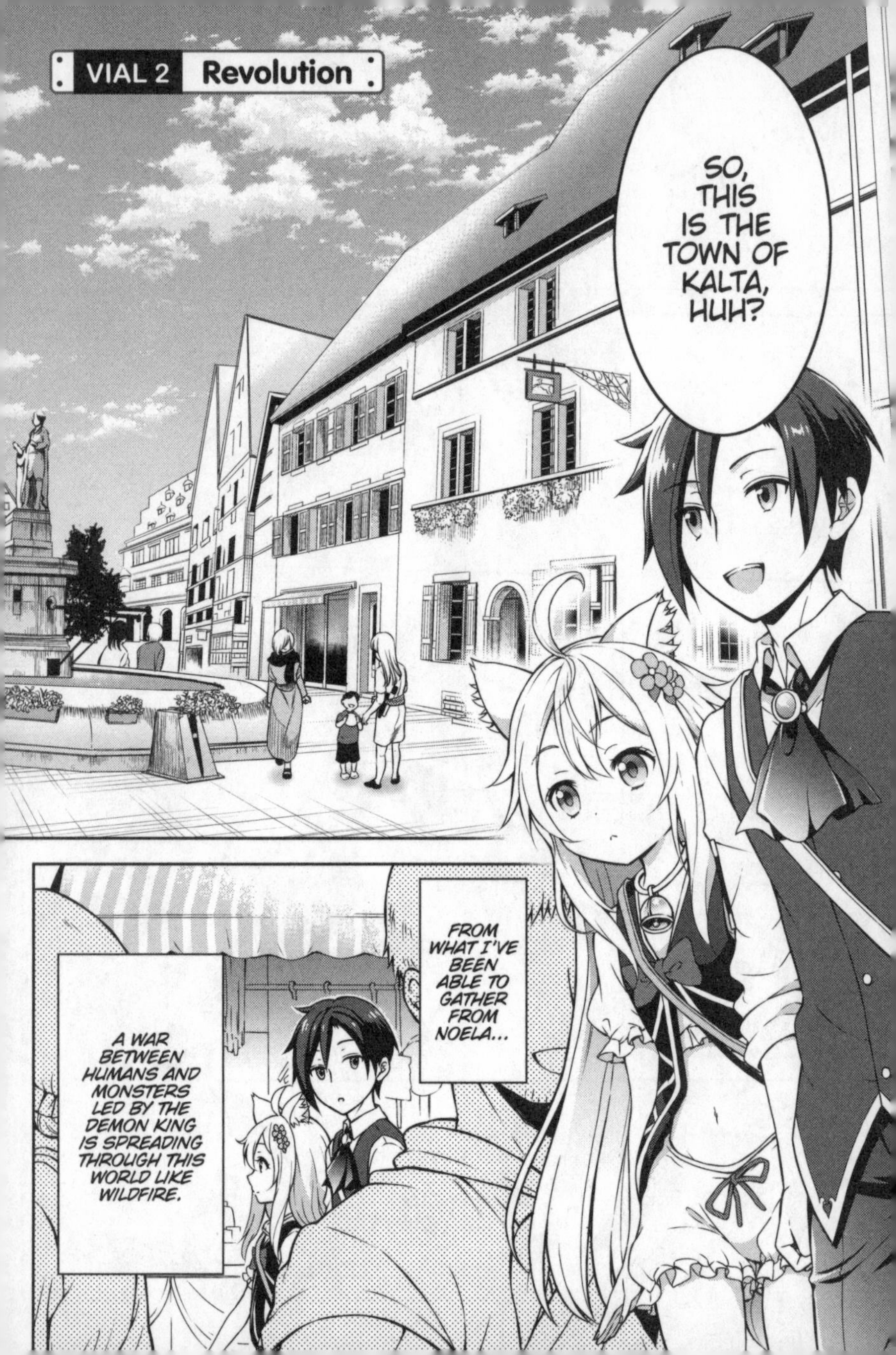
VIAL 2 Revolution
SO, THIS IS THE TOWN OF KALTA, HUH?
FROM WHAT I'VE BEEN ABLE TO GATHER FROM NOELA...
A WAR BETWEEN HUMANS AND MONSTERS LED BY THE DEMON KING IS SPREADING THROUGH THIS WORLD LIKE WILDFIRE.

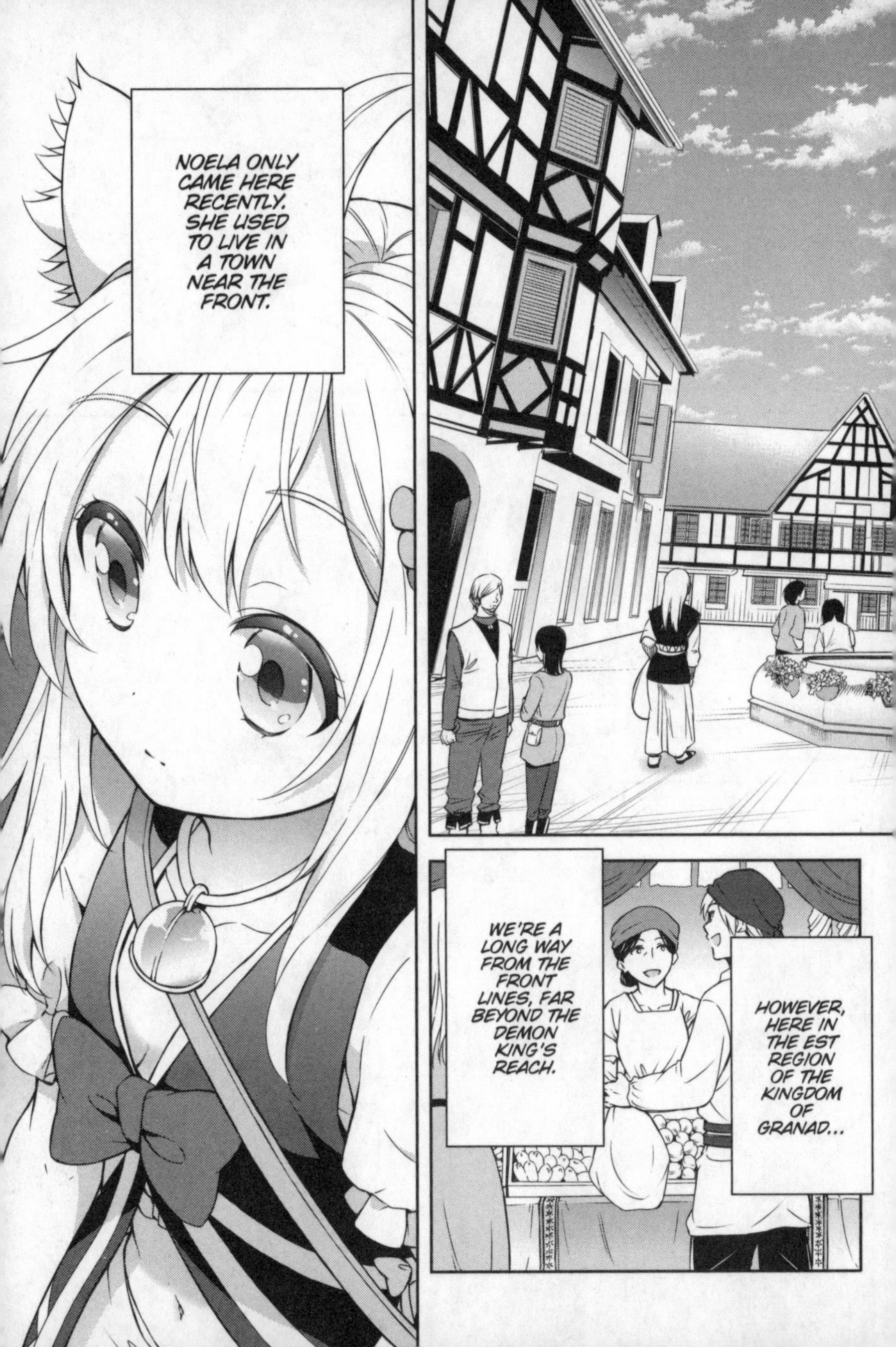
HOWEVER, HERE IN THE EST REGION OF THE KINGDOM OF GRANAD...
WE'RE A LONG WAY FROM THE FRONT LINES, FAR BEYOND THE DEMON KING'S REACH.
NOELA ONLY CAME HERE RECENTLY. SHE USED TO LIVE IN A TOWN NEAR THE FRONT.

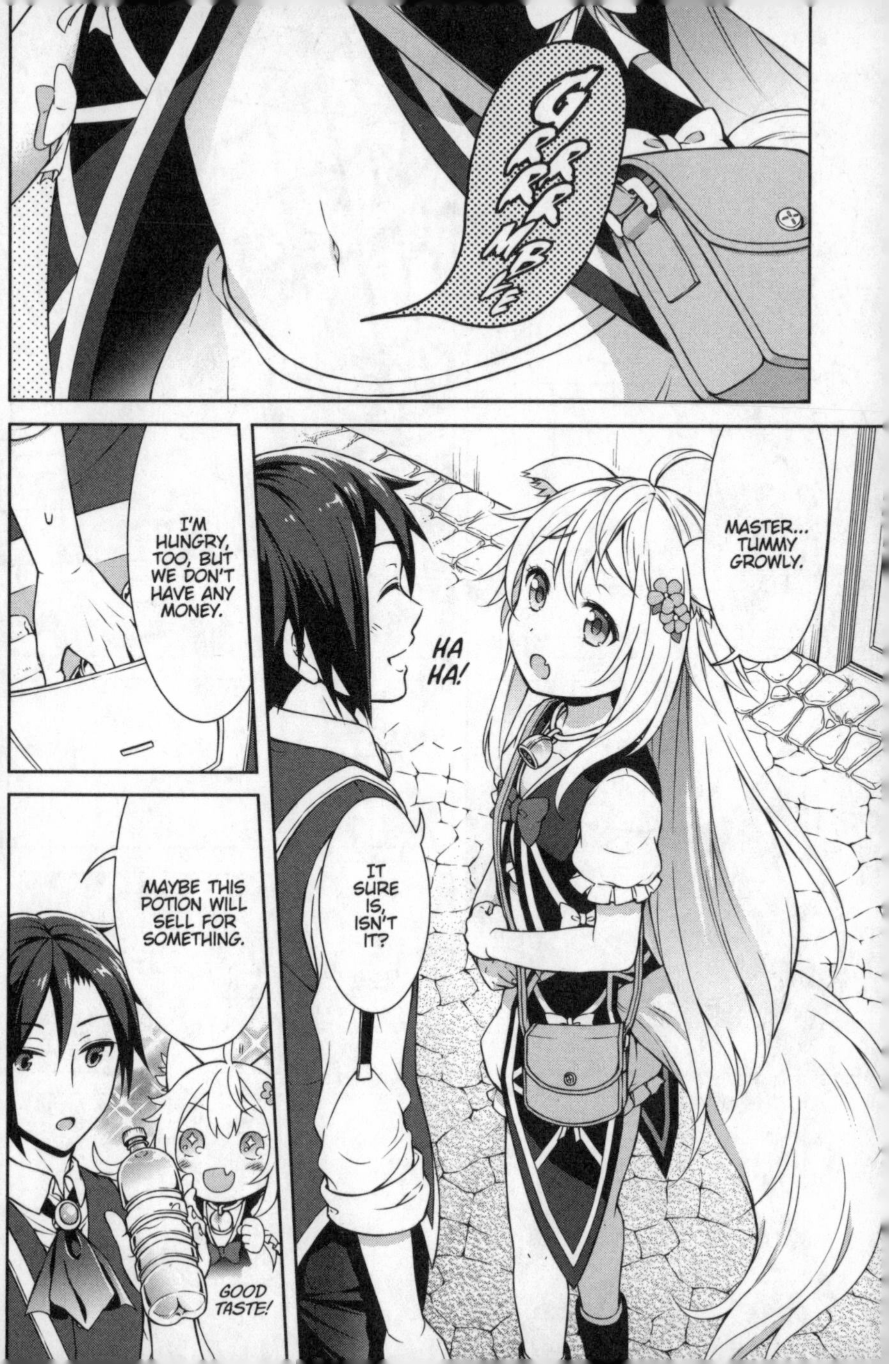
GRRRRMBLE
MASTER... TUMMY GROWLY.
HA HA!
IT SURE IS, ISN'T IT?
I'M HUNGRY, TOO, BUT WE DON'T HAVE ANY MONEY.
MAYBE THIS POTION WILL SELL FOR SOMETHING.
GOOD TASTE!

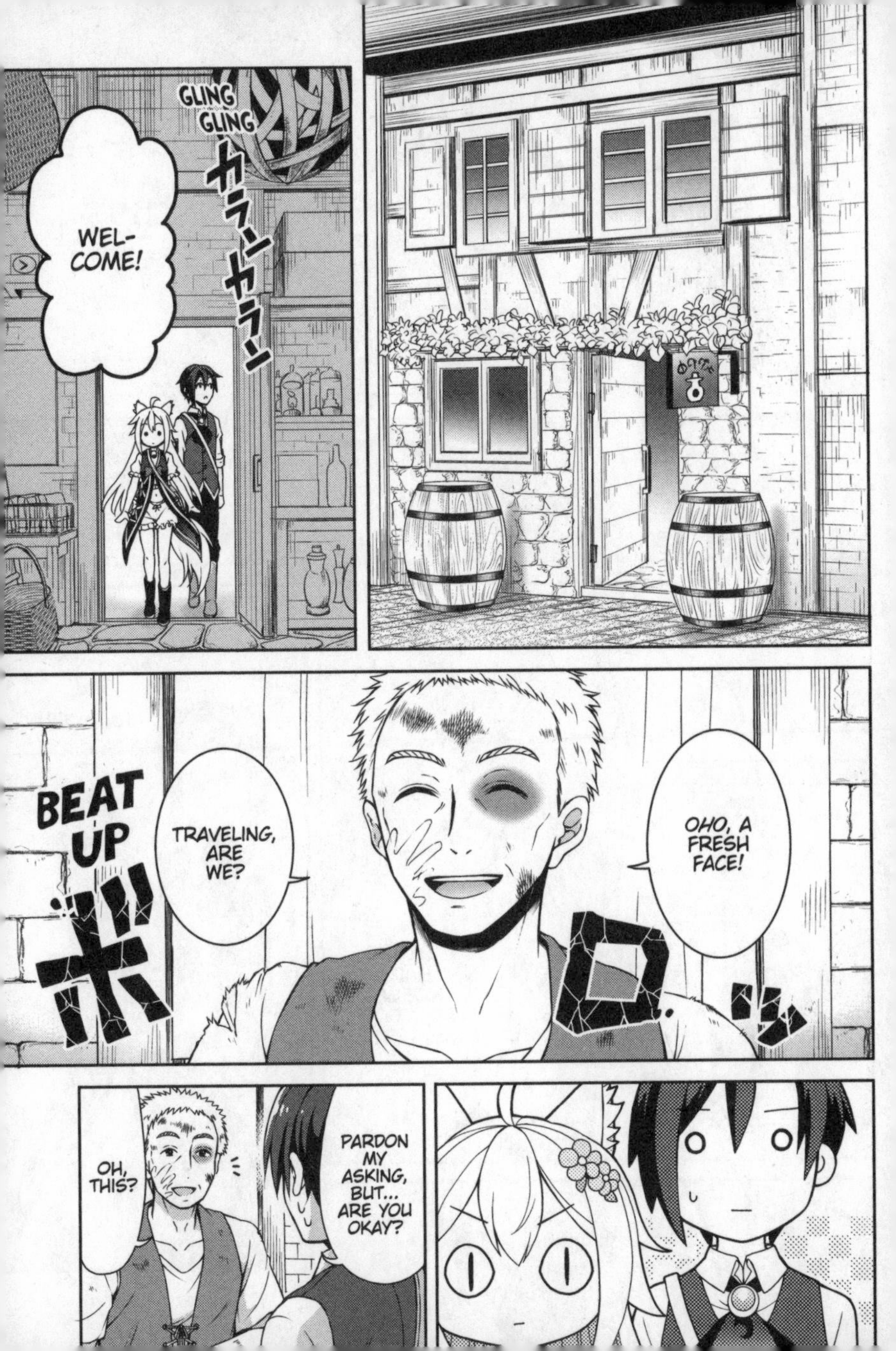
GLING GLING
WEL-COME!
OHO, A FRESH FACE!
TRAVELING, ARE WE?
BEAT UP
ボロッ
PARDON MY ASKING, BUT... ARE YOU OKAY?
OH, THIS?

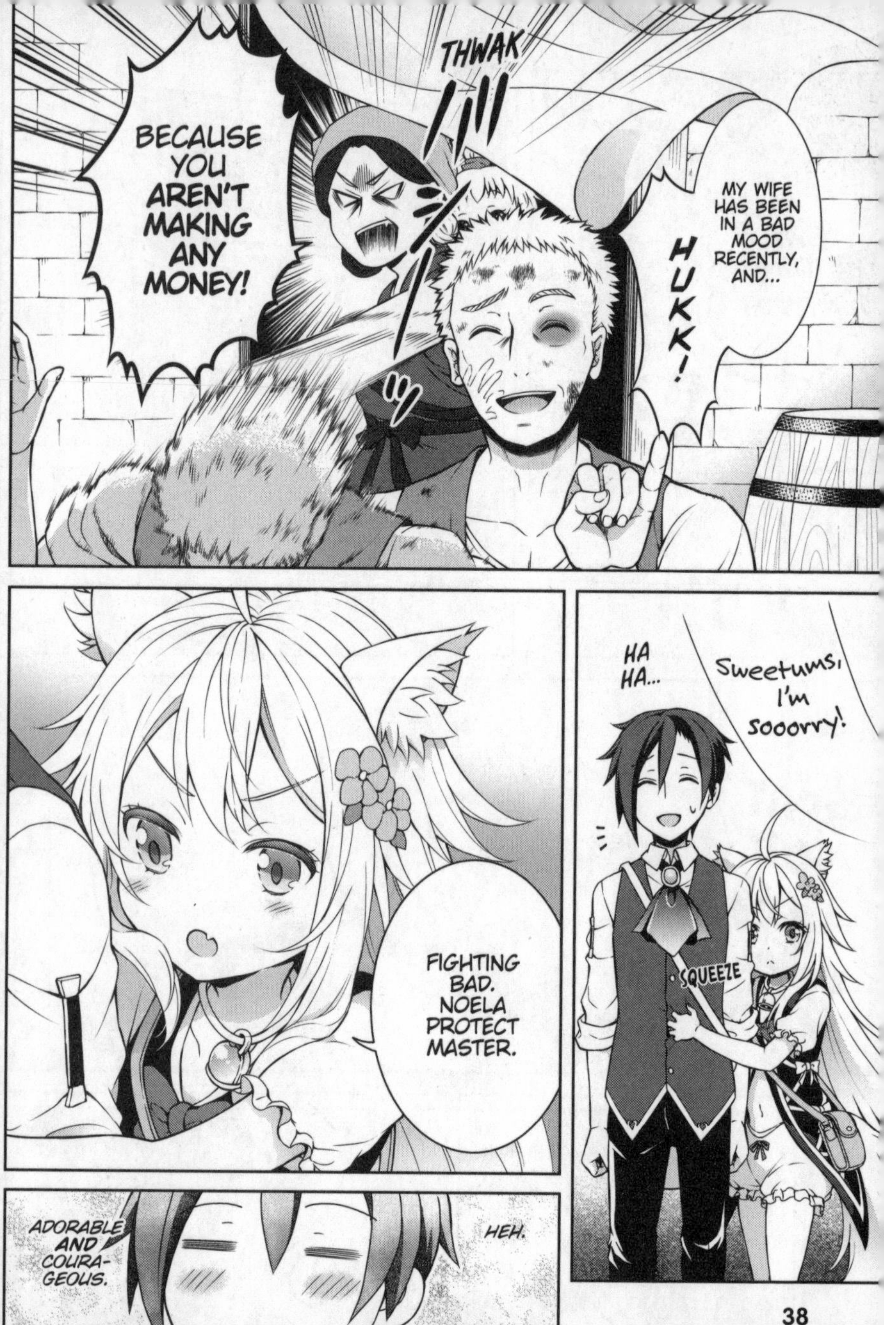
MY WIFE HAS BEEN IN A BAD MOOD RECENTLY, AND...
HUKK!
THWAK
BECAUSE YOU AREN'T MAKING ANY MONEY!
Sweetums, I'm sooorry!
HA HA...
SQUEEZE
FIGHTING BAD. NOELA PROTECT MASTER.
HEH.
ADORABLE AND COURAGEOUS.

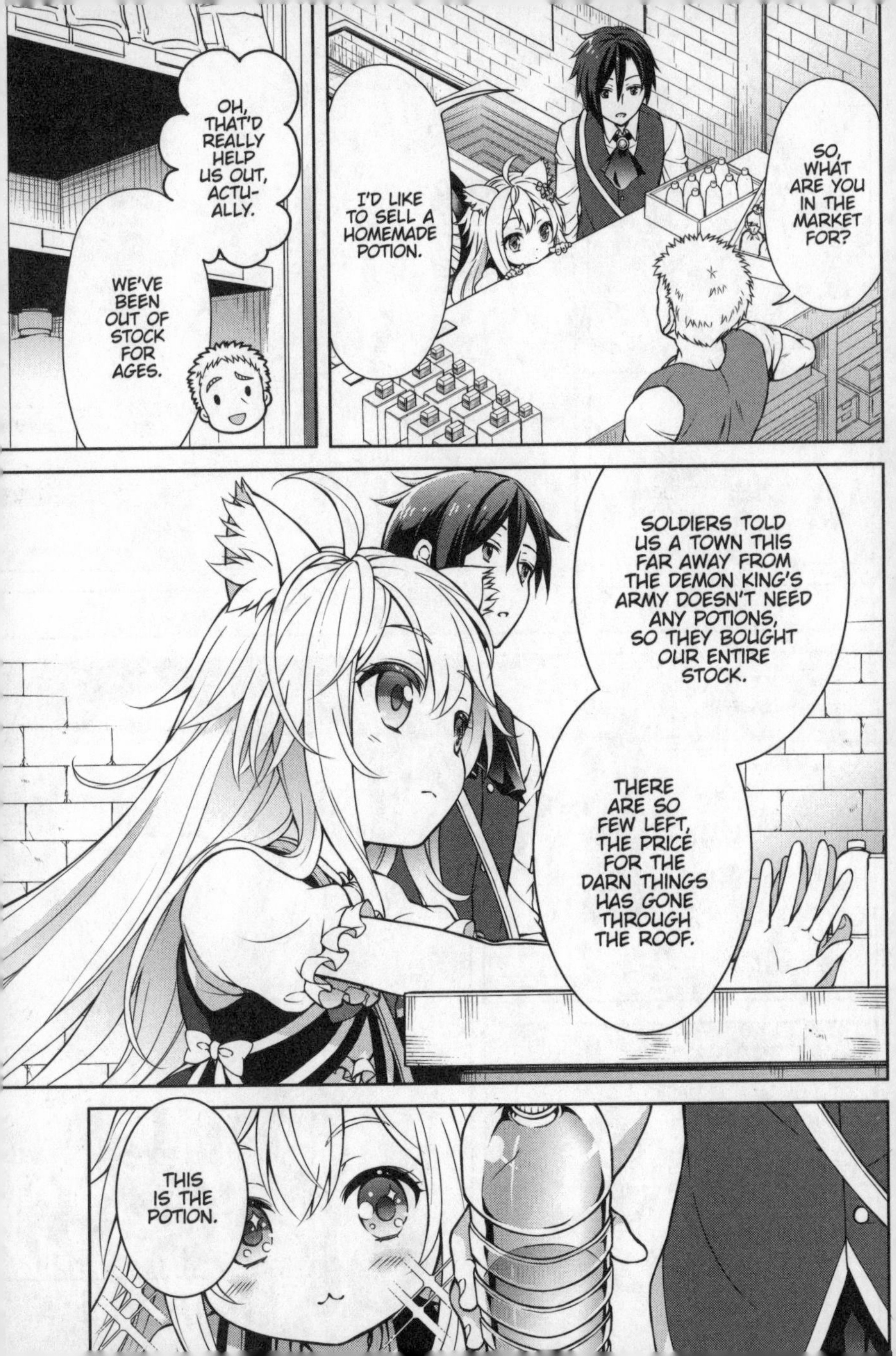
SO, WHAT ARE YOU IN THE MARKET FOR?
I'D LIKE TO SELL A HOMEMADE POTION.
OH, THAT'D REALLY HELP US OUT, ACTUALLY.
WE'VE BEEN OUT OF STOCK FOR AGES.
SOLDIERS TOLD US A TOWN THIS FAR AWAY FROM THE DEMON KING'S ARMY DOESN'T NEED ANY POTIONS, SO THEY BOUGHT OUR ENTIRE STOCK.
THERE ARE SO FEW LEFT, THE PRICE FOR THE DARN THINGS HAS GONE THROUGH THE ROOF.
THIS IS THE POTION.

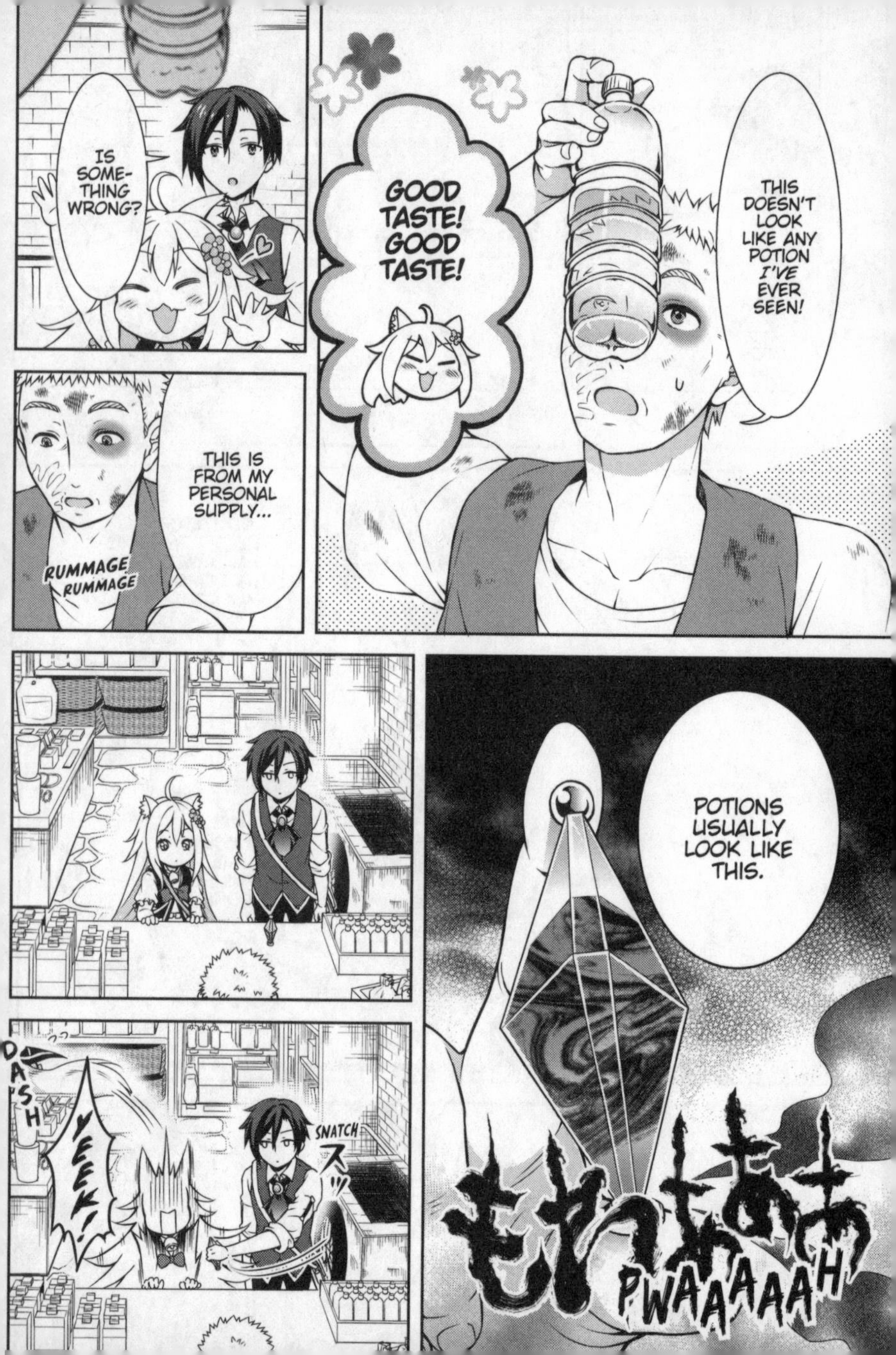
THIS DOESN'T LOOK LIKE ANY POTION I'VE EVER SEEN!
GOOD TASTE! GOOD TASTE!
IS SOME-THING WRONG?
THIS IS FROM MY PERSONAL SUPPLY...
RUMMAGE RUMMAGE
POTIONS USUALLY LOOK LIKE THIS.
PWAAAAAAH
DASH
YEEEK!
SNATCH

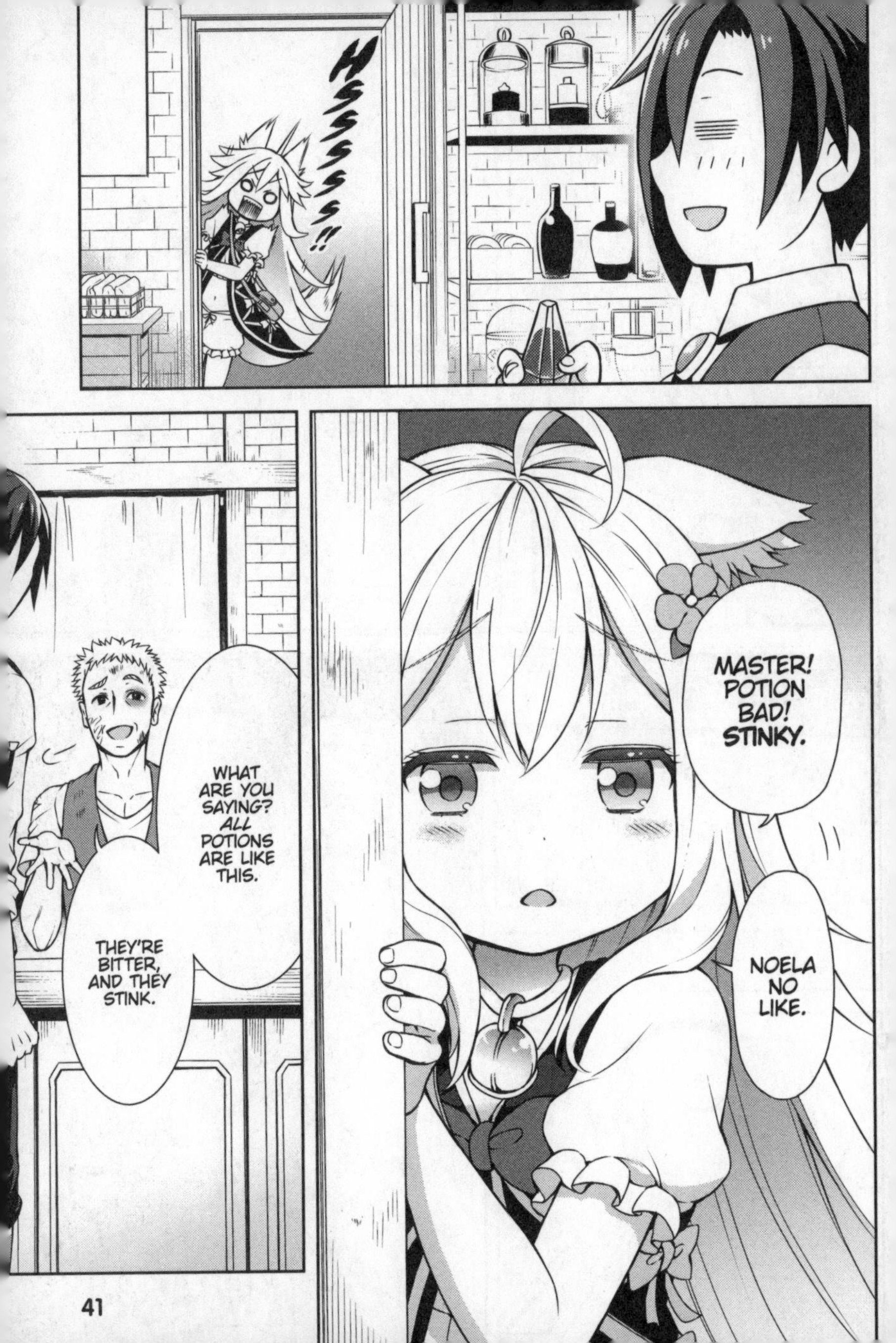
HSSSSSS!!
MASTER! POTION BAD! STINKY.
NOELA NO LIKE.
WHAT ARE YOU SAYING? ALL POTIONS ARE LIKE THIS.
THEY'RE BITTER, AND THEY STINK.

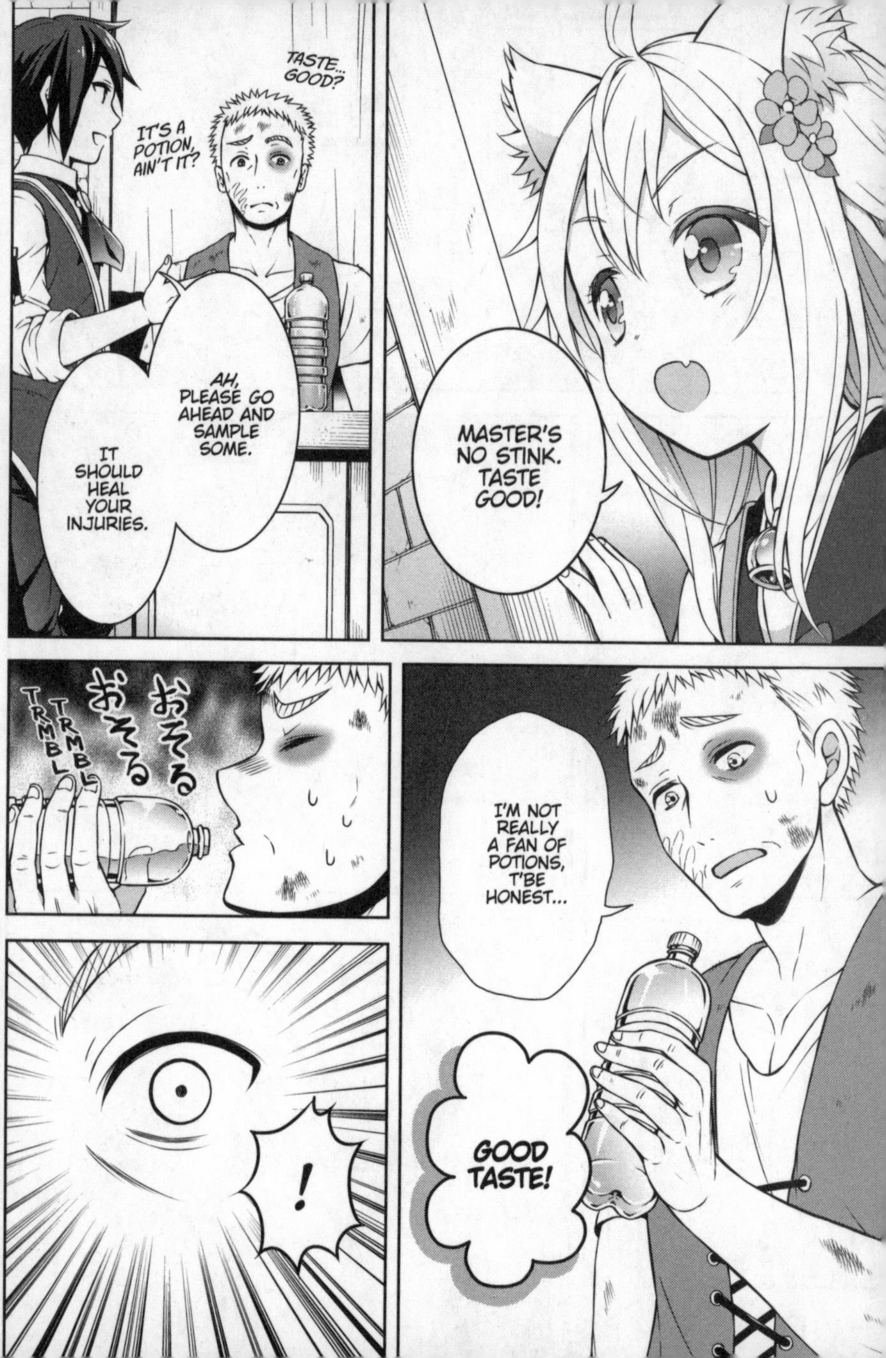
MASTER'S NO STINK. TASTE GOOD!
TASTE... GOOD?
IT'S A POTION, AIN'T IT?
AH, PLEASE GO AHEAD AND SAMPLE SOME.
IT SHOULD HEAL YOUR INJURIES.
I'M NOT REALLY A FAN OF POTIONS, T'BE HONEST...
GOOD TASTE!
おそるおそる
TRMBL TRMBL
!

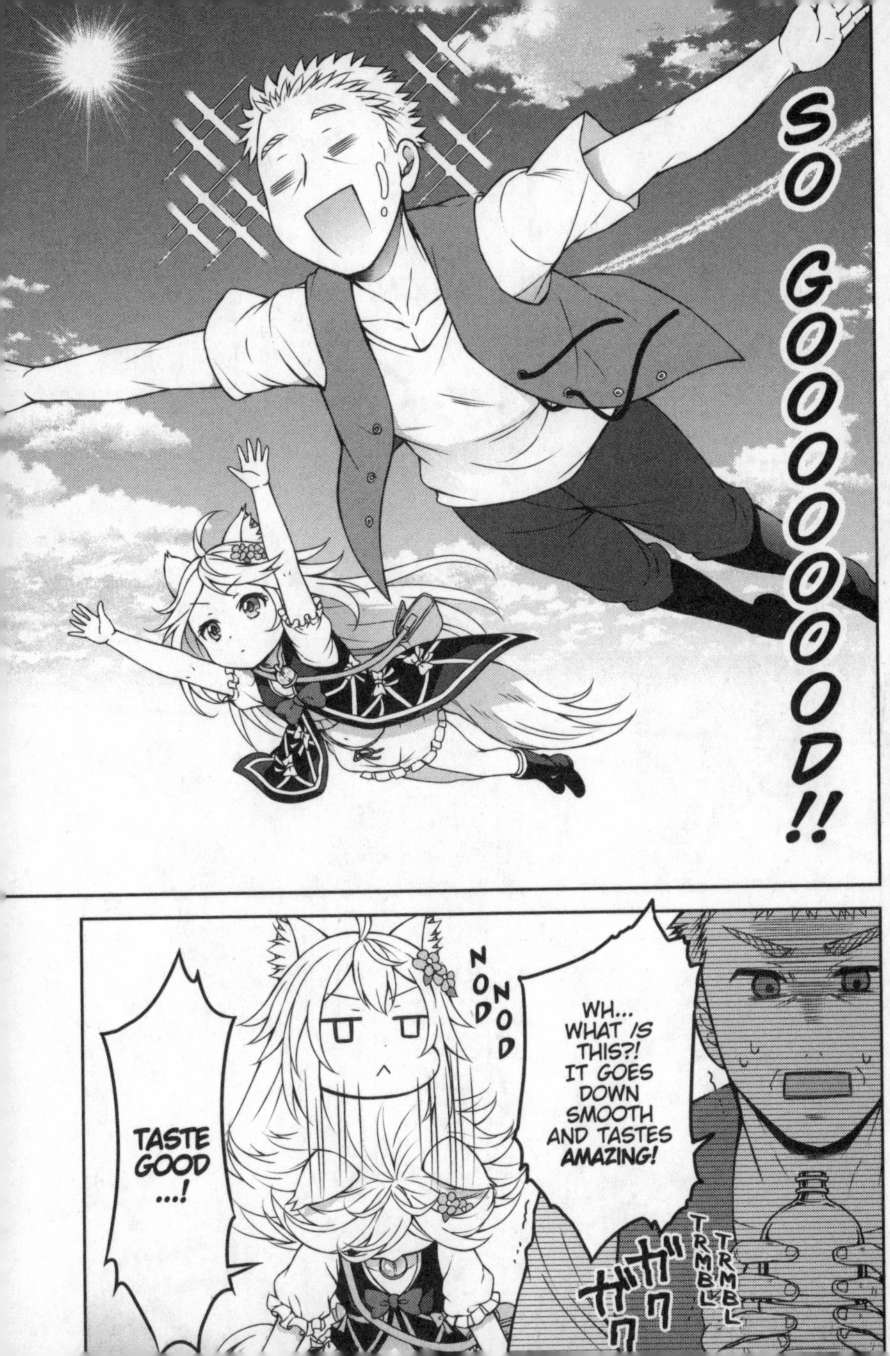
SO GOOOOOOOOD!!
WH... WHAT IS THIS?! IT GOES DOWN SMOOTH AND TASTES AMAZING!
TRMBL TRMBL
NOD NOD
TASTE GOOD ...!

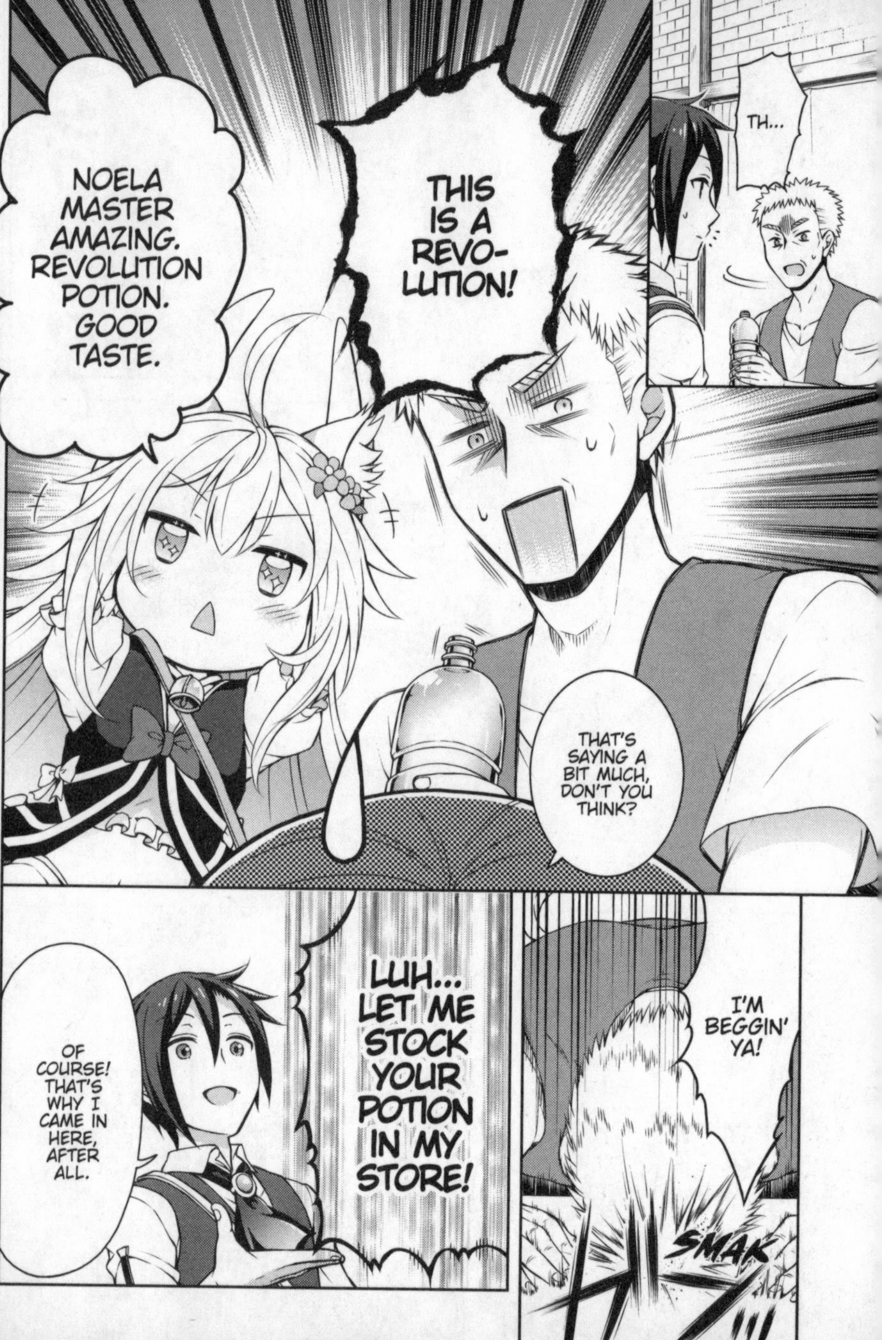
TH...
THIS IS A REVOLUTION!
NOELA MASTER AMAZING. REVOLUTION POTION. GOOD TASTE.
THAT'S SAYING A BIT MUCH, DON'T YOU THINK?
I'M BEGGIN' YA!
SMAK
LUH... LET ME STOCK YOUR POTION IN MY STORE!
OF COURSE! THAT'S WHY I CAME IN HERE, AFTER ALL.

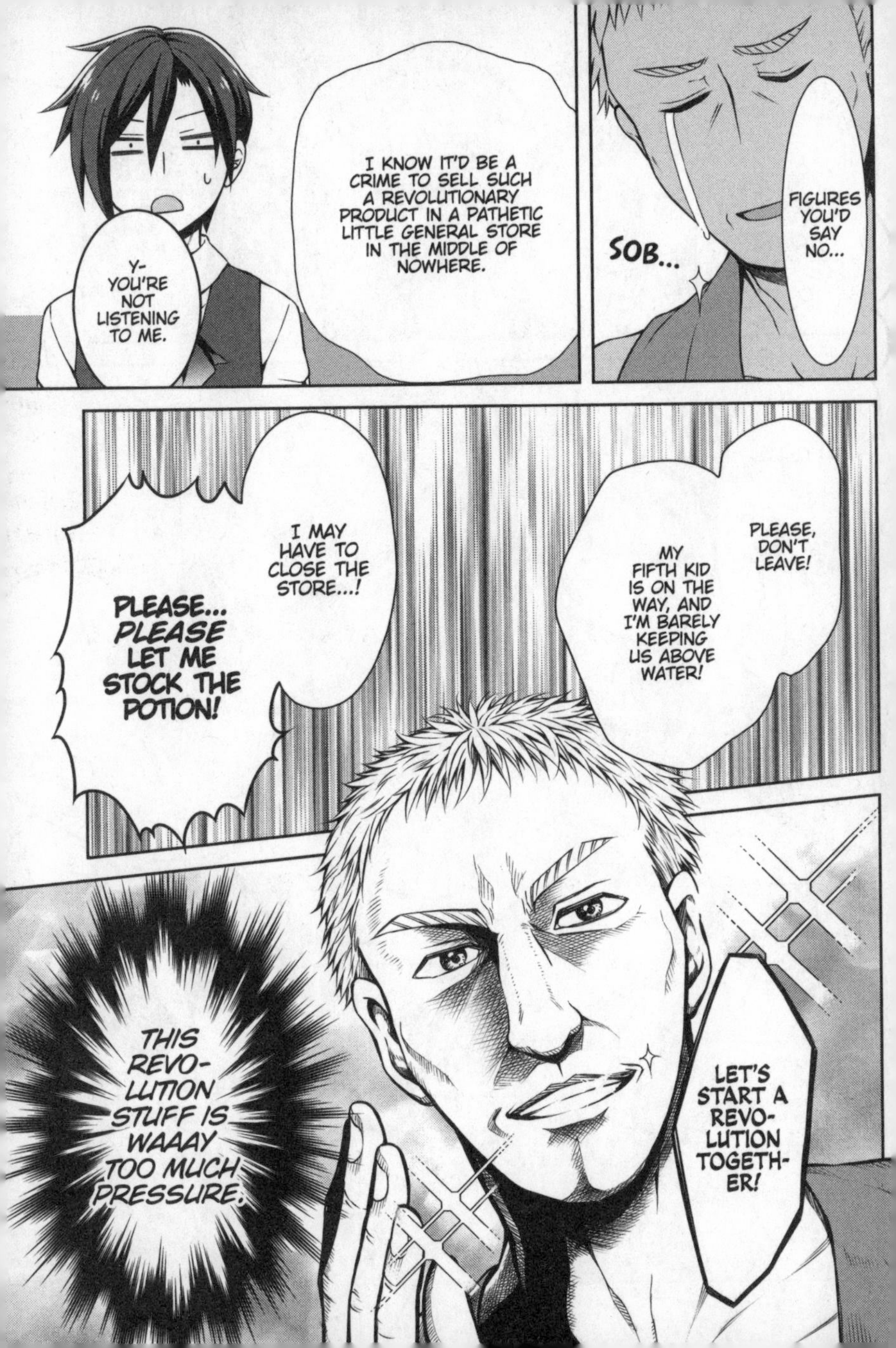
FIGURES YOU'D SAY NO...
SOB...
I KNOW IT'D BE A CRIME TO SELL SUCH A REVOLUTIONARY PRODUCT IN A PATHETIC LITTLE GENERAL STORE IN THE MIDDLE OF NOWHERE.
Y- YOU'RE NOT LISTENING TO ME.
PLEASE, DON'T LEAVE!
MY FIFTH KID IS ON THE WAY, AND I'M BARELY KEEPING US ABOVE WATER!
I MAY HAVE TO CLOSE THE STORE...!
PLEASE... PLEASE LET ME STOCK THE POTION!
LET'S START A REVO-LUTION TOGETH-ER!
THIS REVO-LUTION STUFF IS WAAAY TOO MUCH PRESSURE.

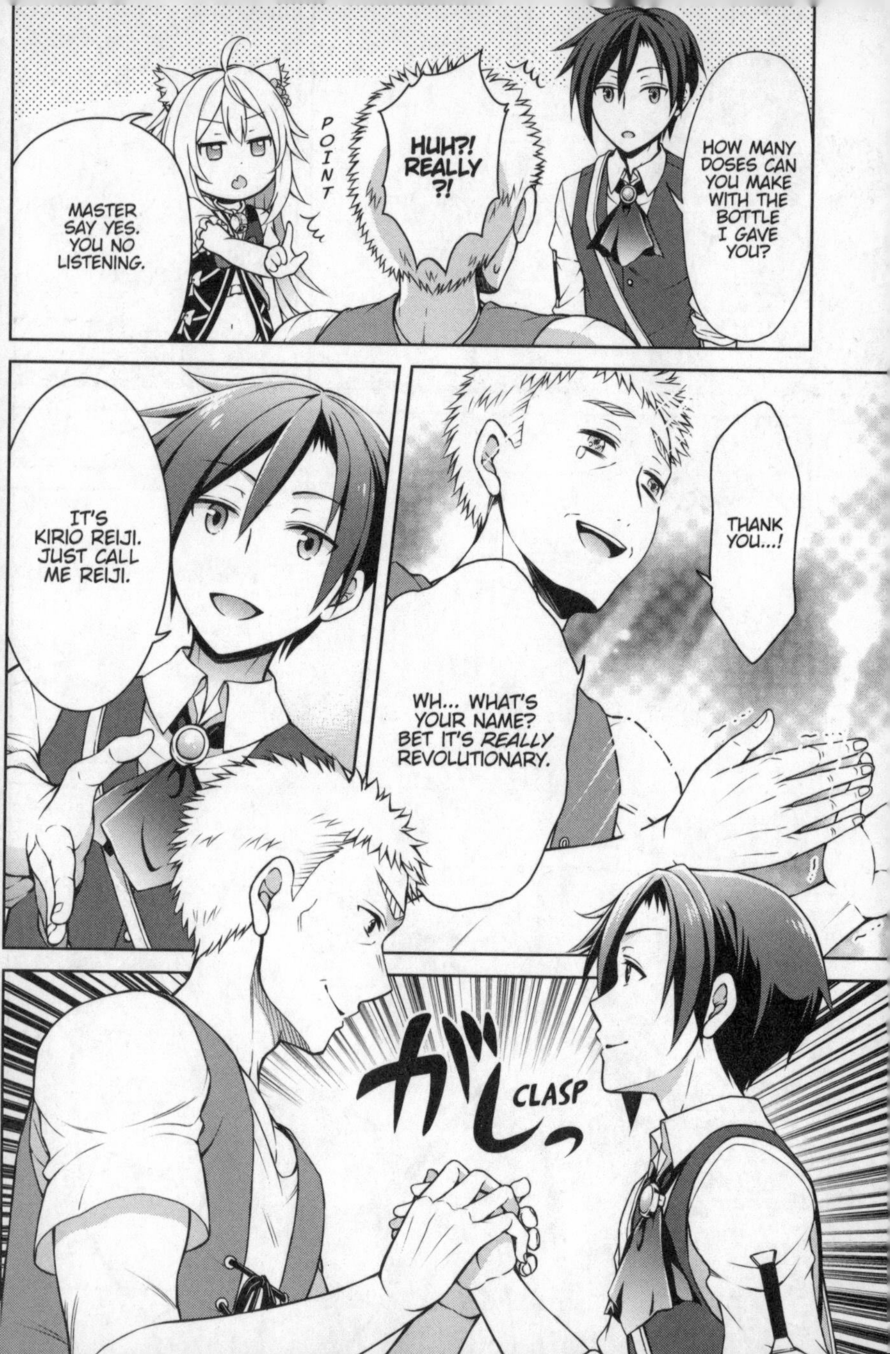
HOW MANY DOSES CAN YOU MAKE WITH THE BOTTLE I GAVE YOU?
HUH?! REALLY?!
POINT
MASTER SAY YES. YOU NO LISTENING.
THANK YOU...!
WH... WHAT'S YOUR NAME? BET IT'S *REALLY* REVOLUTIONARY.
IT'S KIRIO REIJI. JUST CALL ME REIJI.
がしっ
CLASP

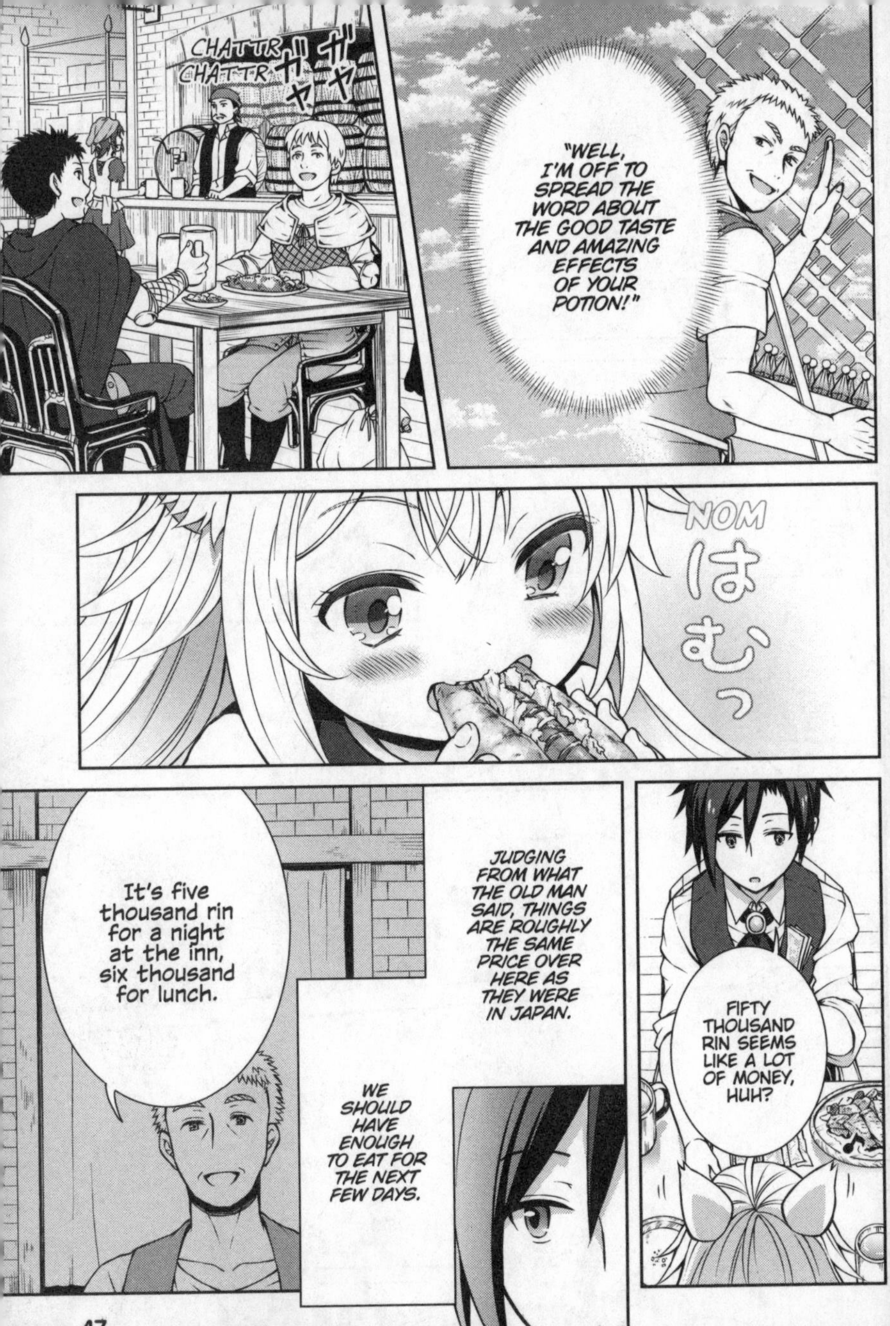
"WELL, I'M OFF TO SPREAD THE WORD ABOUT THE GOOD TASTE AND AMAZING EFFECTS OF YOUR POTION!"
CHATTR CHATTR
ガヤガヤ
NOM
はむっ
FIFTY THOUSAND RIN SEEMS LIKE A LOT OF MONEY, HUH?
It's five thousand rin for a night at the inn, six thousand for lunch.
JUDGING FROM WHAT THE OLD MAN SAID, THINGS ARE ROUGHLY THE SAME PRICE OVER HERE AS THEY WERE IN JAPAN.
WE SHOULD HAVE ENOUGH TO EAT FOR THE NEXT FEW DAYS.

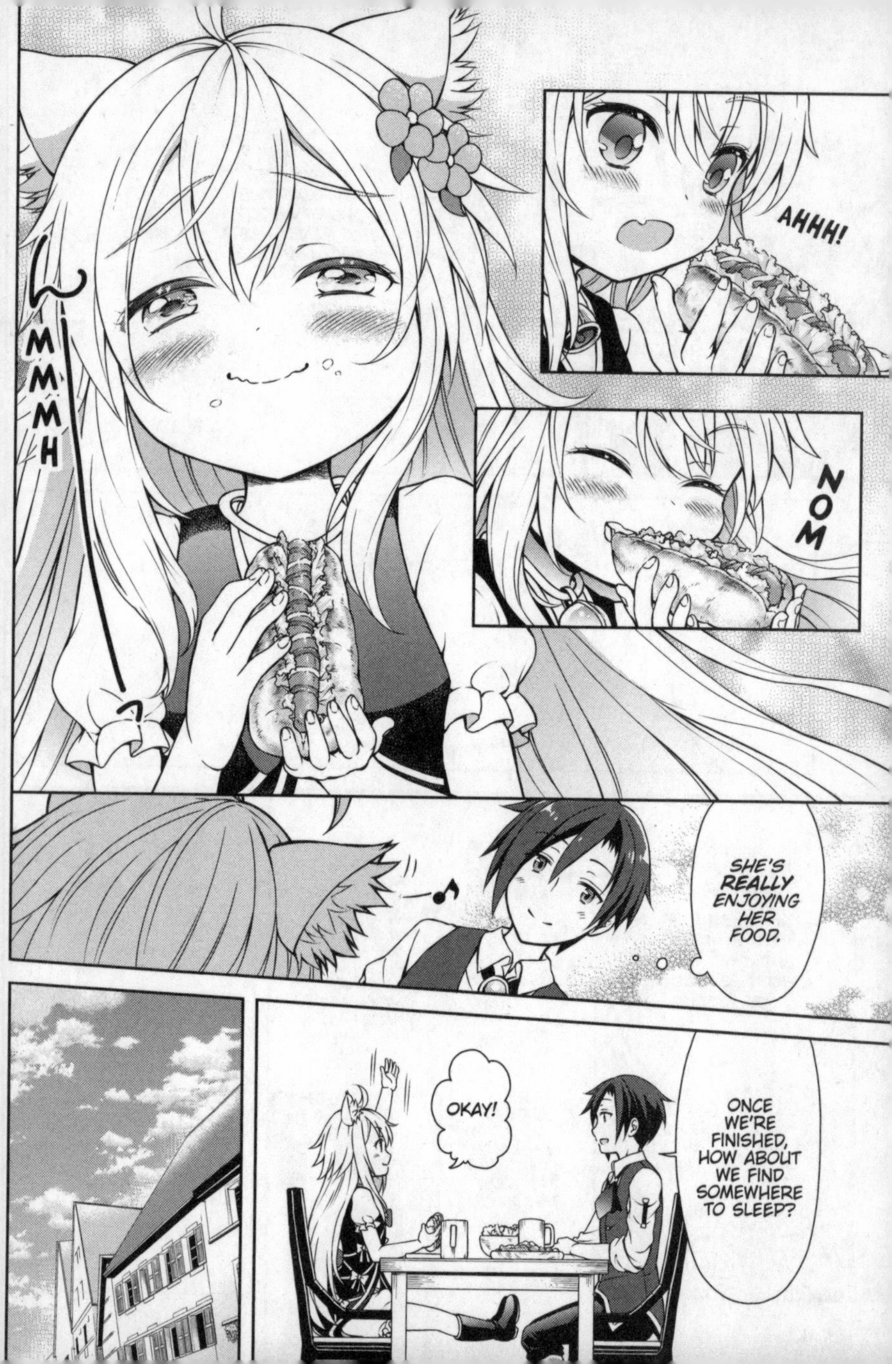
AHHH!
NOM
MMMMH
SHE'S REALLY ENJOYING HER FOOD.
ONCE WE'RE FINISHED, HOW ABOUT WE FIND SOMEWHERE TO SLEEP?
OKAY!

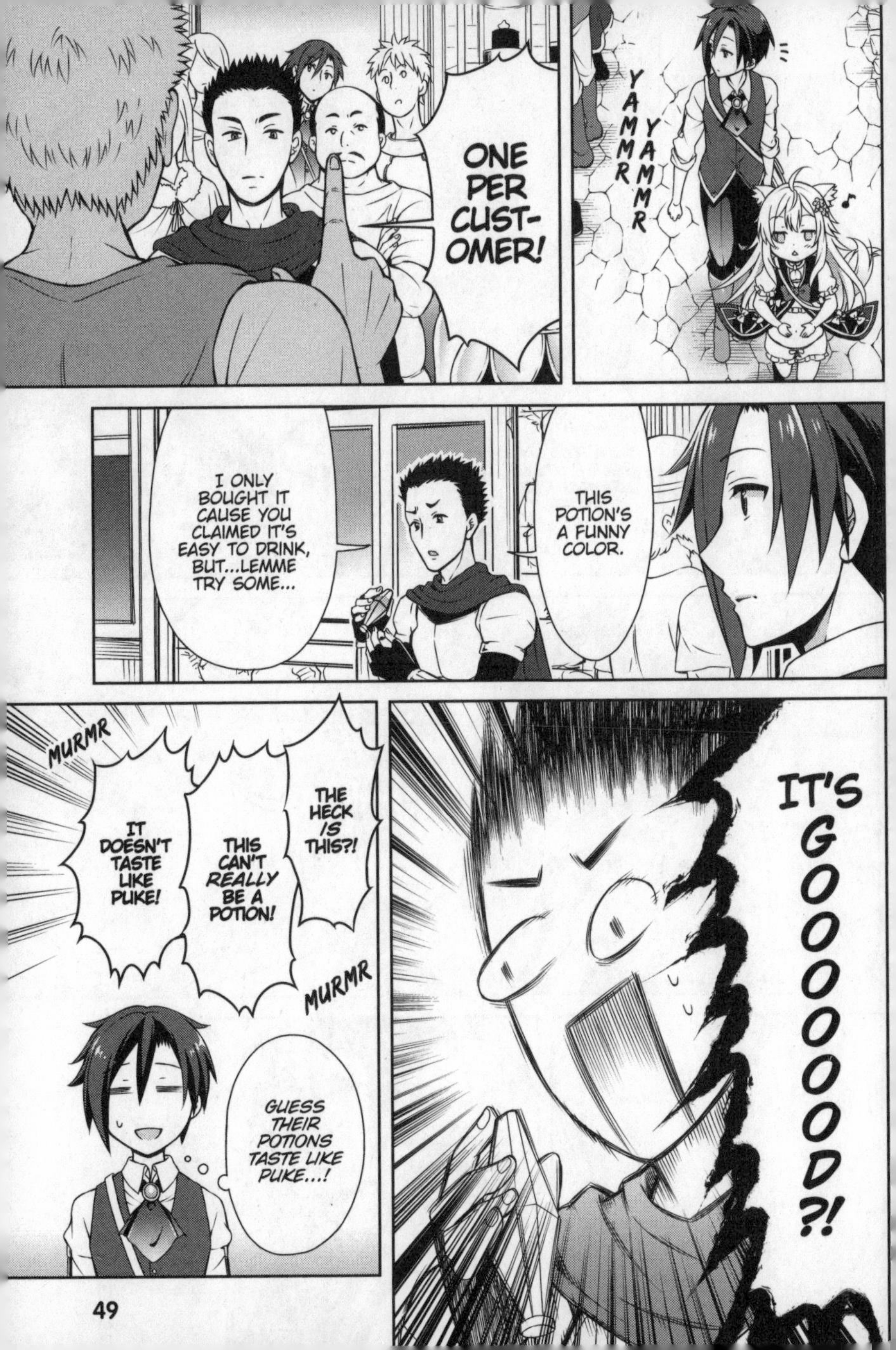

YAMMR YAMMR
ONE PER CUSTOMER!
THIS POTION'S A FUNNY COLOR.
I ONLY BOUGHT IT CAUSE YOU CLAIMED IT'S EASY TO DRINK, BUT...LEMME TRY SOME...
IT'S GOOOOOOOOD?!
THE HECK *IS* THIS?!
THIS CAN'T *REALLY* BE A POTION!
IT DOESN'T TASTE LIKE PUKE!
MURMR
MURMR
GUESS THEIR POTIONS TASTE LIKE PUKE...!

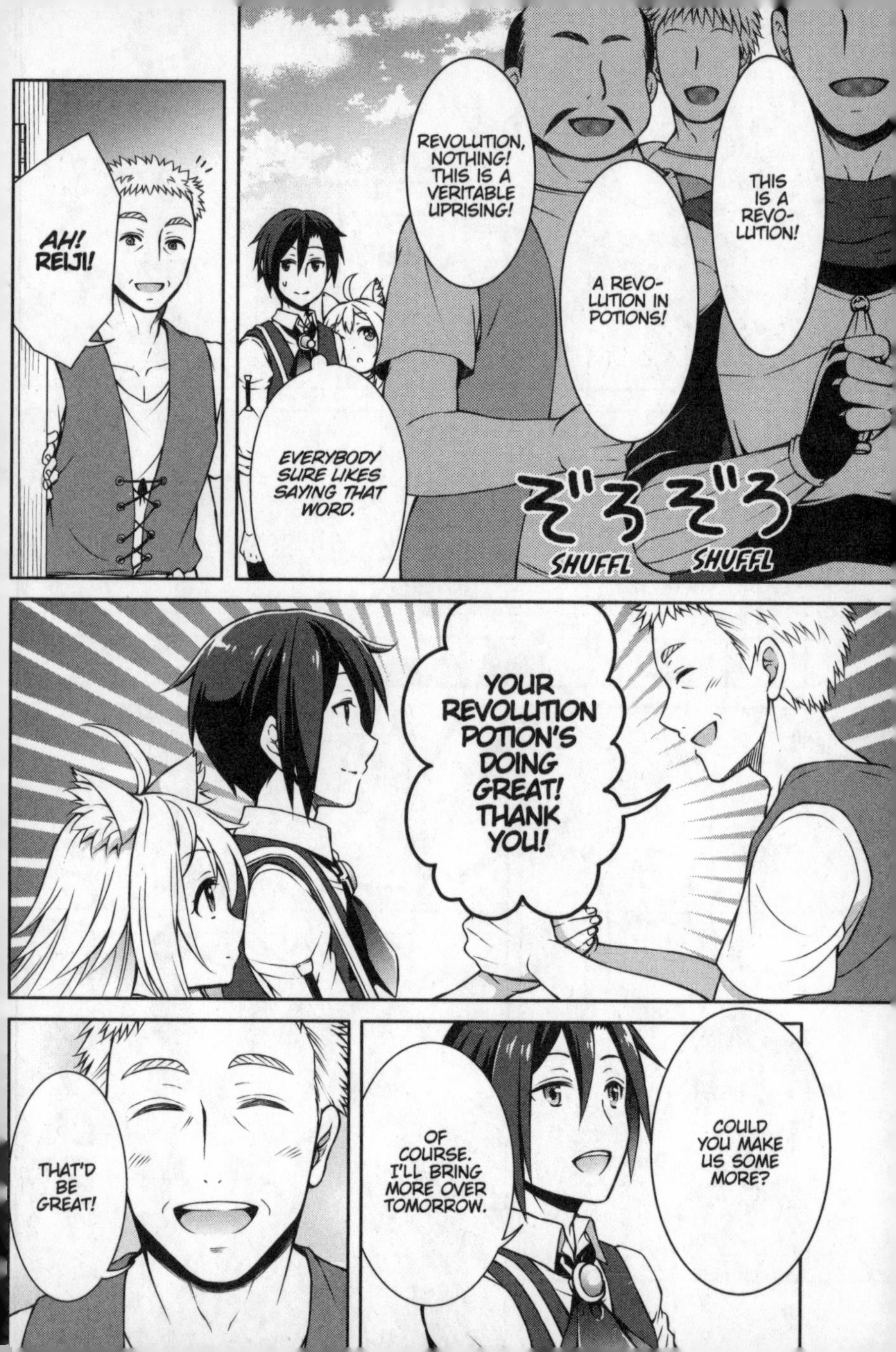
REVOLUTION, NOTHING! THIS IS A VERITABLE UPRISING!
THIS IS A REVO-LUTION!
A REVO-LUTION IN POTIONS!
ぞろぞろ
SHUFFL SHUFFL
EVERYBODY SURE LIKES SAYING THAT WORD.
AH! REIJI!
YOUR REVOLUTION POTION'S DOING GREAT! THANK YOU!
COULD YOU MAKE US SOME MORE?
OF COURSE. I'LL BRING MORE OVER TOMORROW.
THAT'D BE GREAT!

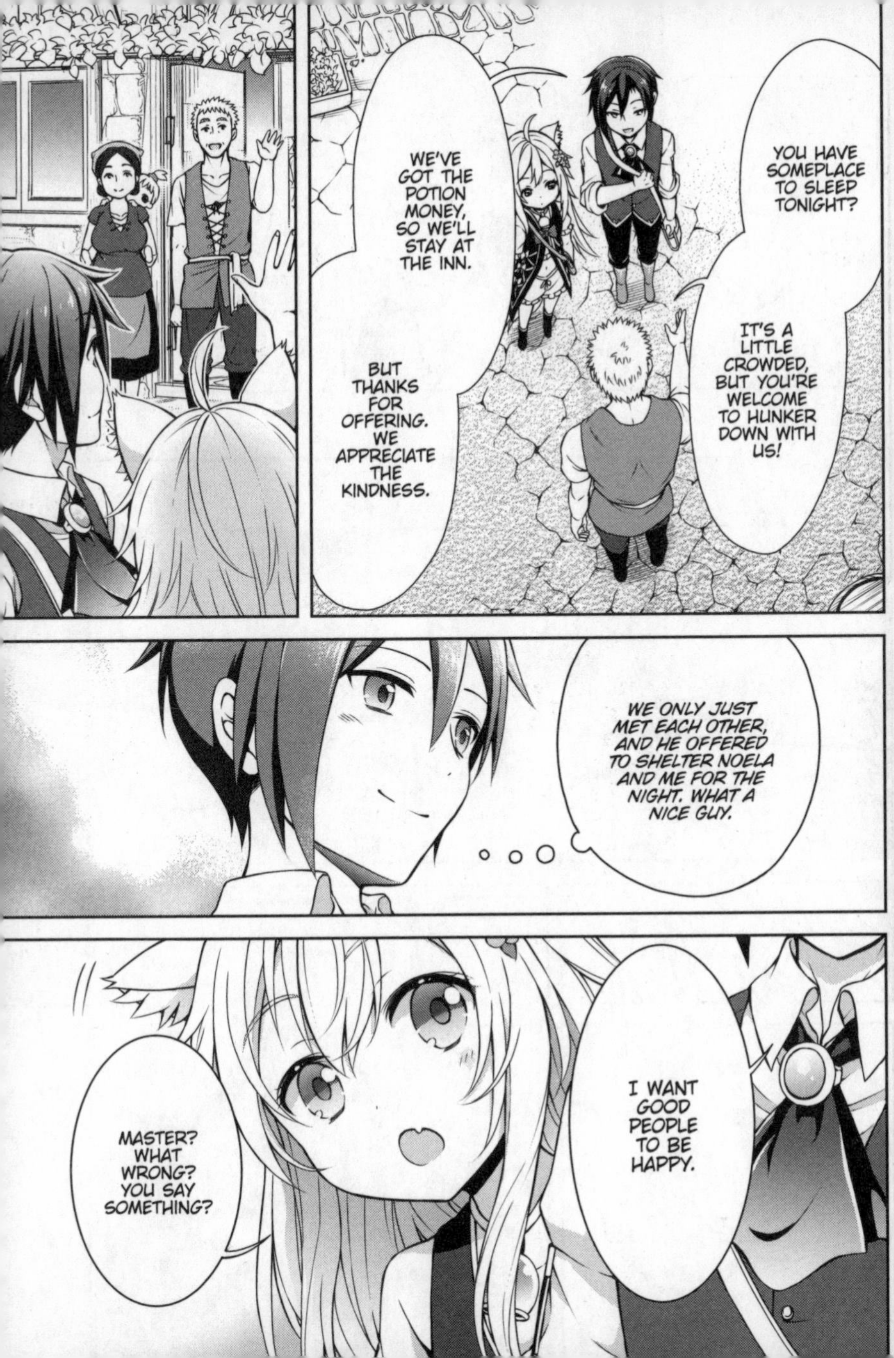
YOU HAVE SOMEPLACE TO SLEEP TONIGHT?
IT'S A LITTLE CROWDED, BUT YOU'RE WELCOME TO HUNKER DOWN WITH US!
WE'VE GOT THE POTION MONEY, SO WE'LL STAY AT THE INN.
BUT THANKS FOR OFFERING. WE APPRECIATE THE KINDNESS.
WE ONLY JUST MET EACH OTHER, AND HE OFFERED TO SHELTER NOELA AND ME FOR THE NIGHT. WHAT A NICE GUY.
I WANT GOOD PEOPLE TO BE HAPPY.
MASTER? WHAT WRONG? YOU SAY SOMETHING?

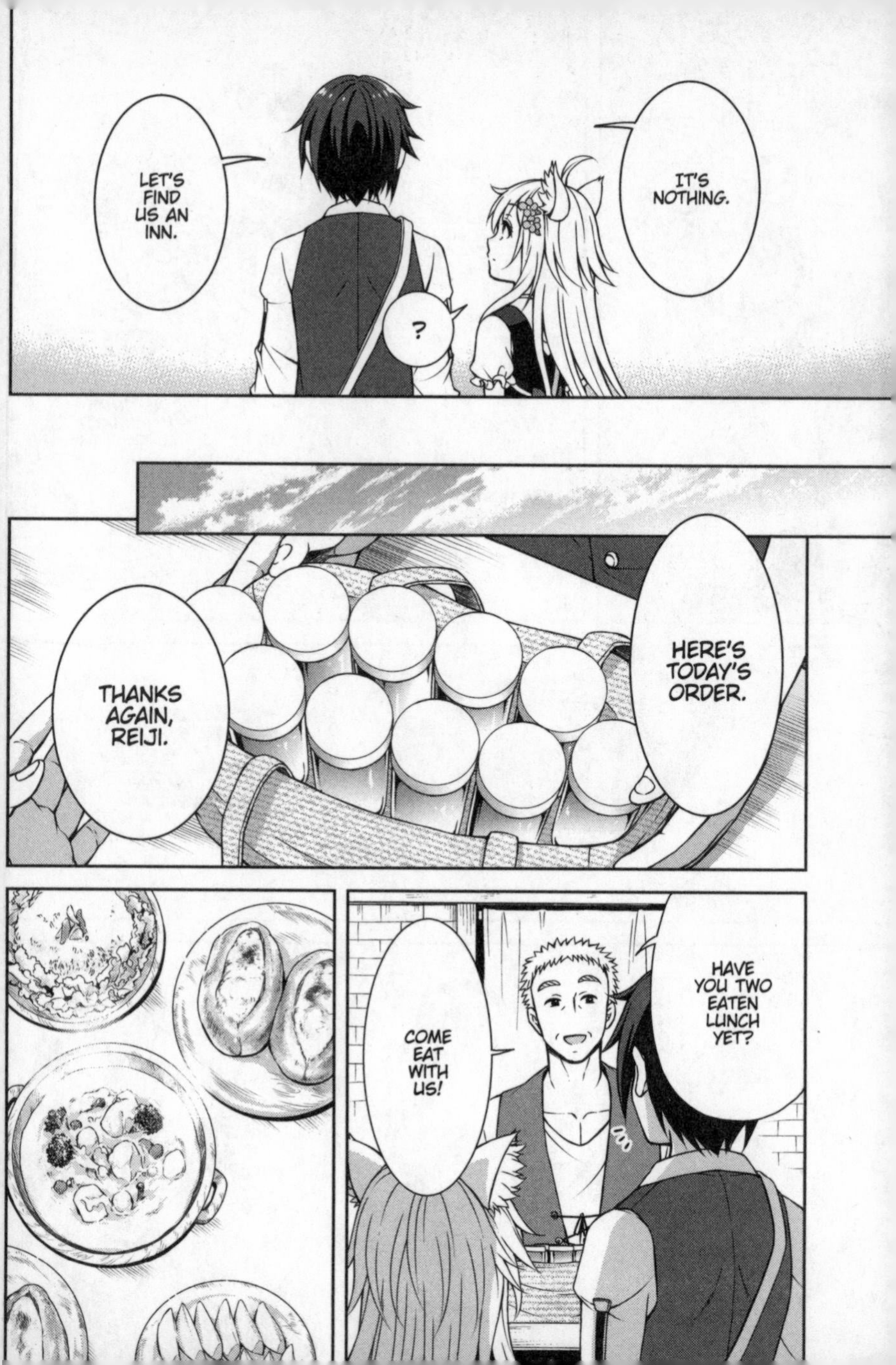
IT'S NOTHING.
?
LET'S FIND US AN INN.
HERE'S TODAY'S ORDER.
THANKS AGAIN, REIJI.
HAVE YOU TWO EATEN LUNCH YET?
COME EAT WITH US!

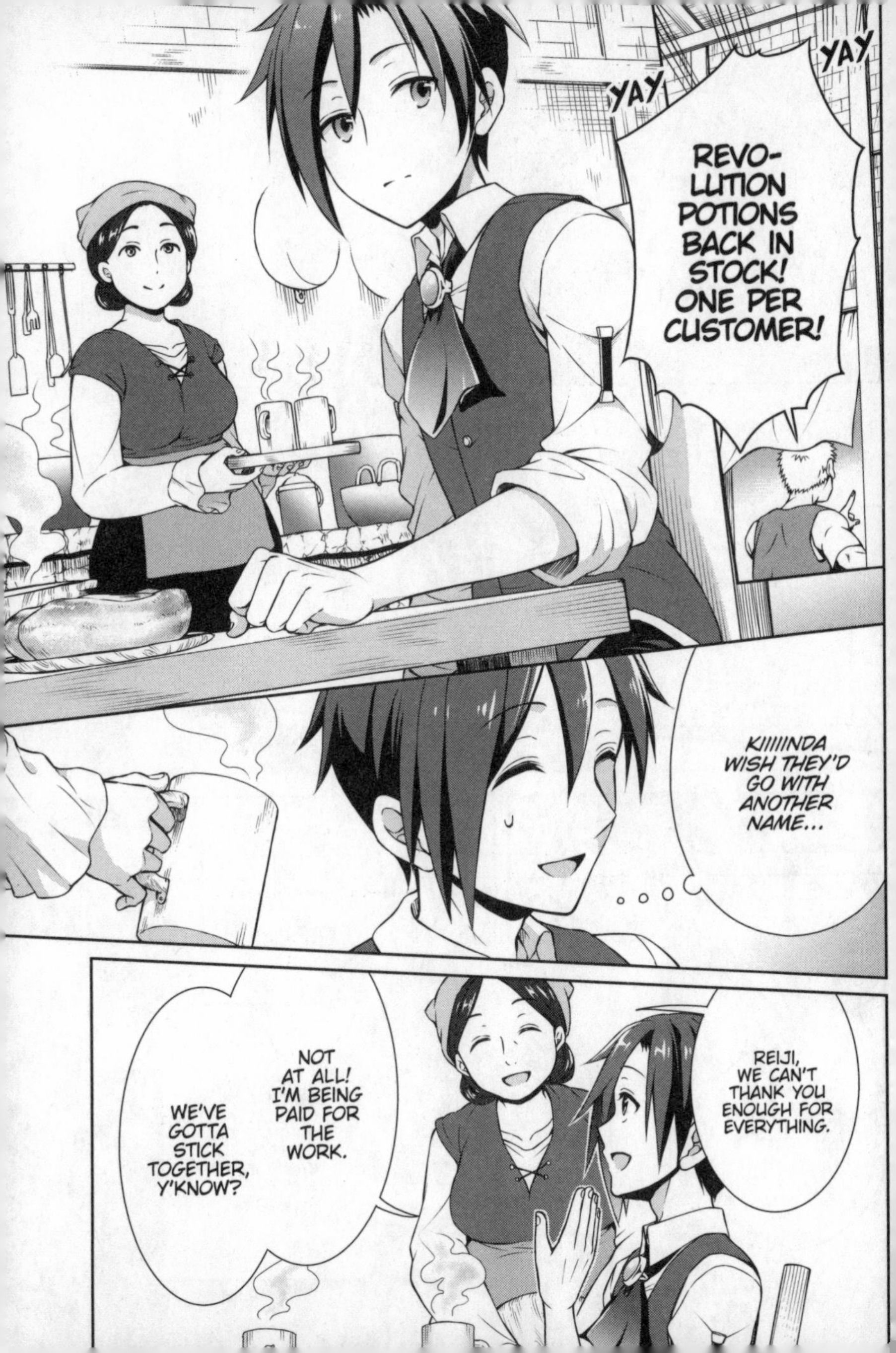
YAY
YAY
REVO-LUTION POTIONS BACK IN STOCK! ONE PER CUSTOMER!
KIIIIINDA WISH THEY'D GO WITH ANOTHER NAME...
REIJI, WE CAN'T THANK YOU ENOUGH FOR EVERYTHING.
NOT AT ALL! I'M BEING PAID FOR THE WORK.
WE'VE GOTTA STICK TOGETHER, Y'KNOW?

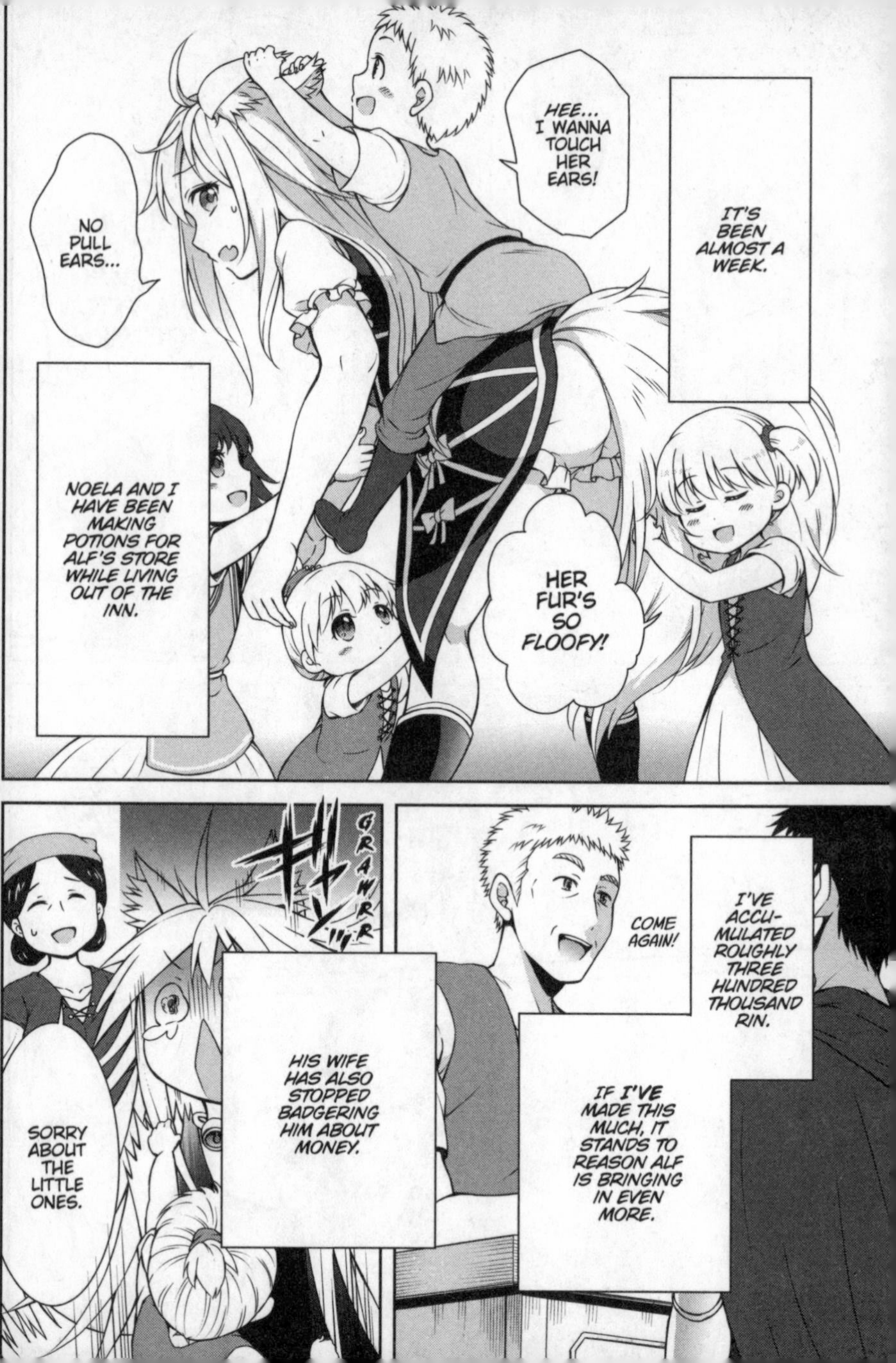
IT'S BEEN ALMOST A WEEK.
HEE... I WANNA TOUCH HER EARS!
NO PULL EARS...
NOELA AND I HAVE BEEN MAKING POTIONS FOR ALF'S STORE WHILE LIVING OUT OF THE INN.
HER FUR'S SO FLOOFY!
I'VE ACCU-MULATED ROUGHLY THREE HUNDRED THOUSAND RIN.
COME AGAIN!
IF I'VE MADE THIS MUCH, IT STANDS TO REASON ALF IS BRINGING IN EVEN MORE.
GRAWRR
HIS WIFE HAS ALSO STOPPED BADGERING HIM ABOUT MONEY.
SORRY ABOUT THE LITTLE ONES.

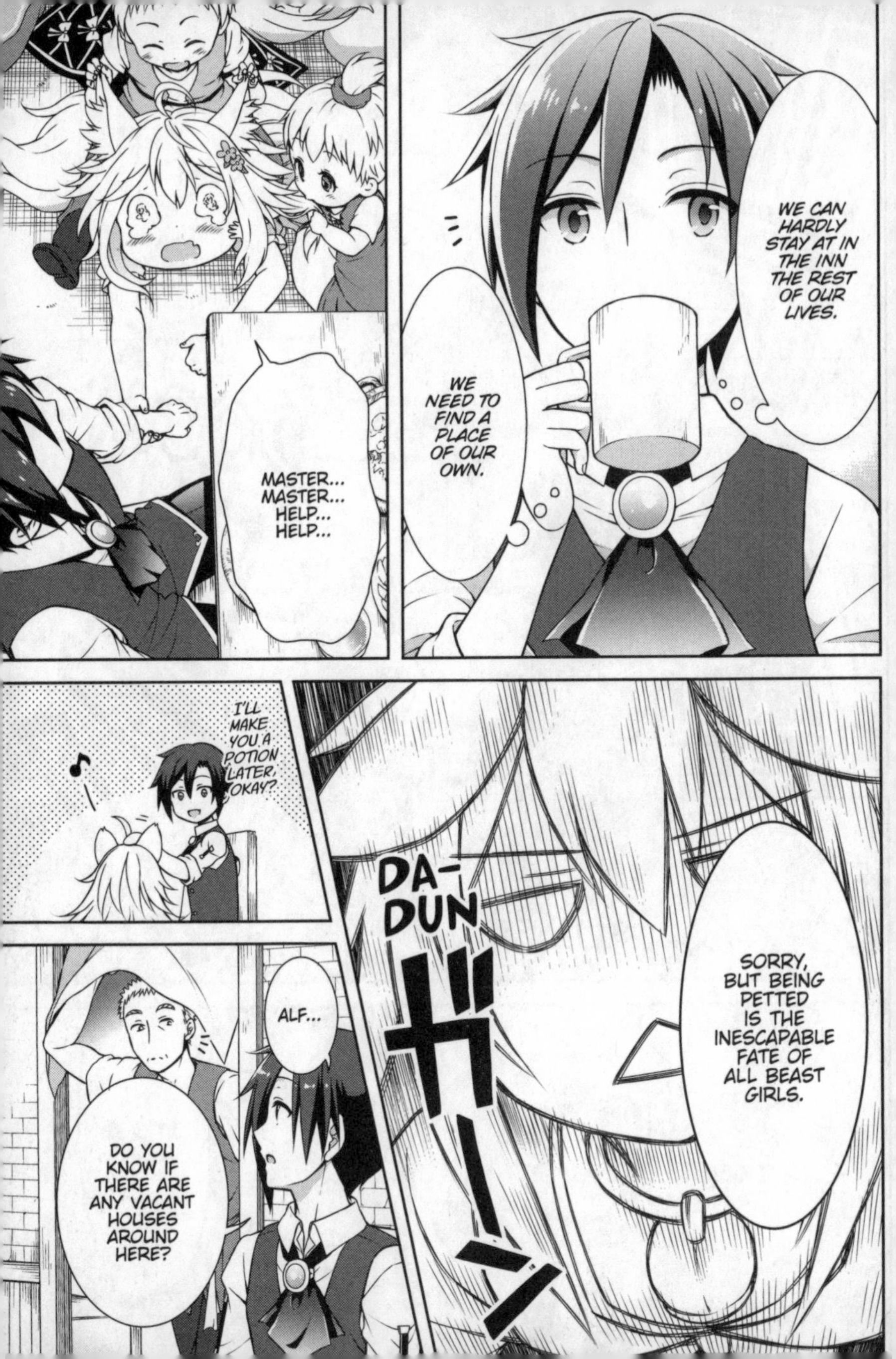
WE CAN HARDLY STAY AT IN THE INN THE REST OF OUR LIVES.
WE NEED TO FIND A PLACE OF OUR OWN.
MASTER... MASTER... HELP... HELP...
DA-DUN
SORRY, BUT BEING PETTED IS THE INESCAPABLE FATE OF ALL BEAST GIRLS.
I'LL MAKE YOU A POTION LATER, OKAY?
ALF...
DO YOU KNOW IF THERE ARE ANY VACANT HOUSES AROUND HERE?

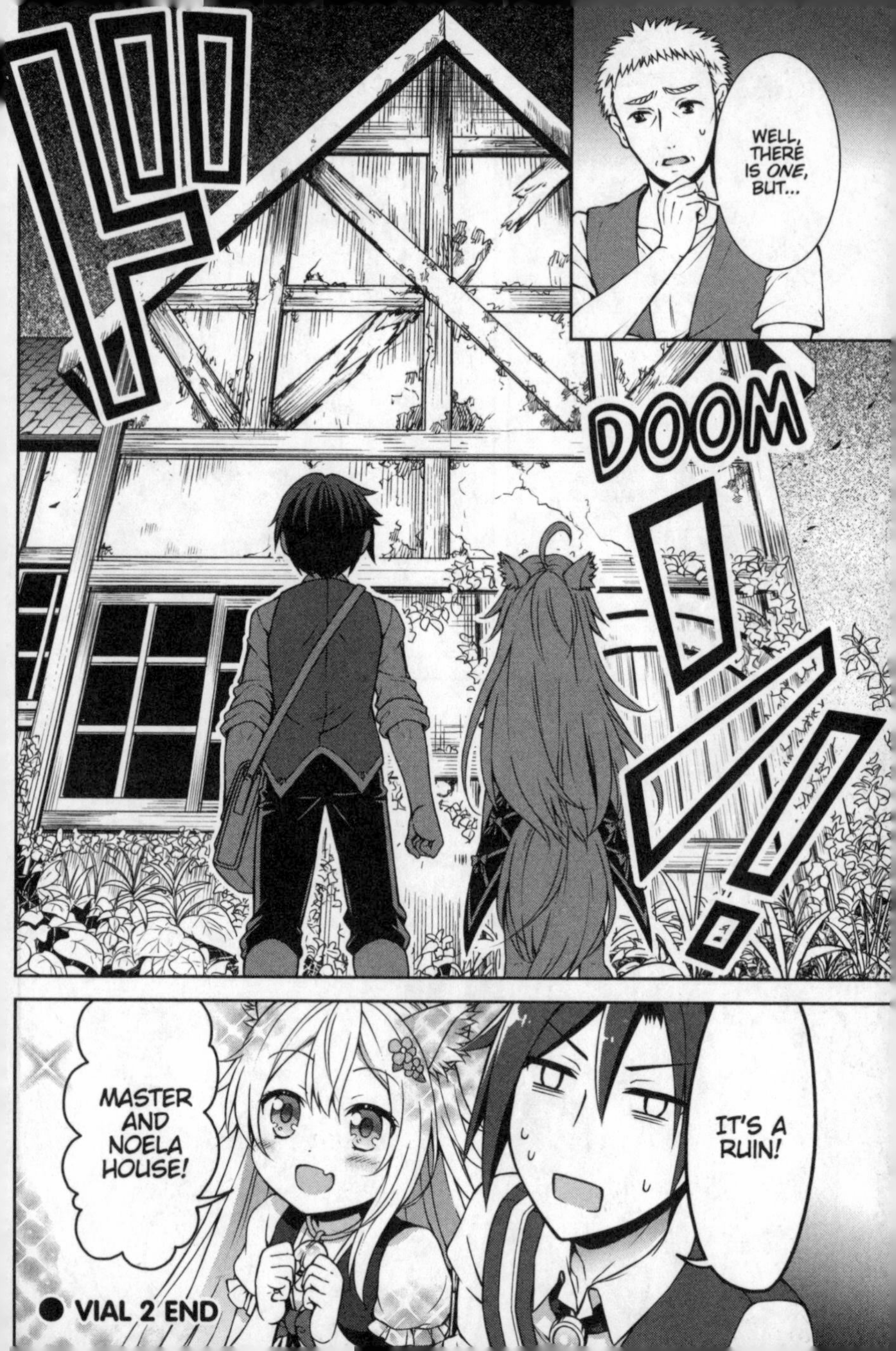
WELL, THERE IS ONE, BUT...
DOOM
IT'S A RUIN!
MASTER AND NOELA HOUSE!
VIAL 2 END

VIAL 3 Sold "As Is"?!

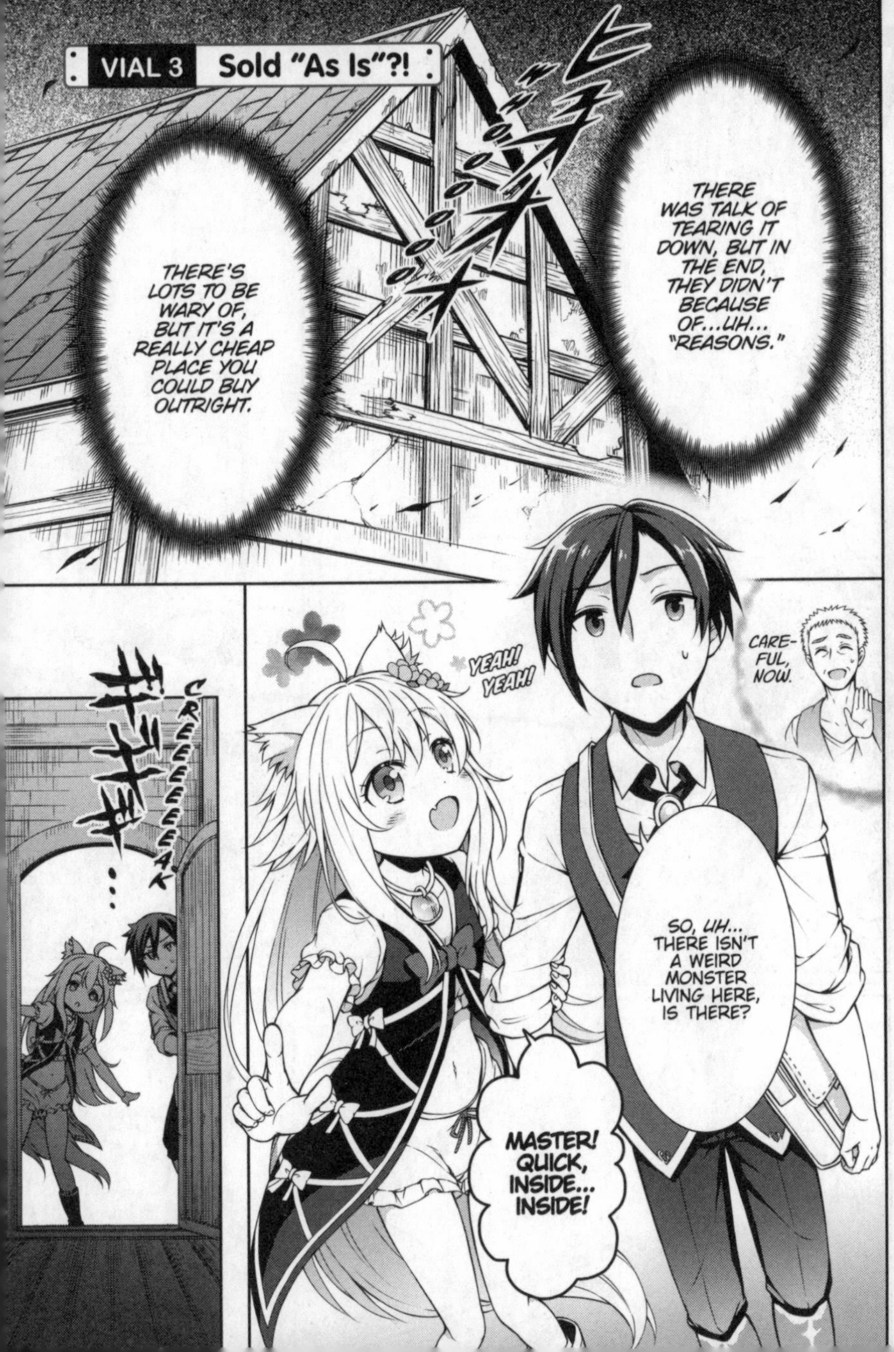
THERE WAS TALK OF TEARING IT DOWN, BUT IN THE END, THEY DIDN'T BECAUSE OF...UH... "REASONS."
THERE'S LOTS TO BE WARY OF, BUT IT'S A REALLY CHEAP PLACE YOU COULD BUY OUTRIGHT.
CARE-FUL, NOW.
YEAH! YEAH!
SO, UH... THERE ISN'T A WEIRD MONSTER LIVING HERE, IS THERE?
MASTER! QUICK, INSIDE... INSIDE!
CREEEEEEEAK
...

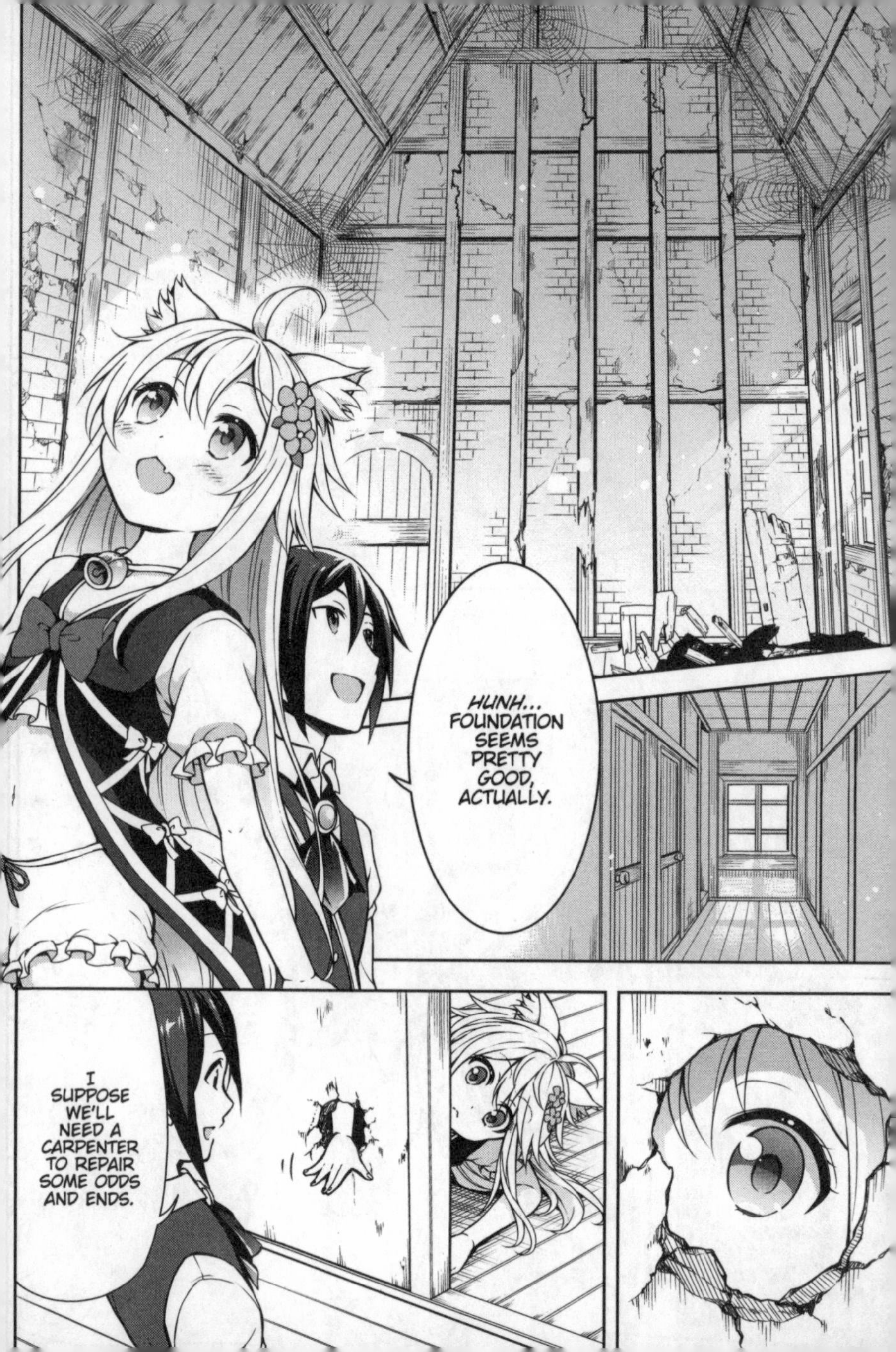
HUNH... FOUNDATION SEEMS PRETTY GOOD, ACTUALLY.
I SUPPOSE WE'LL NEED A CARPENTER TO REPAIR SOME ODDS AND ENDS.

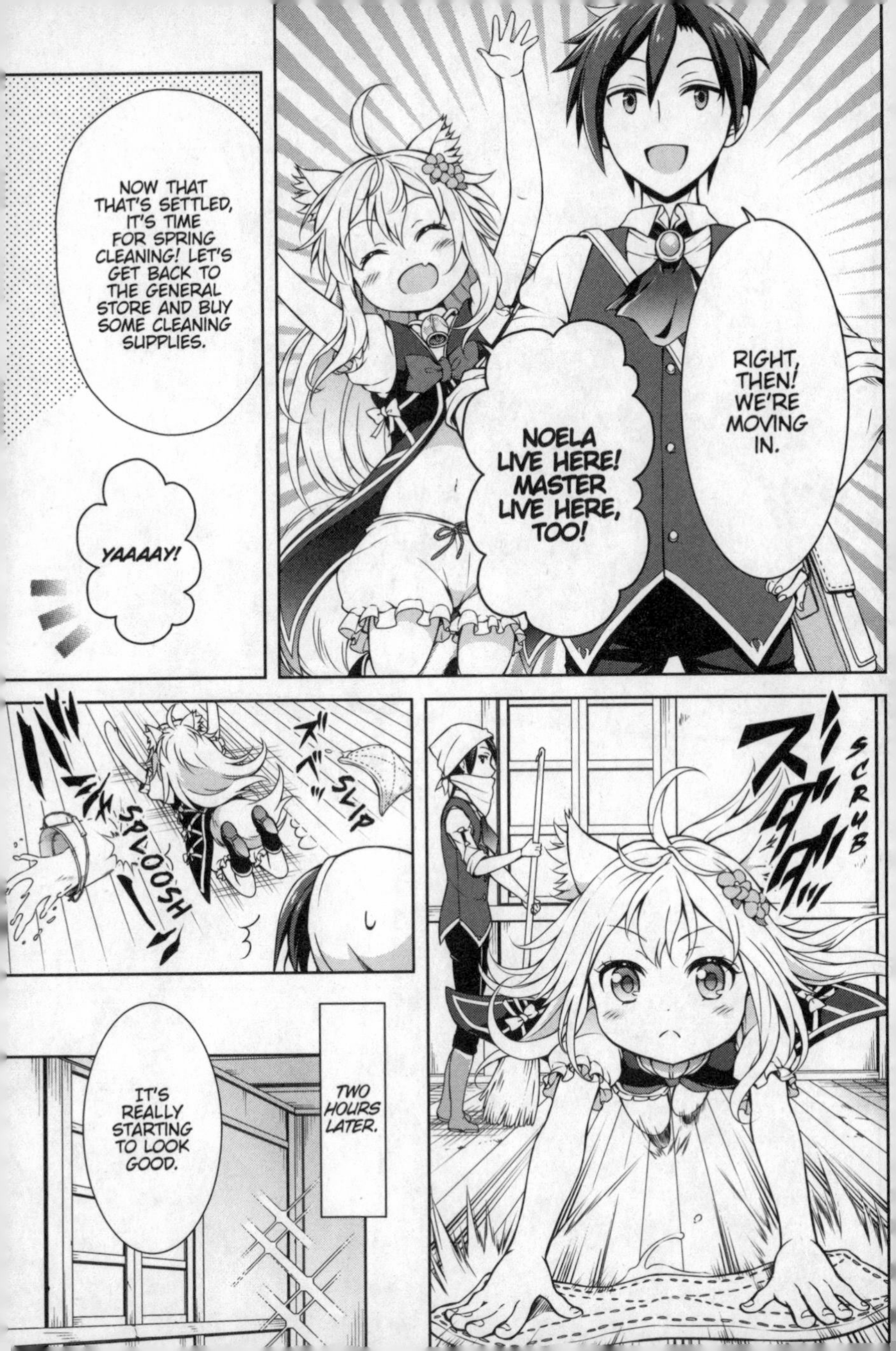
RIGHT, THEN! WE'RE MOVING IN.
NOELA LIVE HERE! MASTER LIVE HERE, TOO!
NOW THAT THAT'S SETTLED, IT'S TIME FOR SPRING CLEANING! LET'S GET BACK TO THE GENERAL STORE AND BUY SOME CLEANING SUPPLIES.
YAAAAY!
SCRUB
SLIP
SPLOOSH
TWO HOURS LATER.
IT'S REALLY STARTING TO LOOK GOOD.

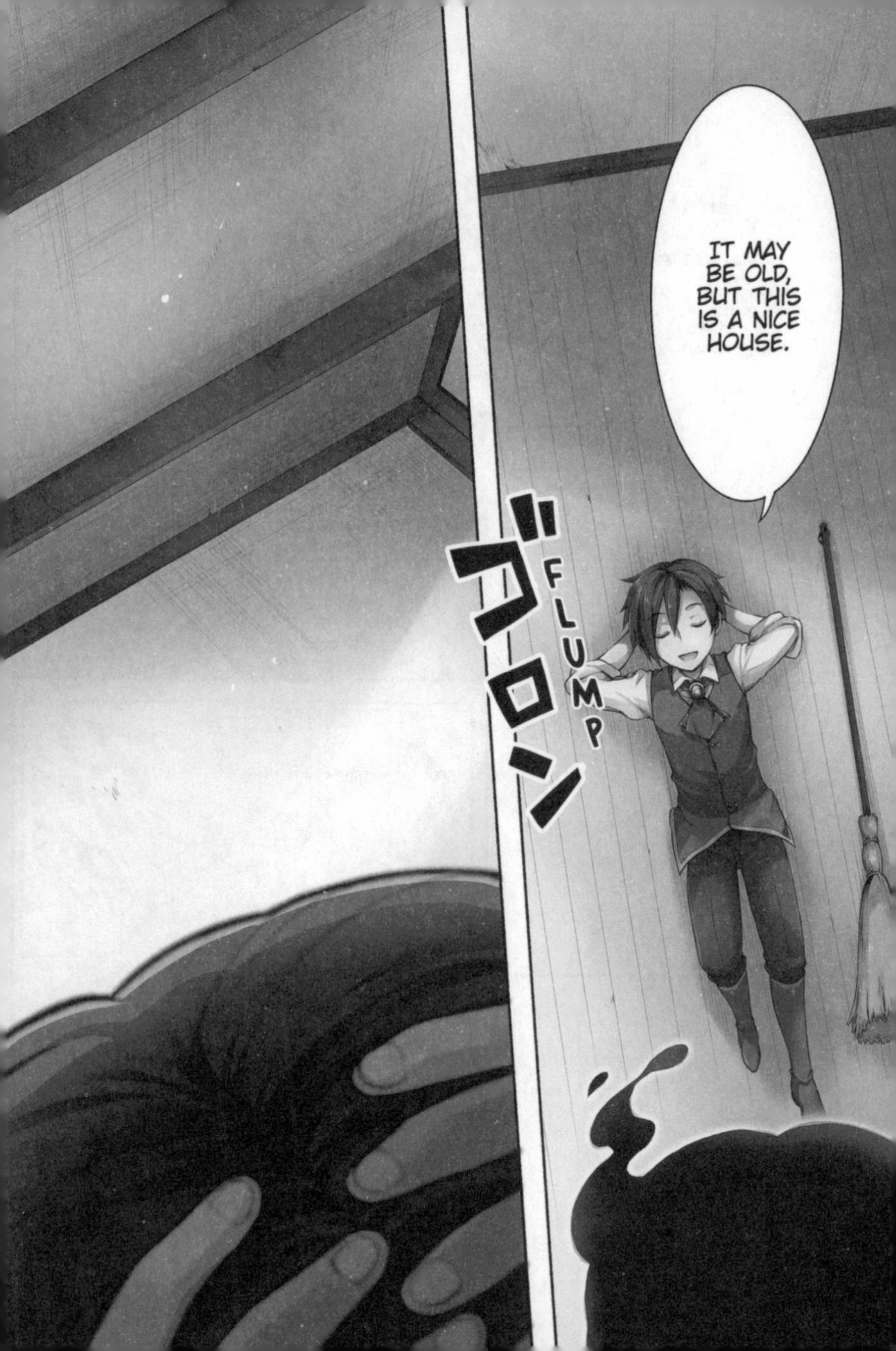
IT MAY BE OLD, BUT THIS IS A NICE HOUSE.
ゴロン
FLUMP

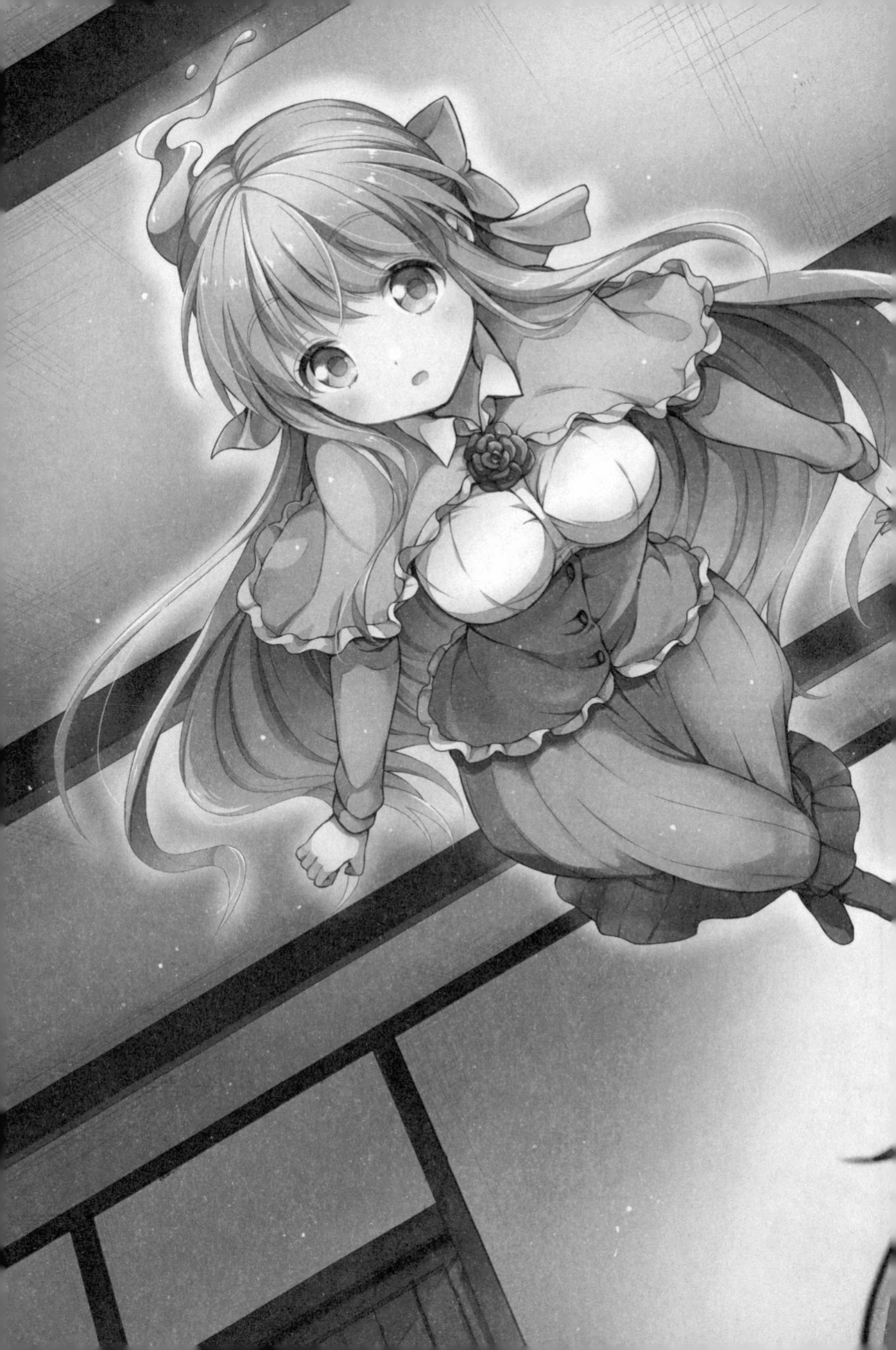

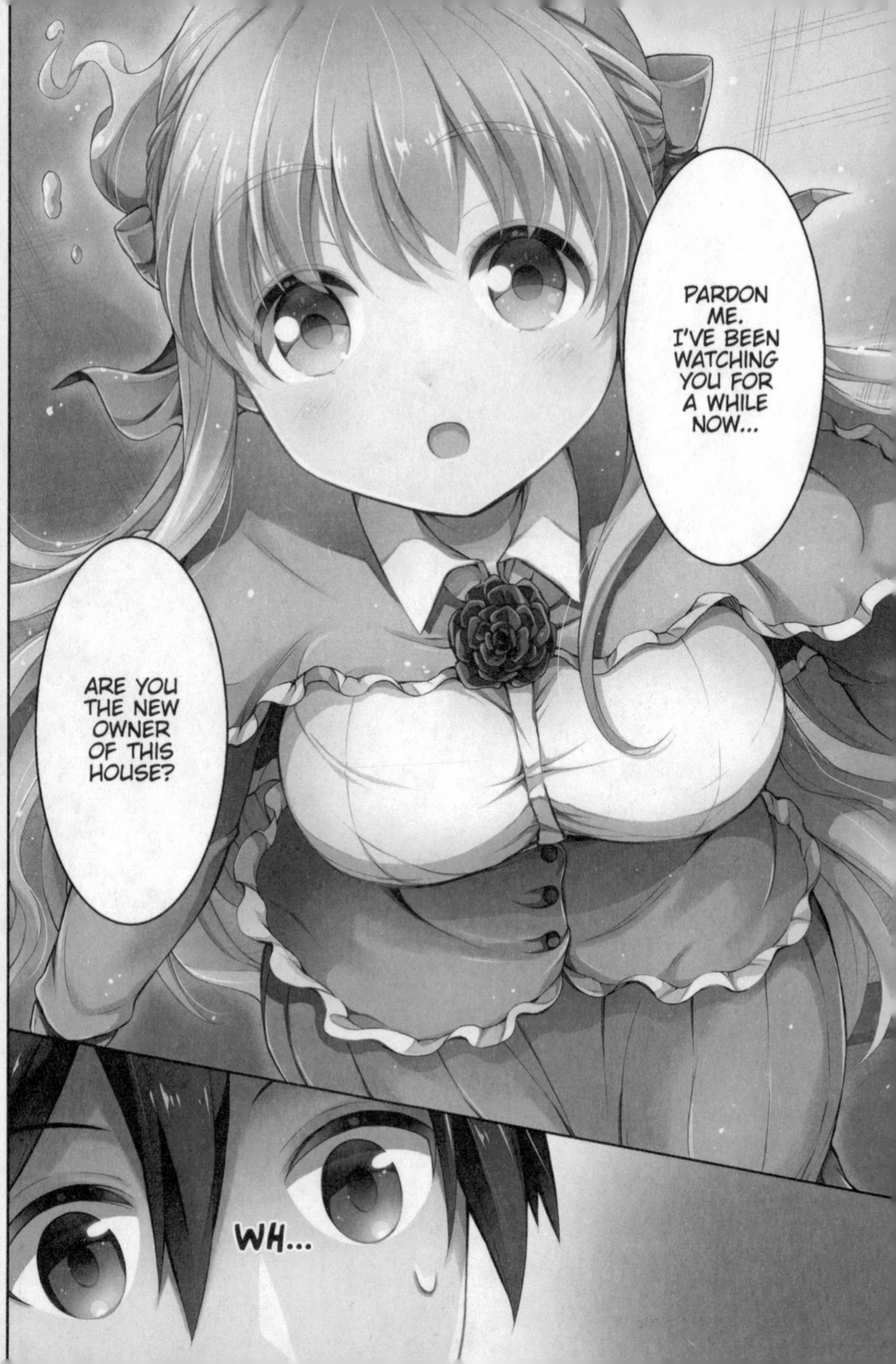
PARDON ME. I'VE BEEN WATCHING YOU FOR A WHILE NOW...
ARE YOU THE NEW OWNER OF THIS HOUSE?
WH...

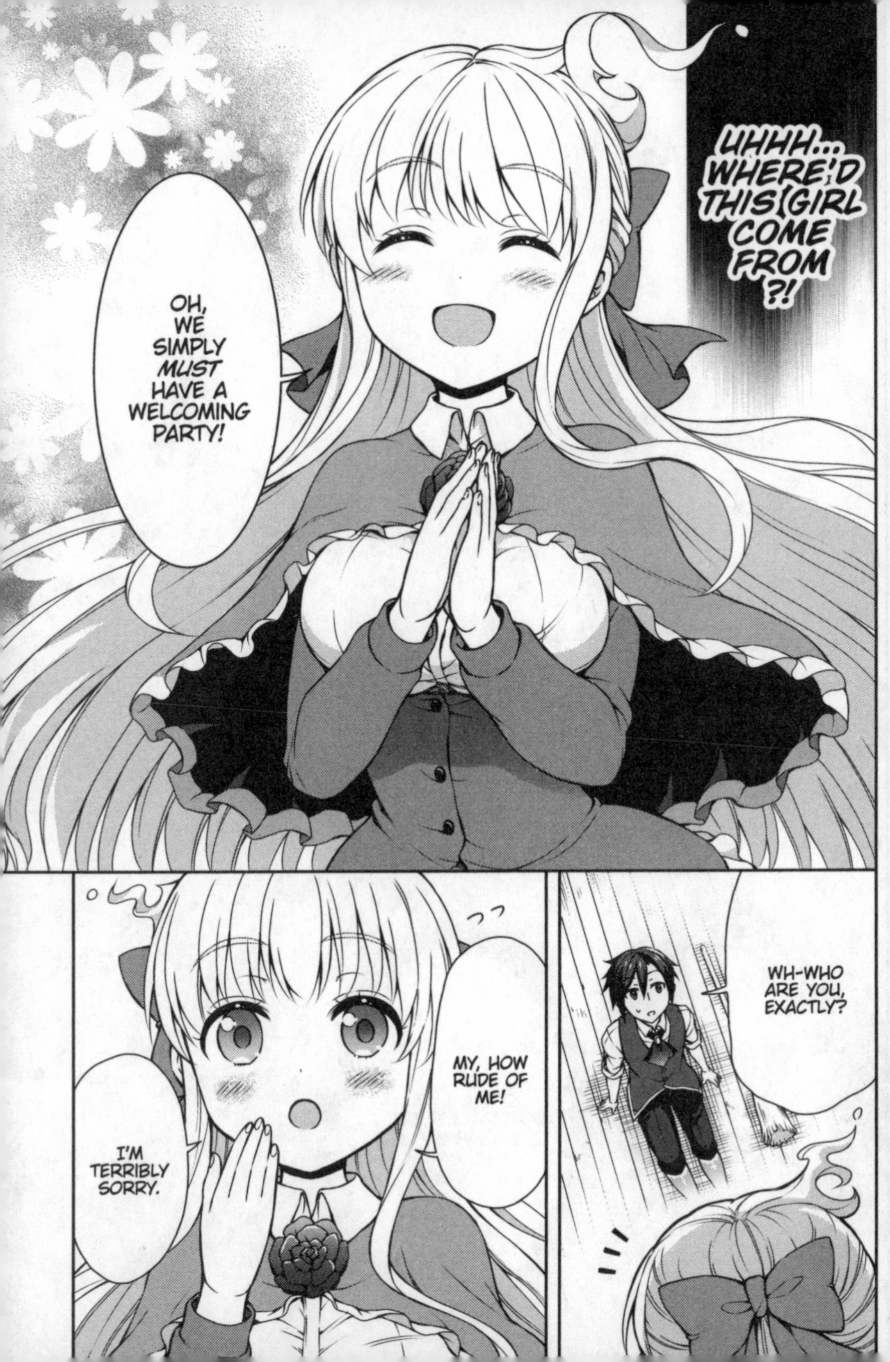
UHHH... WHERE'D THIS GIRL COME FROM?!
OH, WE SIMPLY MUST HAVE A WELCOMING PARTY!
WH-WHO ARE YOU, EXACTLY?
MY, HOW RUDE OF ME!
I'M TERRIBLY SORRY.

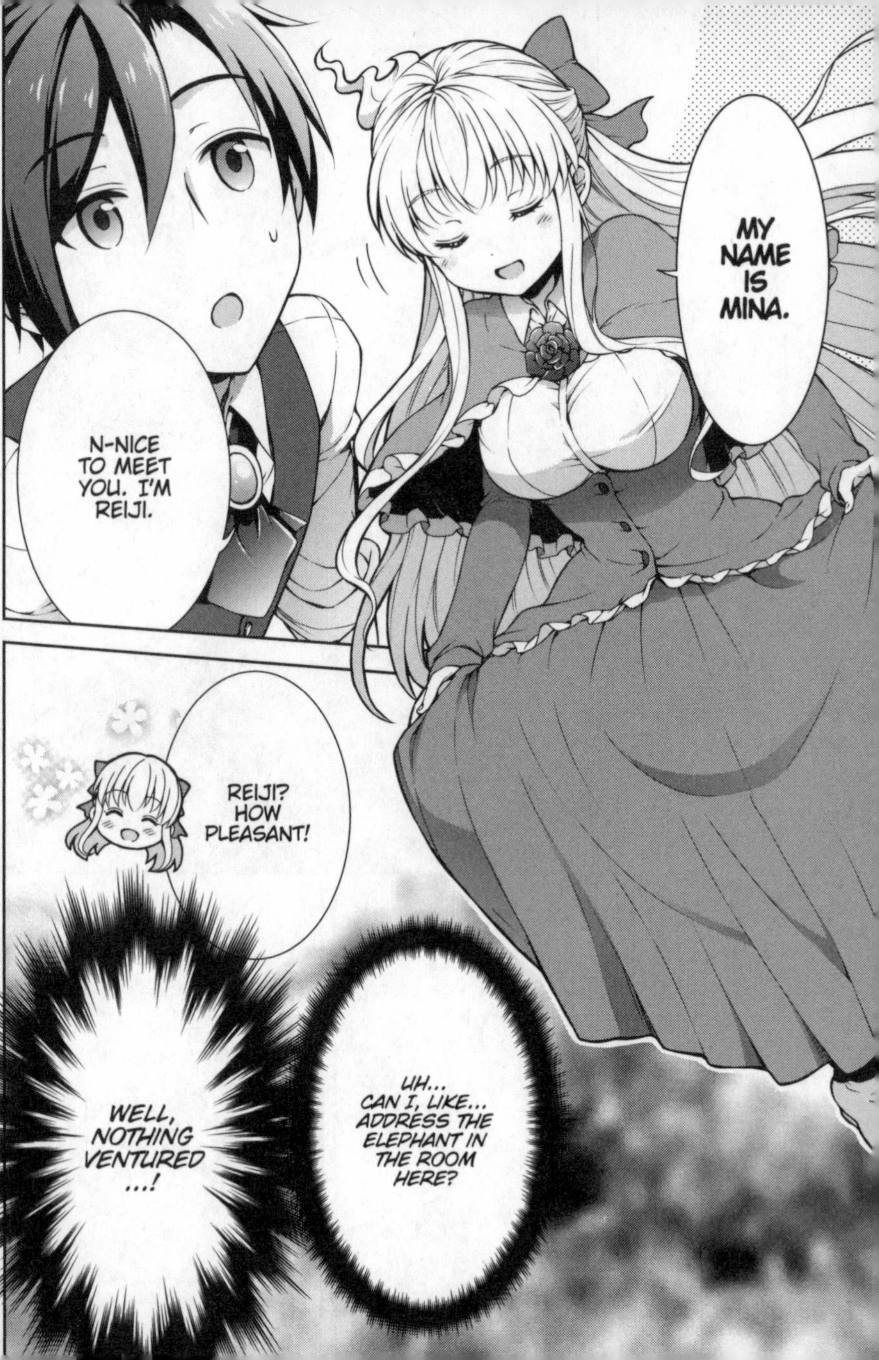
MY NAME IS MINA.
N-NICE TO MEET YOU. I'M REIJI.
REIJI? HOW PLEASANT!
UH... CAN I, LIKE... ADDRESS THE ELEPHANT IN THE ROOM HERE?
WELL, NOTHING VENTURED ...!

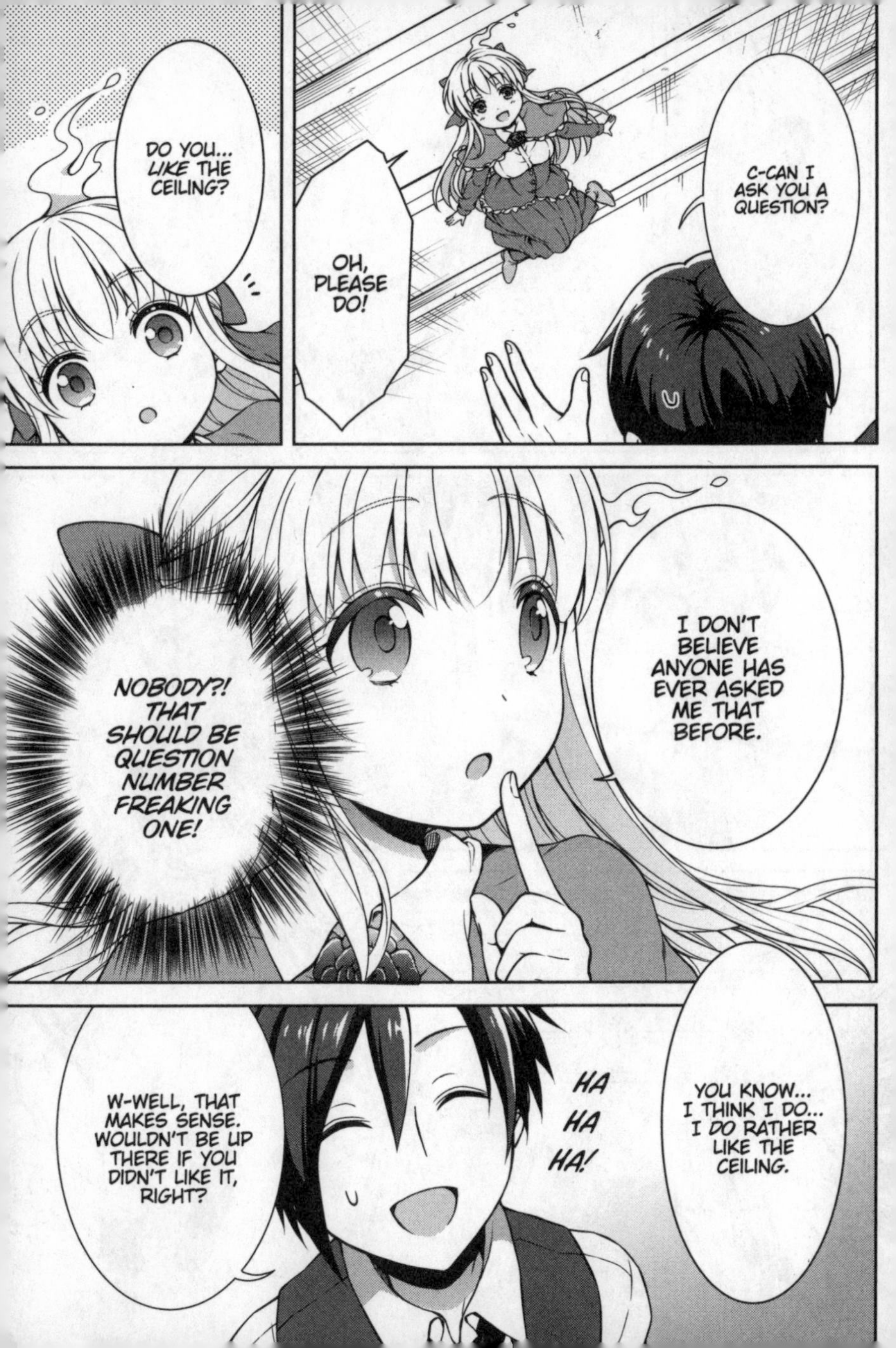
C-CAN I ASK YOU A QUESTION?
OH, PLEASE DO!
DO YOU... LIKE THE CEILING?
I DON'T BELIEVE ANYONE HAS EVER ASKED ME THAT BEFORE.
NOBODY?! THAT SHOULD BE QUESTION NUMBER FREAKING ONE!
YOU KNOW... I THINK I DO... I DO RATHER LIKE THE CEILING.
HA HA HA!
W-WELL, THAT MAKES SENSE. WOULDN'T BE UP THERE IF YOU DIDN'T LIKE IT, RIGHT?

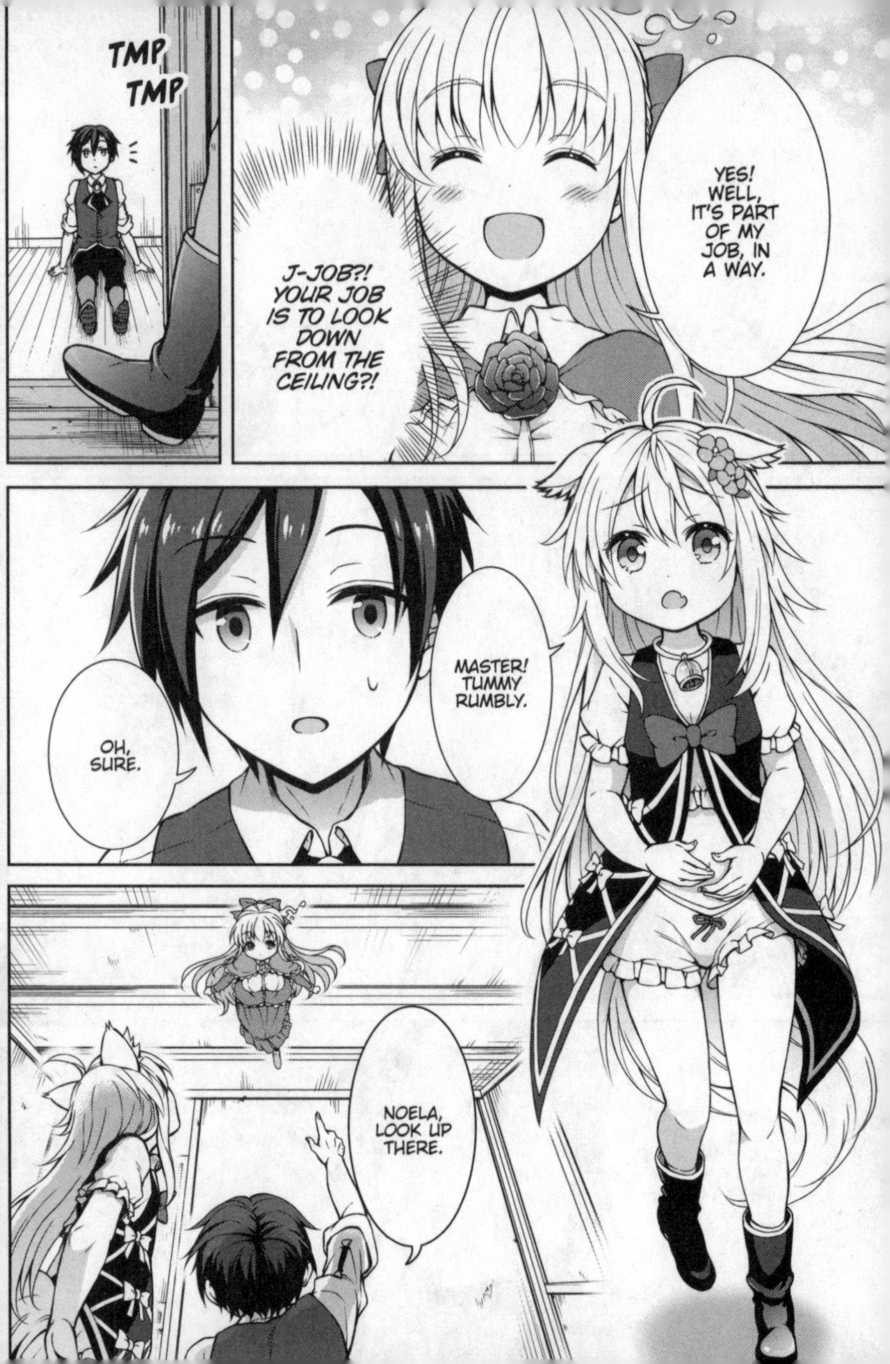
YES! WELL, IT'S PART OF MY JOB, IN A WAY.
J-JOB?! YOUR JOB IS TO LOOK DOWN FROM THE CEILING?!
TMP TMP
MASTER! TUMMY RUMBLY.
OH, SURE.
NOELA, LOOK UP THERE.

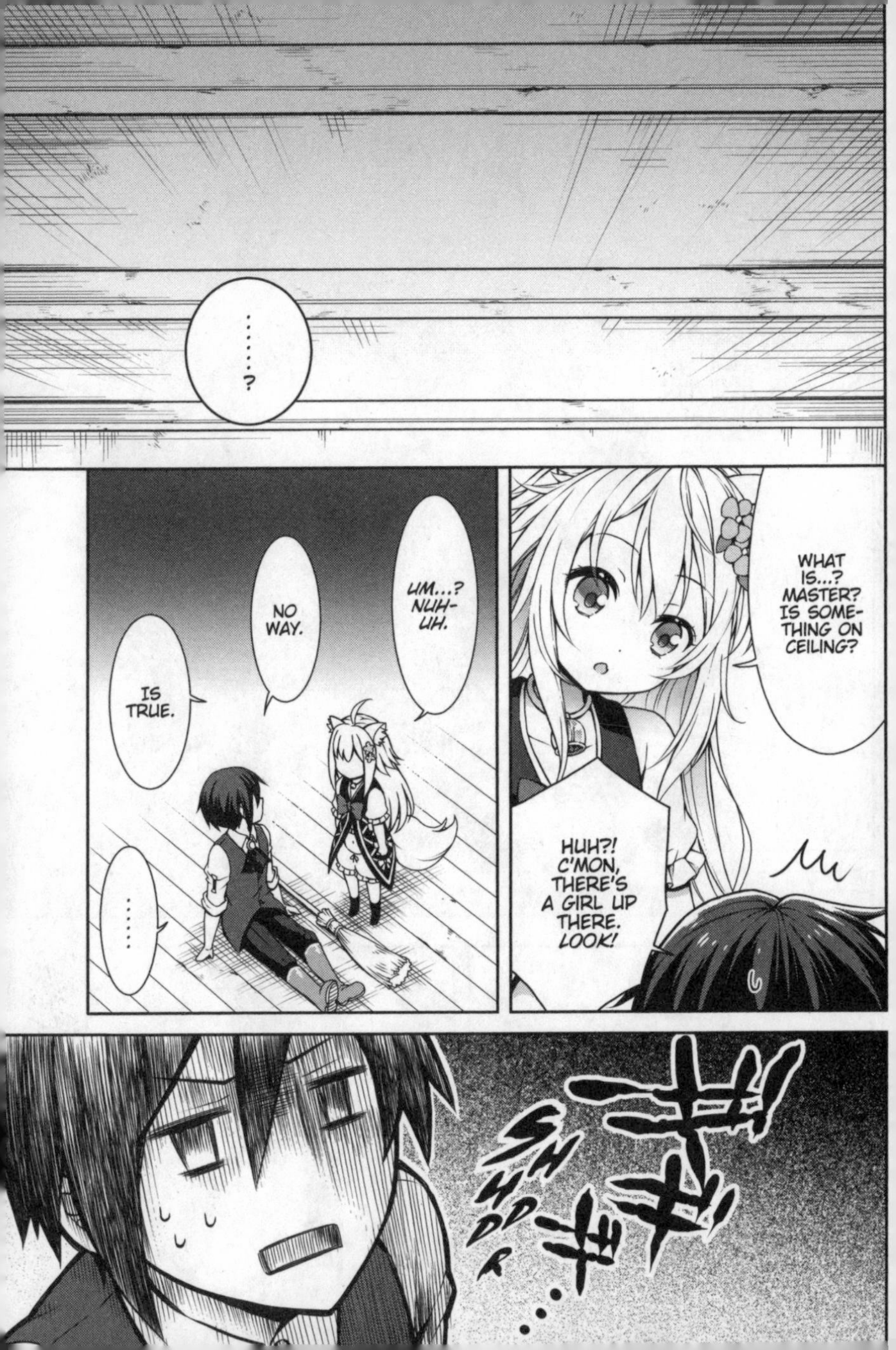
......?
WHAT IS...? MASTER? IS SOMETHING ON CEILING?
HUH?! C'MON, THERE'S A GIRL UP THERE. LOOK!
UM...? NUH-UH.
NO WAY.
IS TRUE.
......
SHUDDR...

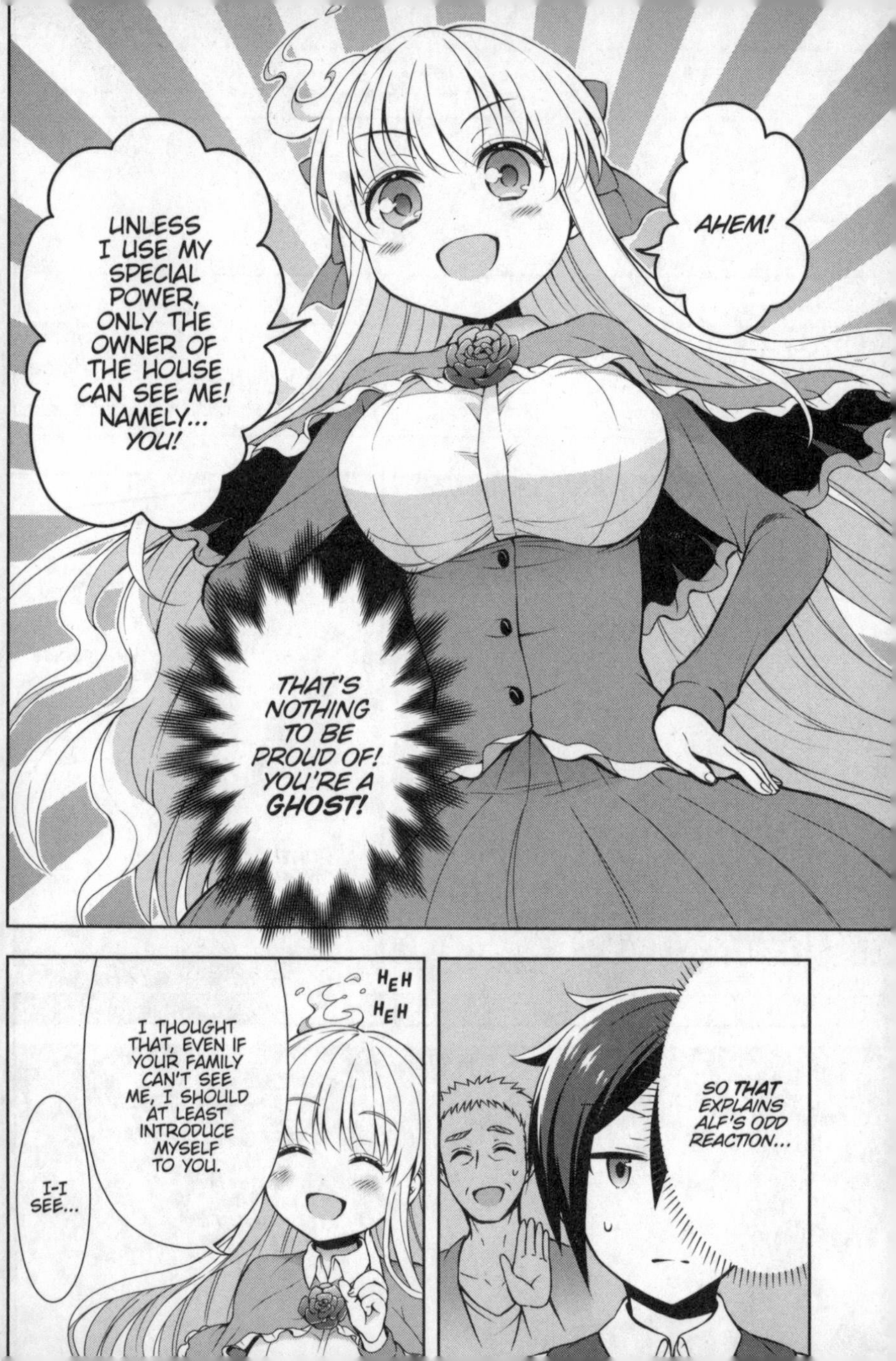
AHEM!
UNLESS I USE MY SPECIAL POWER, ONLY THE OWNER OF THE HOUSE CAN SEE ME! NAMELY... YOU!
THAT'S NOTHING TO BE PROUD OF! YOU'RE A GHOST!
SO THAT EXPLAINS ALF'S ODD REACTION...
HEH HEH
I THOUGHT THAT, EVEN IF YOUR FAMILY CAN'T SEE ME, I SHOULD AT LEAST INTRODUCE MYSELF TO YOU.
I-I SEE...

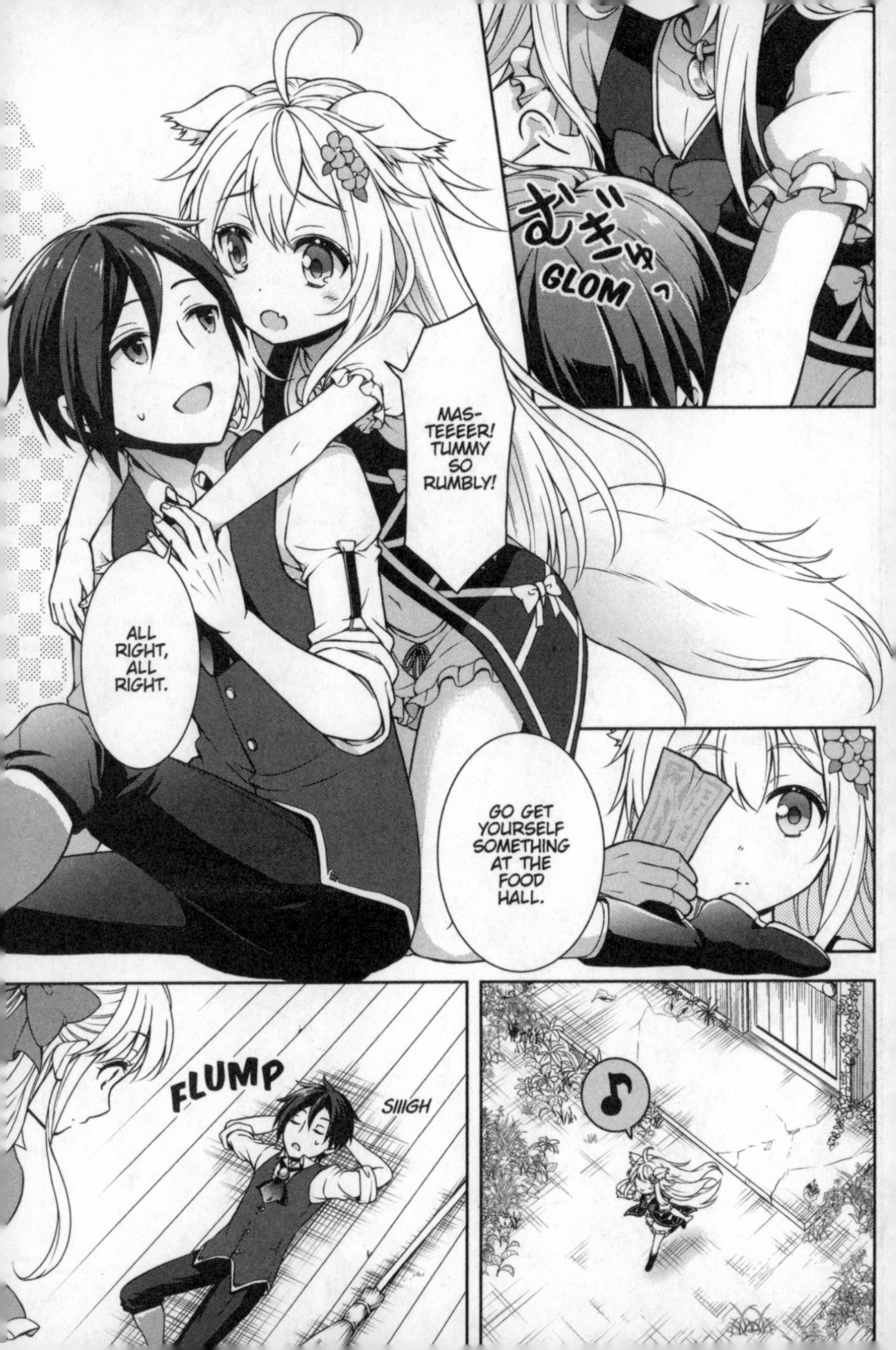
むぎゅっ
GLOM
MAS-TEEEER! TUMMY SO RUMBLY!
ALL RIGHT, ALL RIGHT.
GO GET YOURSELF SOMETHING AT THE FOOD HALL.
FLUMP
SIIGH

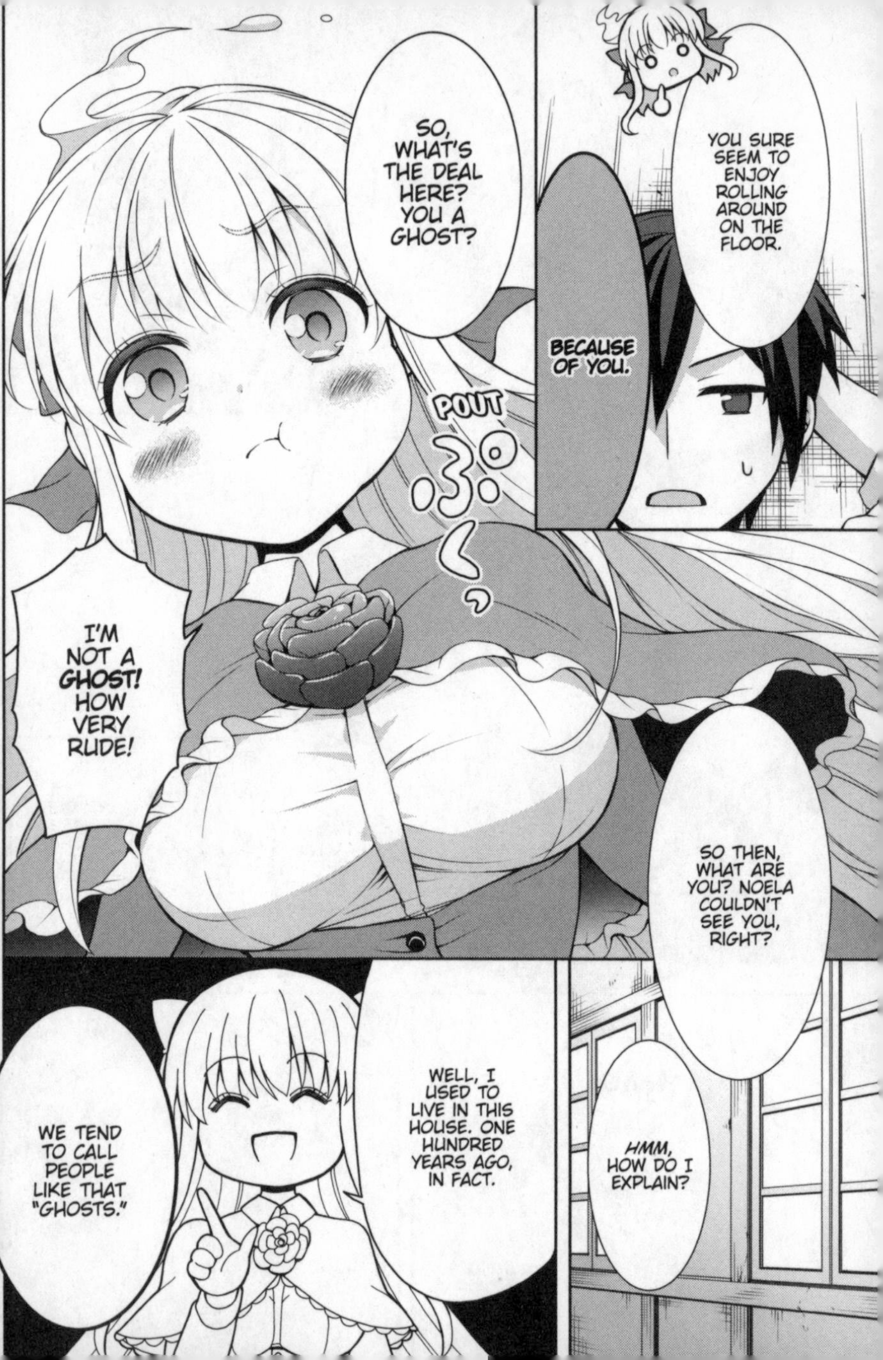
YOU SURE SEEM TO ENJOY ROLLING AROUND ON THE FLOOR.
BECAUSE OF YOU.
SO, WHAT'S THE DEAL HERE? YOU A GHOST?
POUT
I'M NOT A **GHOST!** HOW VERY RUDE!
SO THEN, WHAT ARE YOU? NOELA COULDN'T SEE YOU, RIGHT?
HMM, HOW DO I EXPLAIN?
WELL, I USED TO LIVE IN THIS HOUSE. ONE HUNDRED YEARS AGO, IN FACT.
WE TEND TO CALL PEOPLE LIKE THAT "GHOSTS."

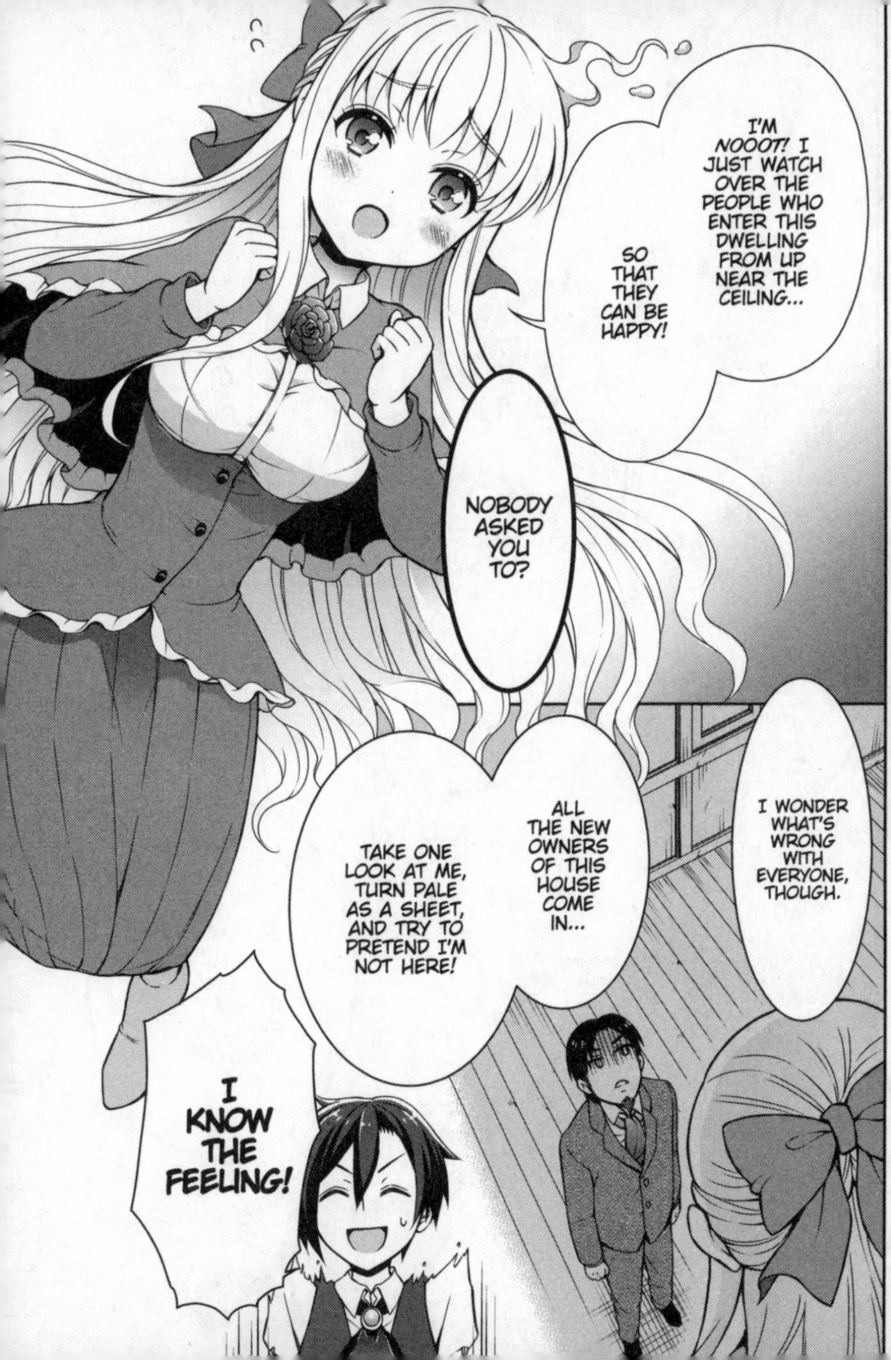
I'M NOOOT! I JUST WATCH OVER THE PEOPLE WHO ENTER THIS DWELLING FROM UP NEAR THE CEILING...
SO THAT THEY CAN BE HAPPY!
NOBODY ASKED YOU TO?
I WONDER WHAT'S WRONG WITH EVERYONE, THOUGH.
ALL THE NEW OWNERS OF THIS HOUSE COME IN...
TAKE ONE LOOK AT ME, TURN PALE AS A SHEET, AND TRY TO PRETEND I'M NOT HERE!
I KNOW THE FEELING!

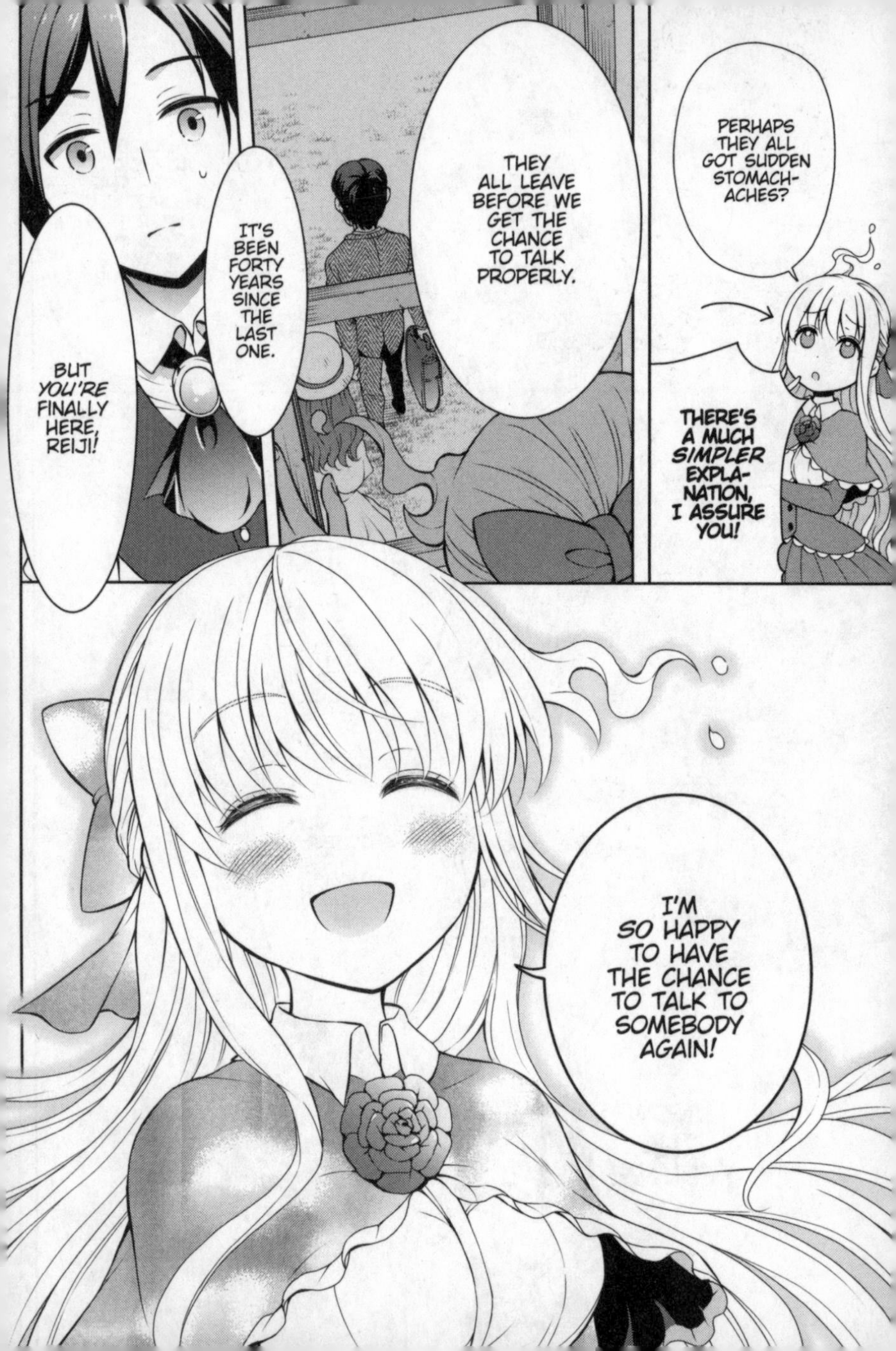
PERHAPS THEY ALL GOT SUDDEN STOMACH-ACHES?
THERE'S A MUCH *SIMPLER* EXPLA-NATION, I ASSURE YOU!
THEY ALL LEAVE BEFORE WE GET THE CHANCE TO TALK PROPERLY.
IT'S BEEN FORTY YEARS SINCE THE LAST ONE.
BUT *YOU'RE* FINALLY HERE, REIJI!
I'M *SO* HAPPY TO HAVE THE CHANCE TO TALK TO SOMEBODY AGAIN!

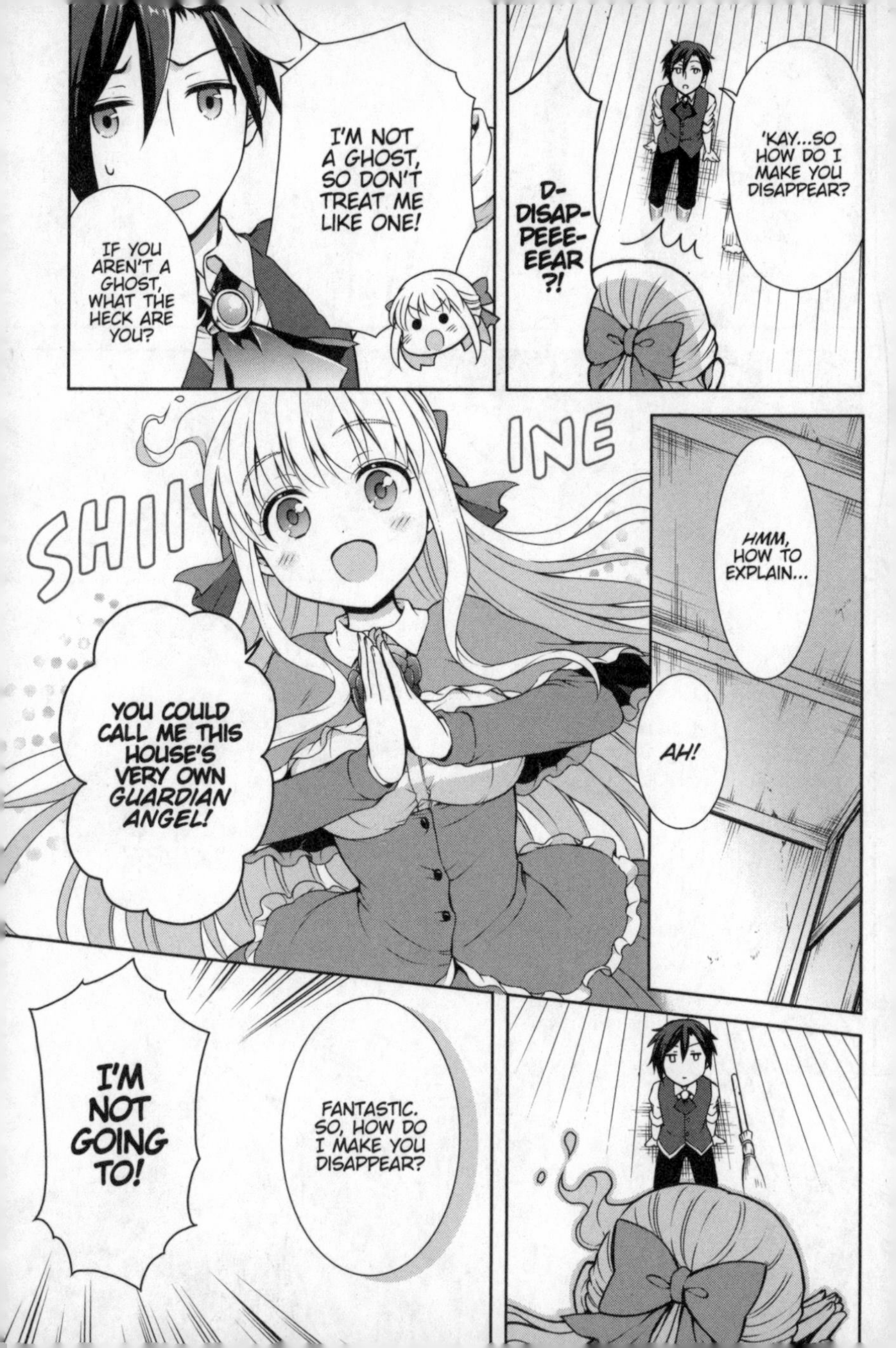
'KAY...SO HOW DO I MAKE YOU DISAPPEAR?
D-DISAP-PEEE-EEAR?!
I'M NOT A GHOST, SO DON'T TREAT ME LIKE ONE!
IF YOU AREN'T A GHOST, WHAT THE HECK ARE YOU?
HMM, HOW TO EXPLAIN...
AH!
SHIIINE
YOU COULD CALL ME THIS HOUSE'S VERY OWN GUARDIAN ANGEL!
FANTASTIC. SO, HOW DO I MAKE YOU DISAPPEAR?
I'M NOT GOING TO!

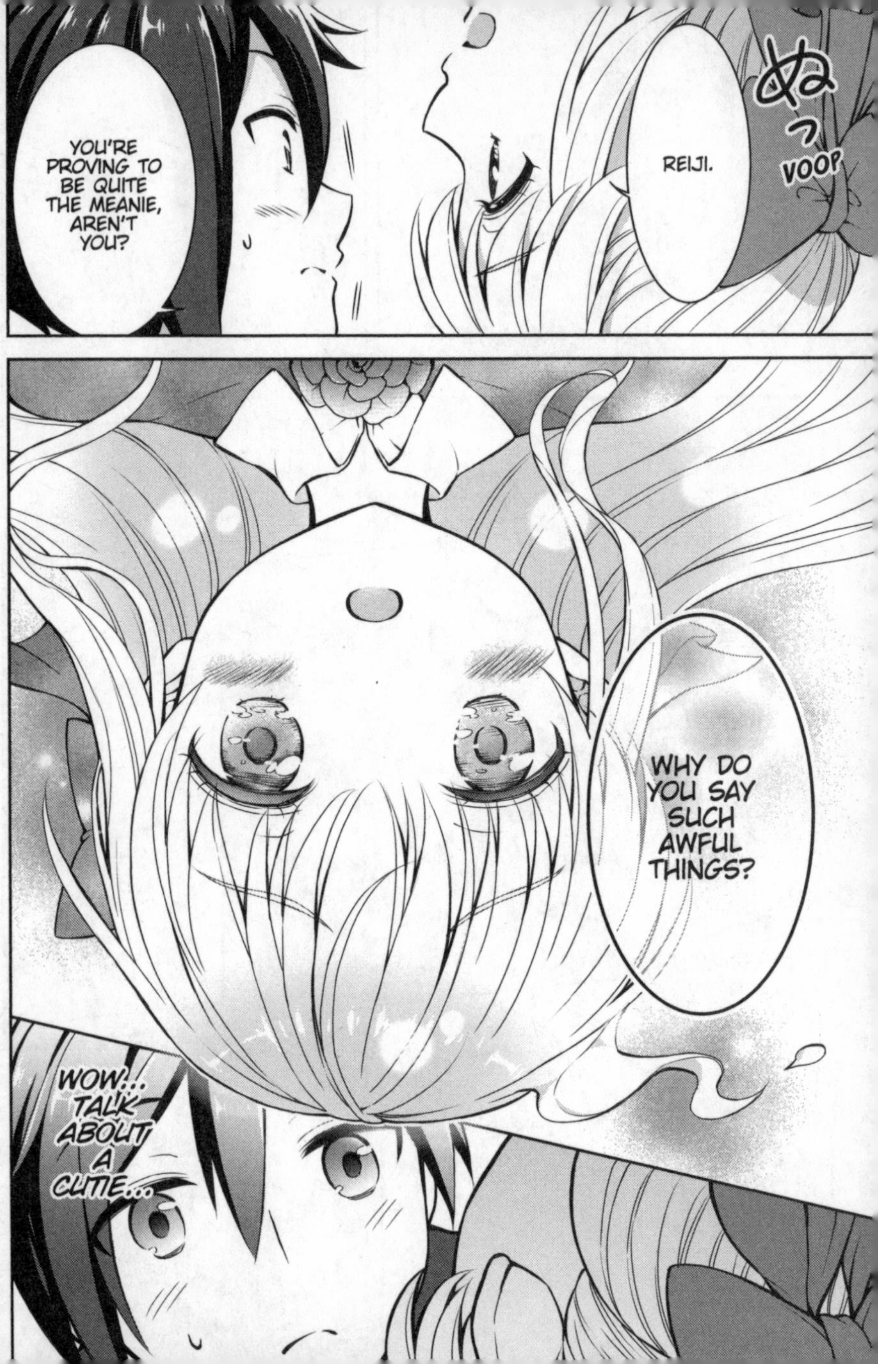

ぬっ
VOOP
REIJI.
YOU'RE PROVING TO BE QUITE THE MEANIE, AREN'T YOU?
WHY DO YOU SAY SUCH AWFUL THINGS?
WOW... TALK ABOUT A CUTIE...

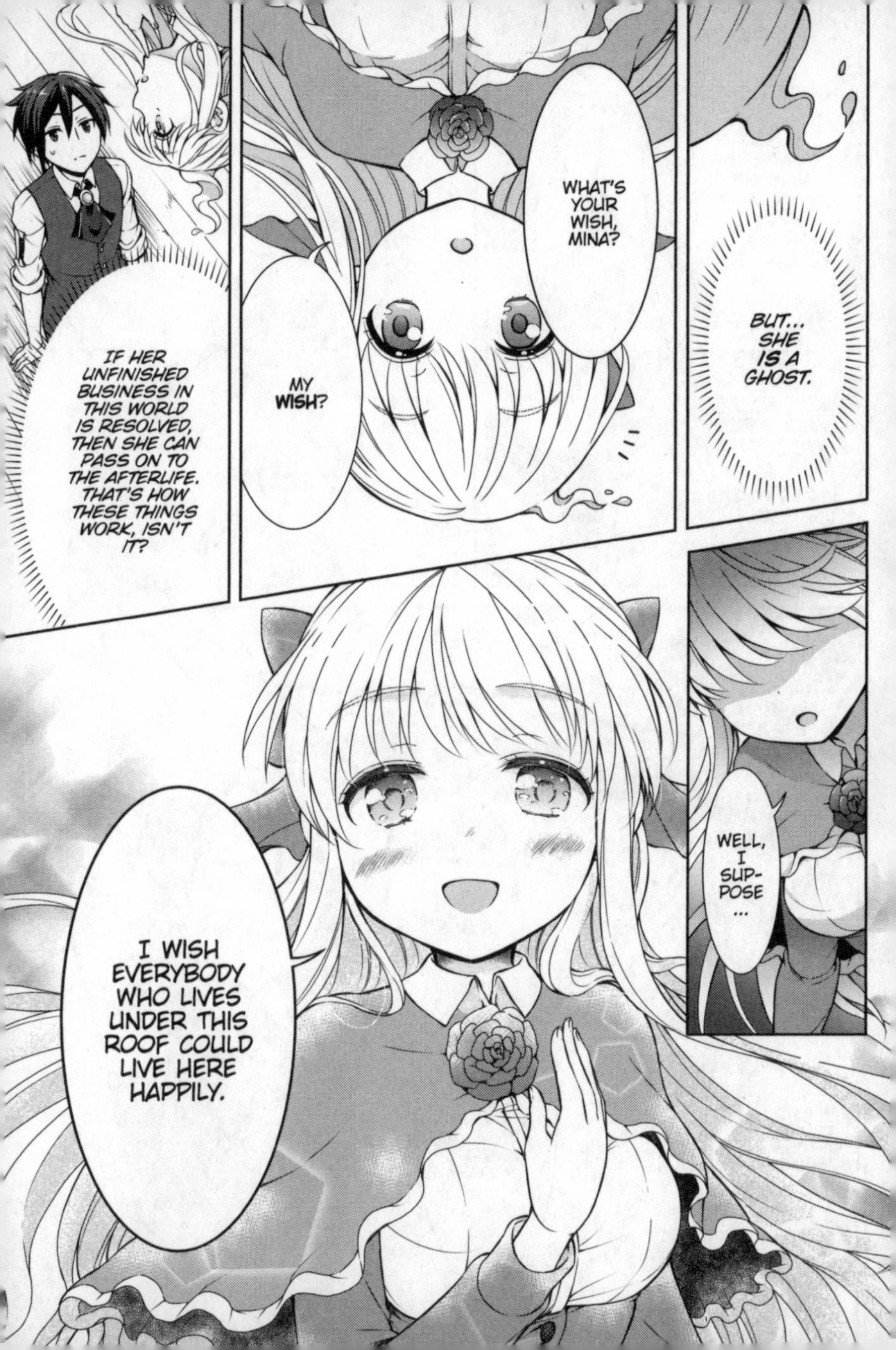
BUT... SHE IS A GHOST.
WHAT'S YOUR WISH, MINA?
MY WISH?
IF HER UNFINISHED BUSINESS IN THIS WORLD IS RESOLVED, THEN SHE CAN PASS ON TO THE AFTERLIFE. THAT'S HOW THESE THINGS WORK, ISN'T IT?
WELL, I SUP-POSE ...
I WISH EVERYBODY WHO LIVES UNDER THIS ROOF COULD LIVE HERE HAPPILY.

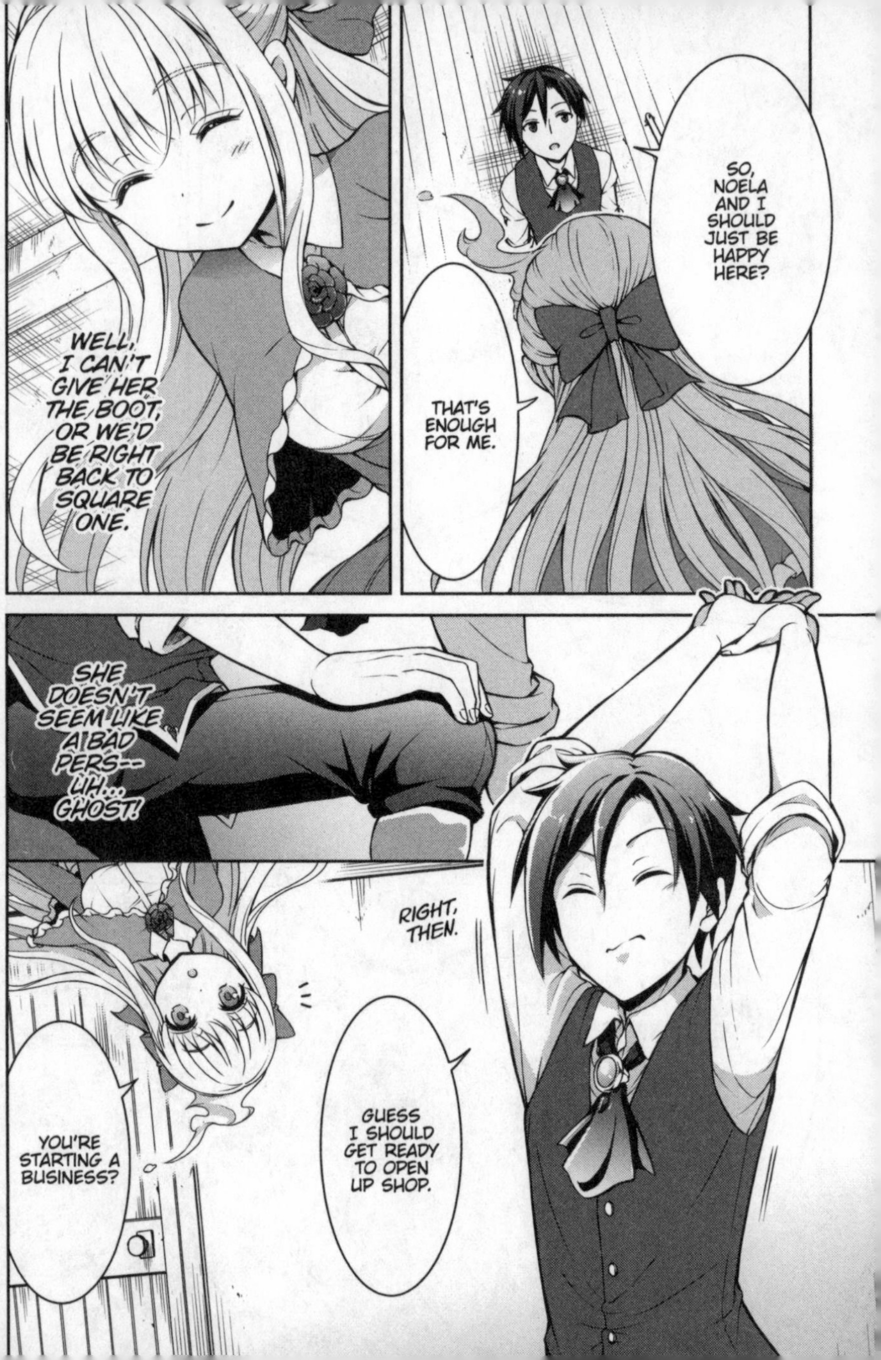

SO, NOELA AND I SHOULD JUST BE HAPPY HERE?
THAT'S ENOUGH FOR ME.
WELL, I CAN'T GIVE HER THE BOOT, OR WE'D BE RIGHT BACK TO SQUARE ONE.
RIGHT, THEN.
GUESS I SHOULD GET READY TO OPEN UP SHOP.
SHE DOESN'T SEEM LIKE A BAD PERS-- UH... GHOST!
YOU'RE STARTING A BUSINESS?

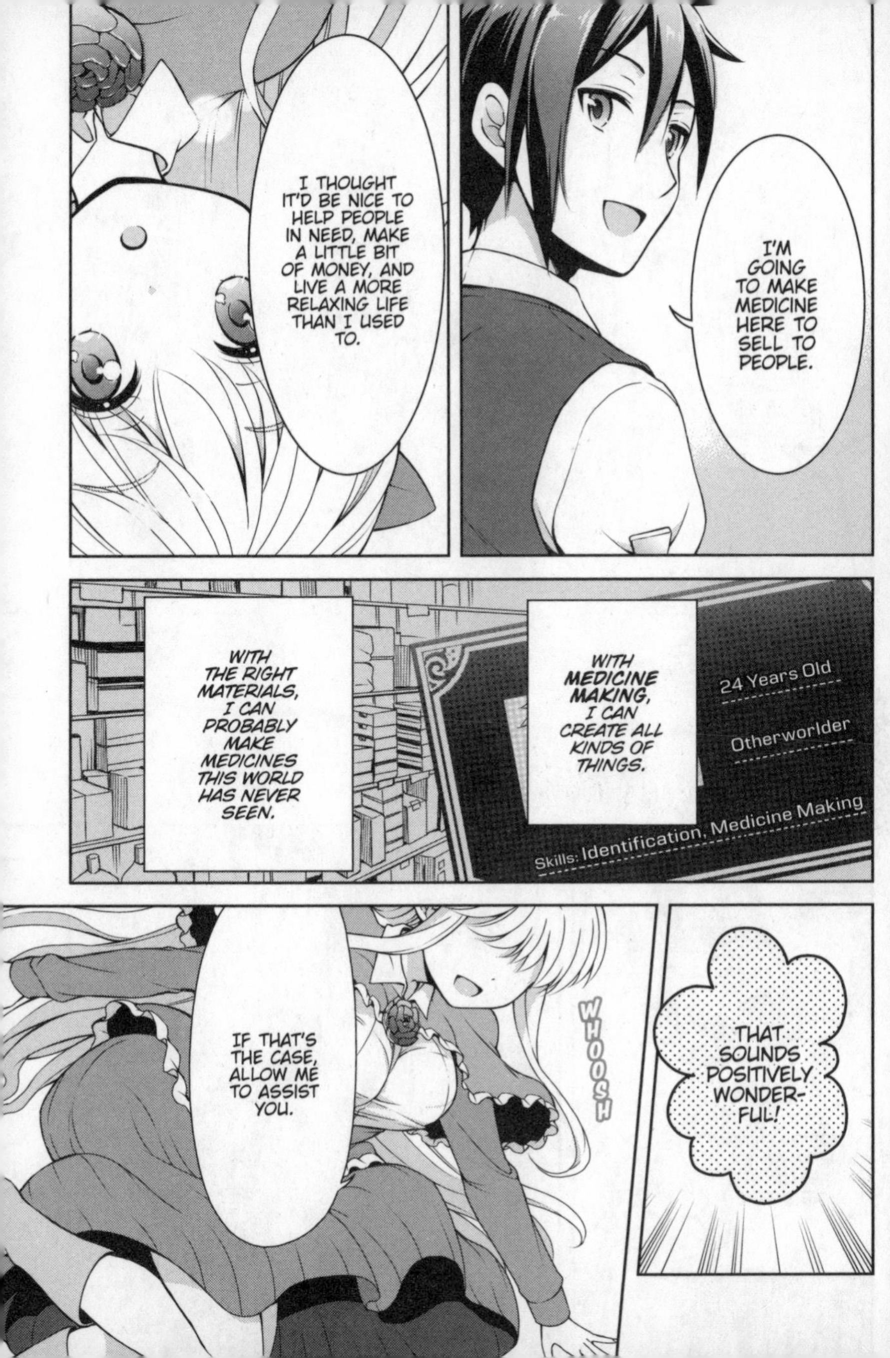
I'M GOING TO MAKE MEDICINE HERE TO SELL TO PEOPLE.
I THOUGHT IT'D BE NICE TO HELP PEOPLE IN NEED, MAKE A LITTLE BIT OF MONEY, AND LIVE A MORE RELAXING LIFE THAN I USED TO.
24 Years Old
Otherworlder
Skills: Identification, Medicine Making
WITH MEDICINE MAKING, I CAN CREATE ALL KINDS OF THINGS.
WITH THE RIGHT MATERIALS, I CAN PROBABLY MAKE MEDICINES THIS WORLD HAS NEVER SEEN.
THAT SOUNDS POSITIVELY WONDERFUL!
WHOOSH
IF THAT'S THE CASE, ALLOW ME TO ASSIST YOU.

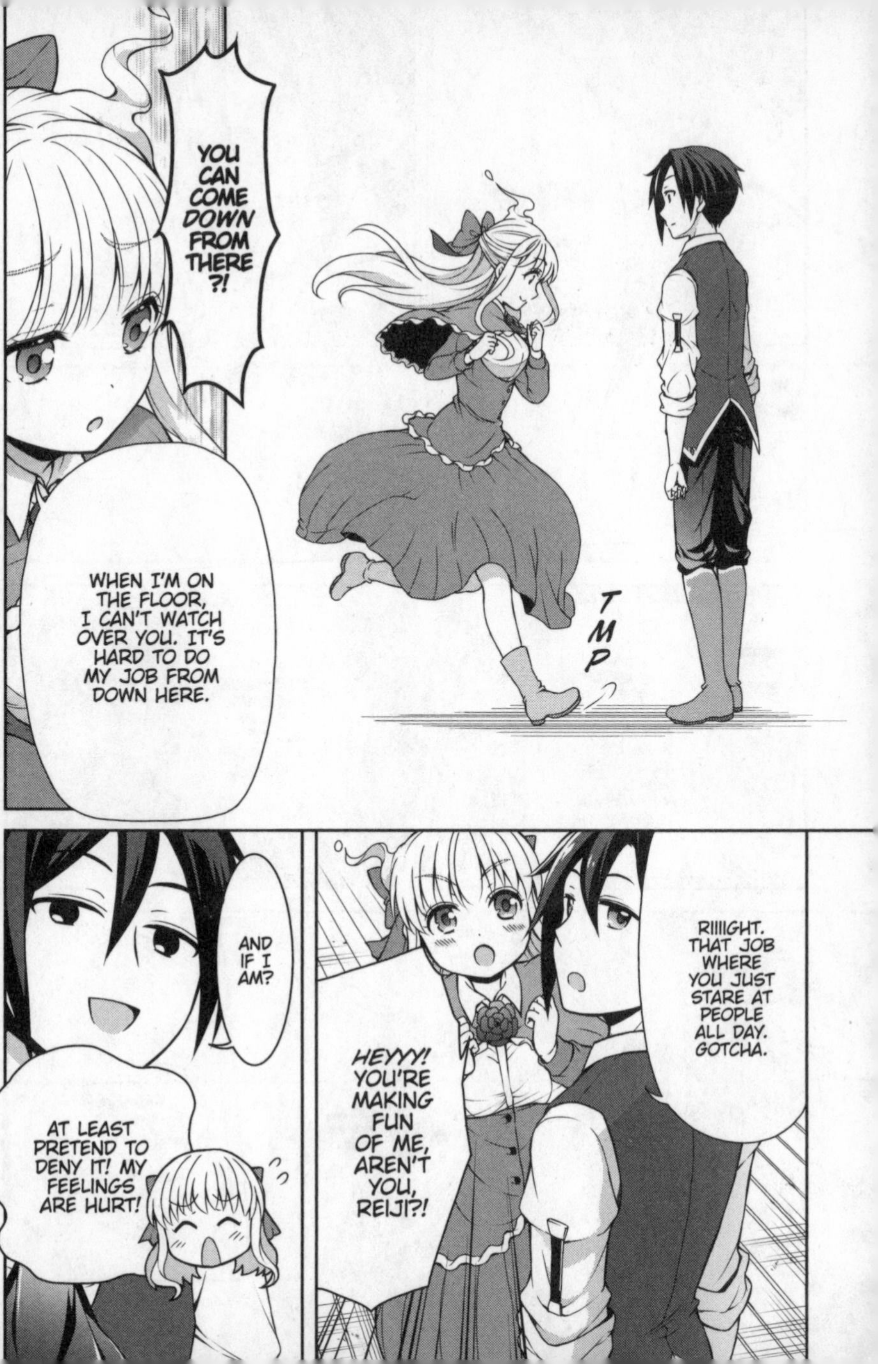
TMP
YOU CAN COME DOWN FROM THERE?!
WHEN I'M ON THE FLOOR, I CAN'T WATCH OVER YOU. IT'S HARD TO DO MY JOB FROM DOWN HERE.
RIIIGHT. THAT JOB WHERE YOU JUST STARE AT PEOPLE ALL DAY. GOTCHA.
HEYYY! YOU'RE MAKING FUN OF ME, AREN'T YOU, REIJI?!
AND IF I AM?
AT LEAST PRETEND TO DENY IT! MY FEELINGS ARE HURT!

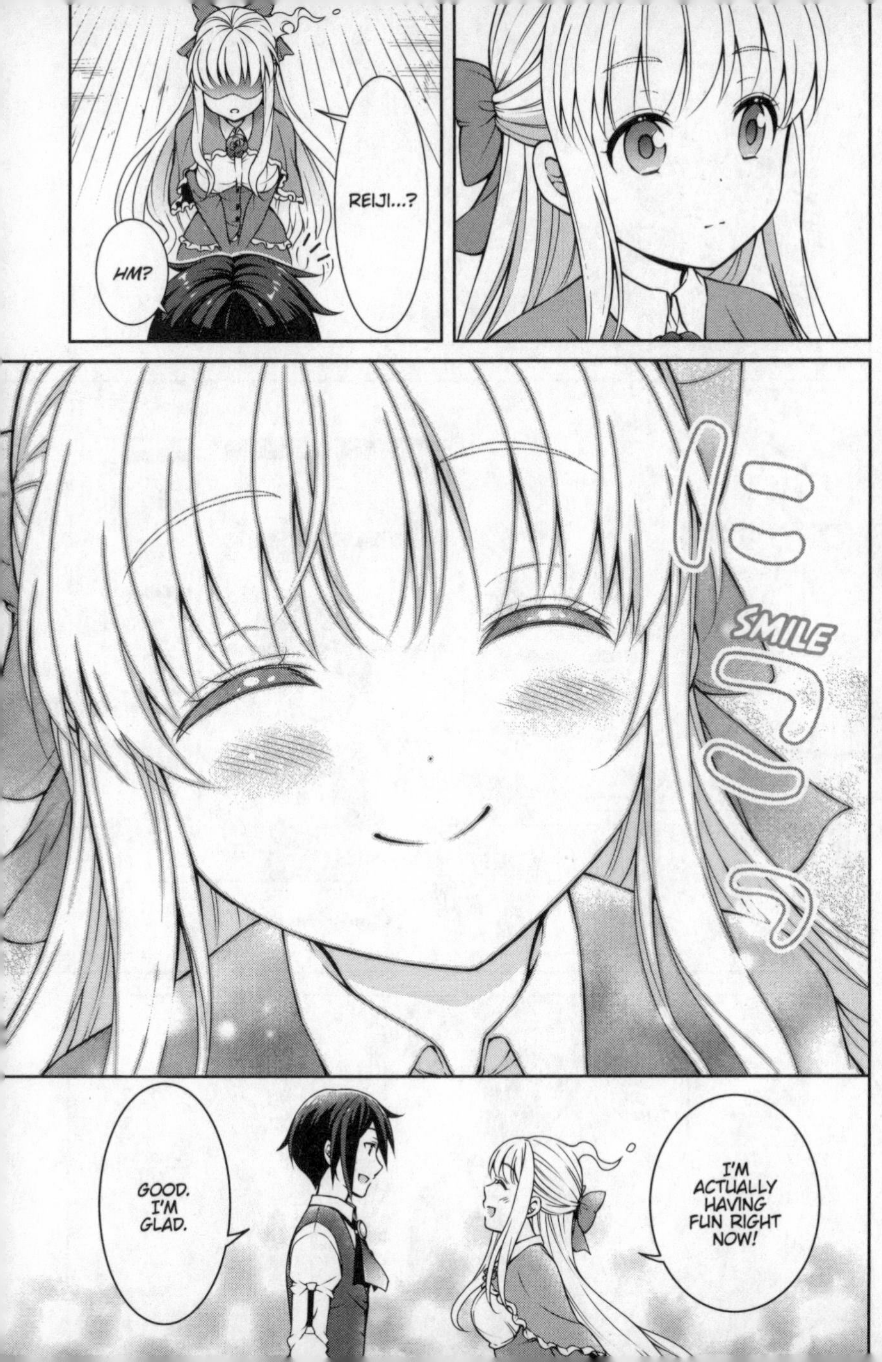
REIJI...?
HM?
SMILE
I'M ACTUALLY HAVING FUN RIGHT NOW!
GOOD. I'M GLAD.

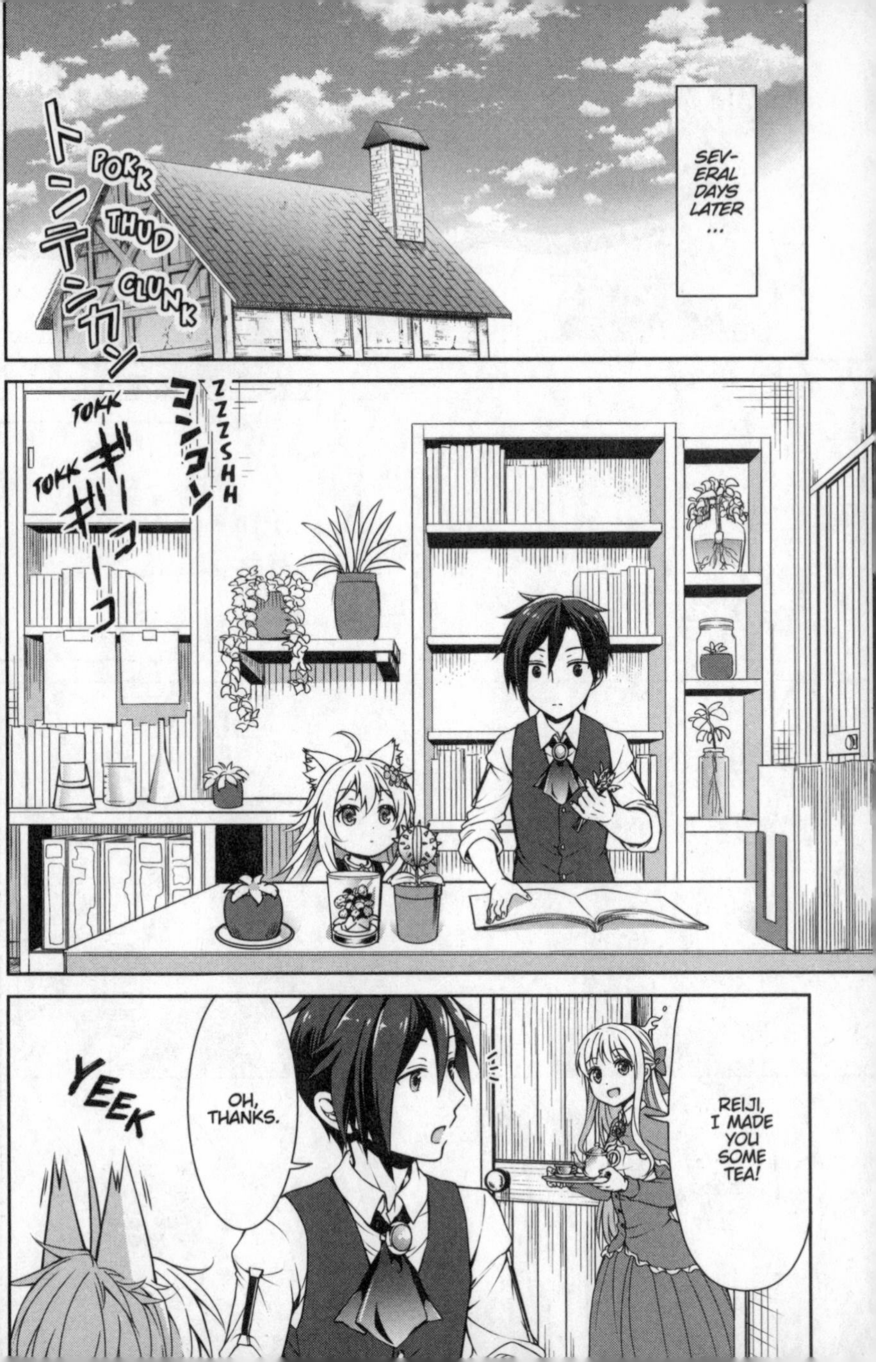
SEV-ERAL DAYS LATER ...
POKK
THUD
CLUNK
トンテンカン
ZZZSHH
コンコン
TOKK
TOKK
ギーコギーコ
REIJI, I MADE YOU SOME TEA!
OH, THANKS.
YEEK

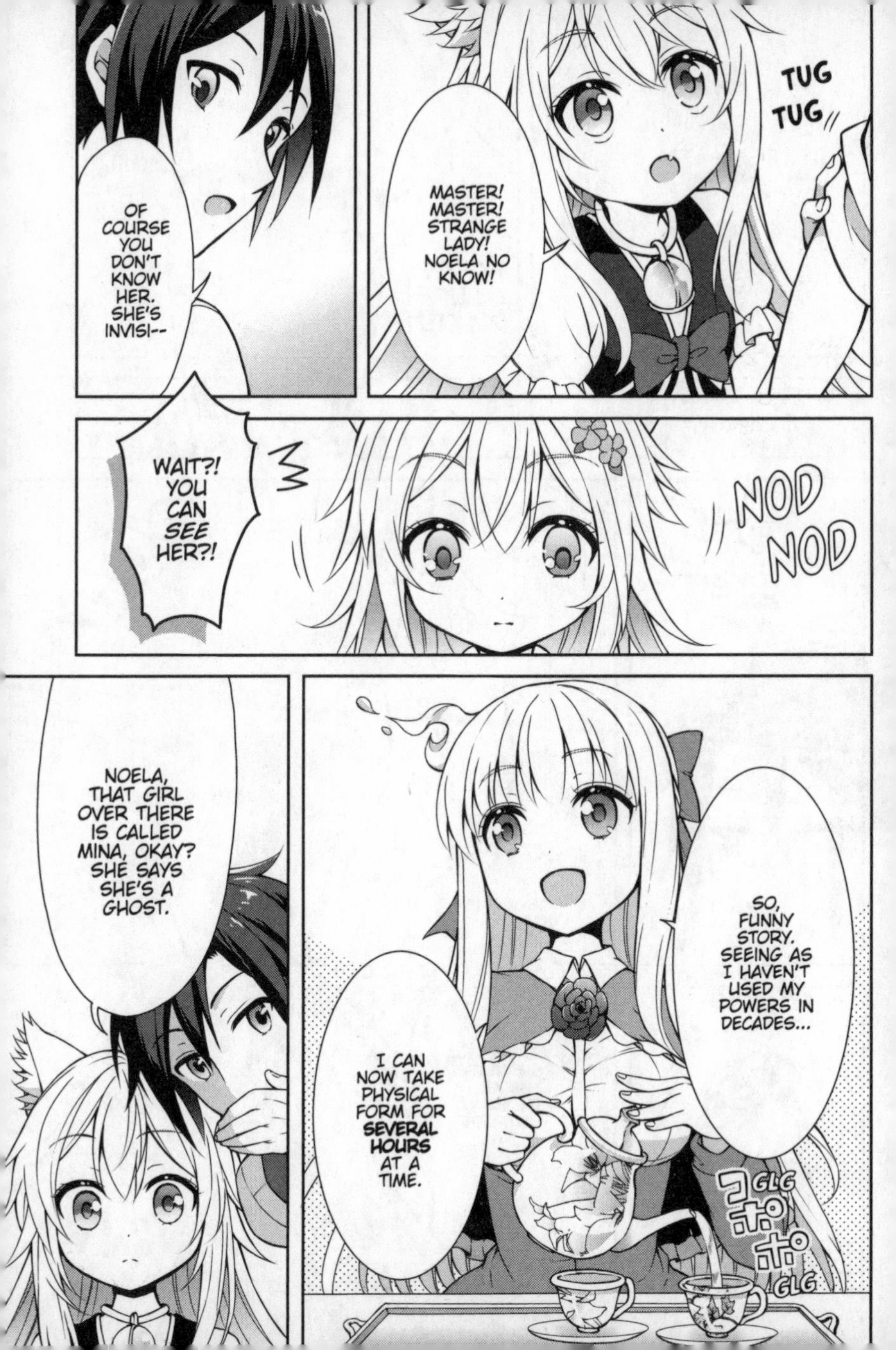
TUG TUG
MASTER! MASTER! STRANGE LADY! NOELA NO KNOW!
OF COURSE YOU DON'T KNOW HER. SHE'S INVISI--
WAIT?! YOU CAN SEE HER?!
NOD NOD
SO, FUNNY STORY. SEEING AS I HAVEN'T USED MY POWERS IN DECADES...
I CAN NOW TAKE PHYSICAL FORM FOR **SEVERAL HOURS** AT A TIME.
GLG
コポポ
GLG
NOELA, THAT GIRL OVER THERE IS CALLED MINA, OKAY? SHE SAYS SHE'S A GHOST.

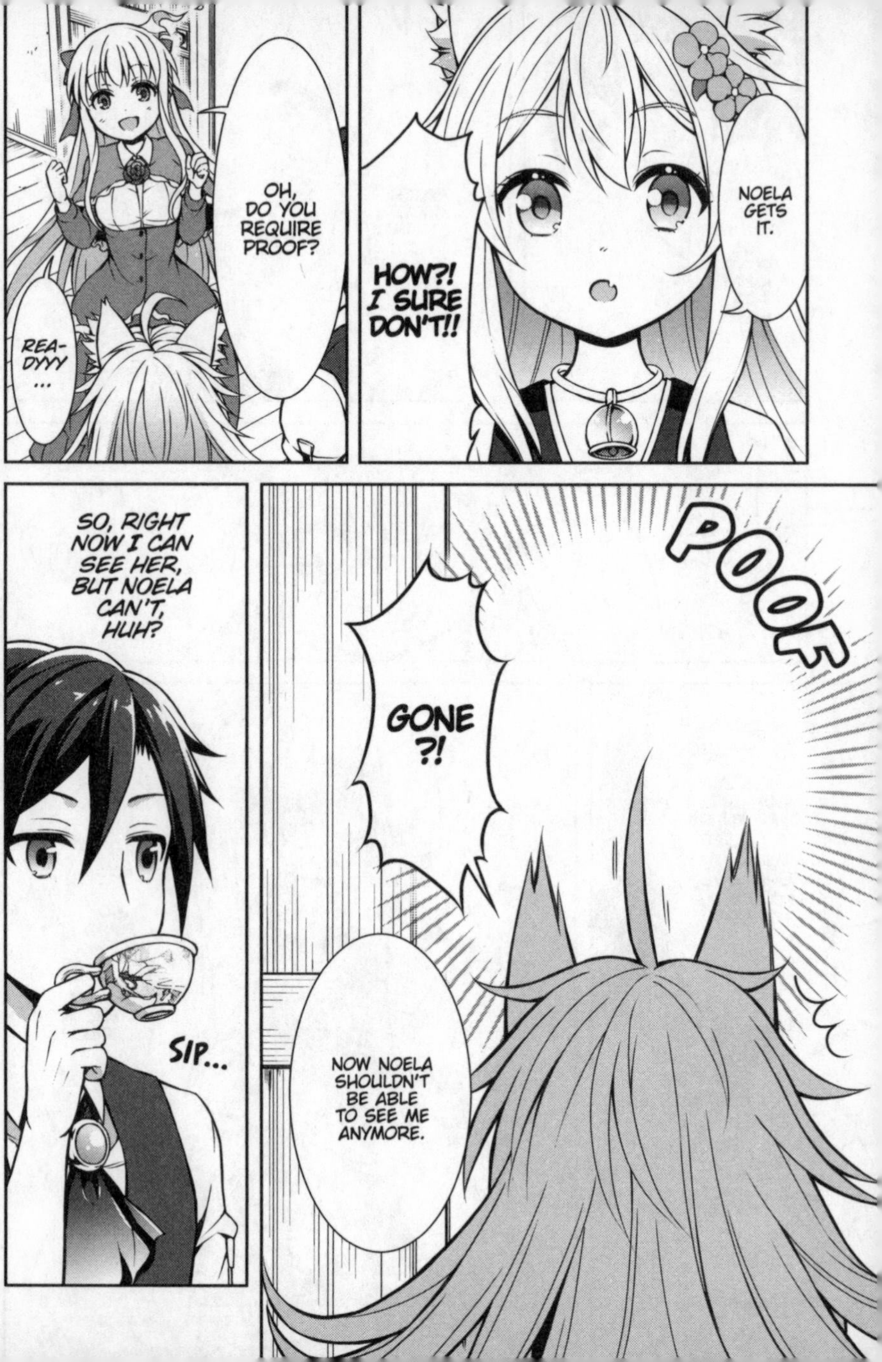
NOELA GETS IT.
HOW?! I SURE DON'T!!
OH, DO YOU REQUIRE PROOF?
REA-DYYY...
POOF
GONE?!
NOW NOELA SHOULDN'T BE ABLE TO SEE ME ANYMORE.
SO, RIGHT NOW I CAN SEE HER, BUT NOELA CAN'T, HUH?
SIP...

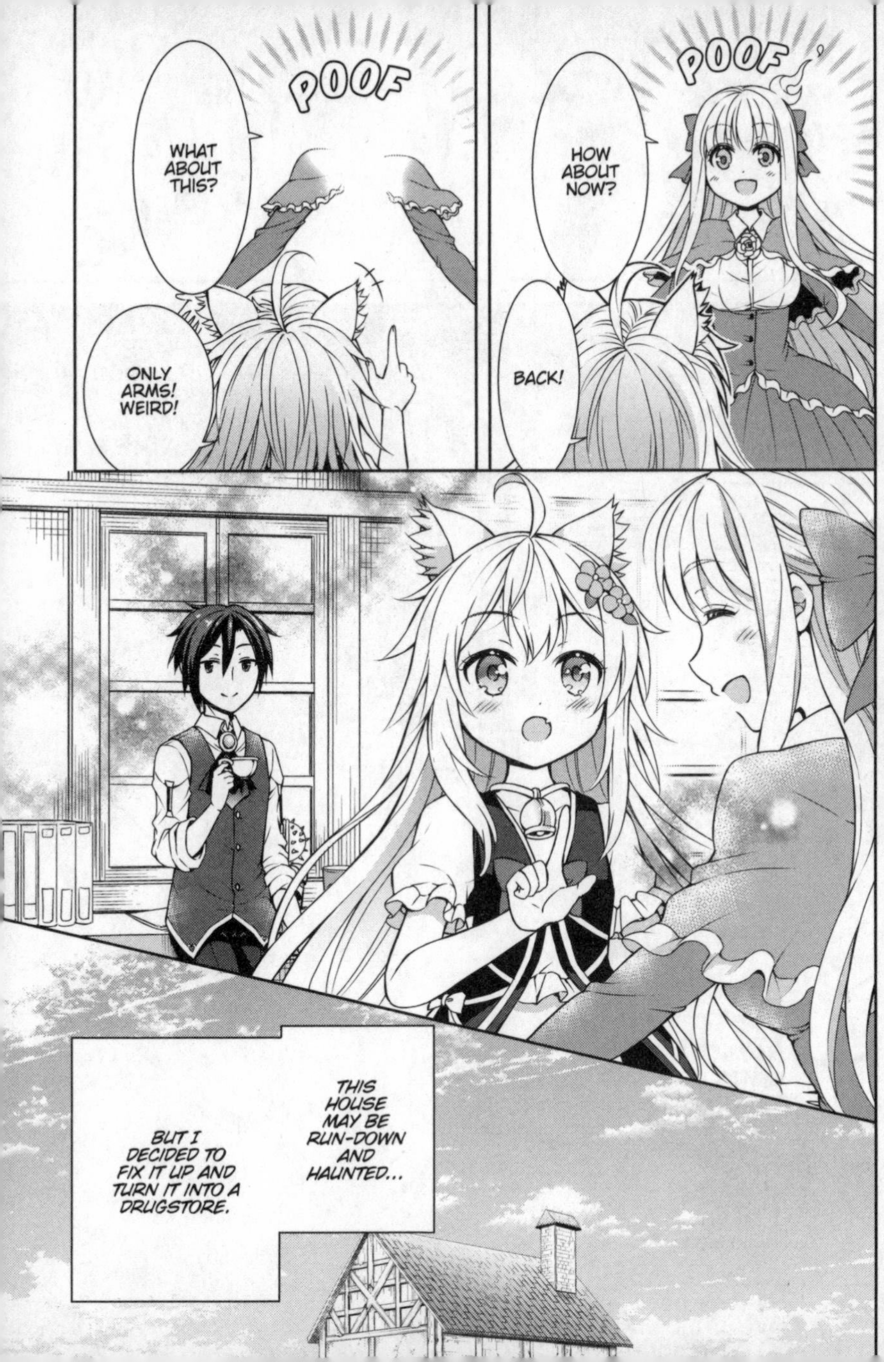
POOF
HOW ABOUT NOW?
BACK!
POOF
WHAT ABOUT THIS?
ONLY ARMS! WEIRD!
THIS HOUSE MAY BE RUN-DOWN AND HAUNTED...
BUT I DECIDED TO FIX IT UP AND TURN IT INTO A DRUGSTORE.

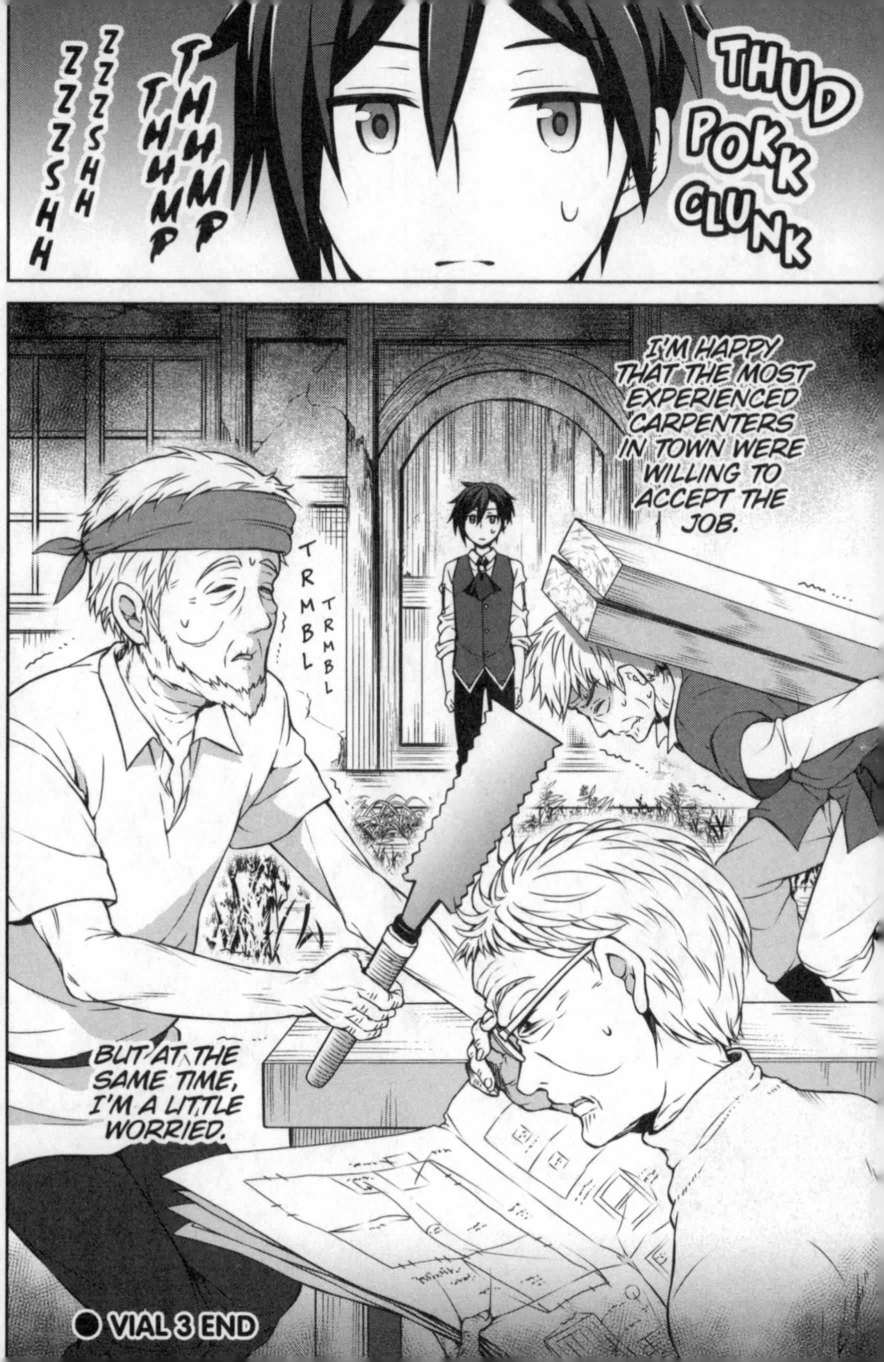
THUD
POKK
CLUNK
THUMP THUMP
ZZZSHH ZZZSHH
I'M HAPPY THAT THE MOST EXPERIENCED CARPENTERS IN TOWN WERE WILLING TO ACCEPT THE JOB.
TRMBL TRMBL
BUT AT THE SAME TIME, I'M A LITTLE WORRIED.
VIAL 3 END

DRUGSTORE in Another World

The Slow Life of a
~ Cheat Pharmacist ~

DRUGSTORE
iN ANOTHER WORLD
~ The Slow Life of a ~
Cheat Pharmacist

VIAL 4 Research & Development

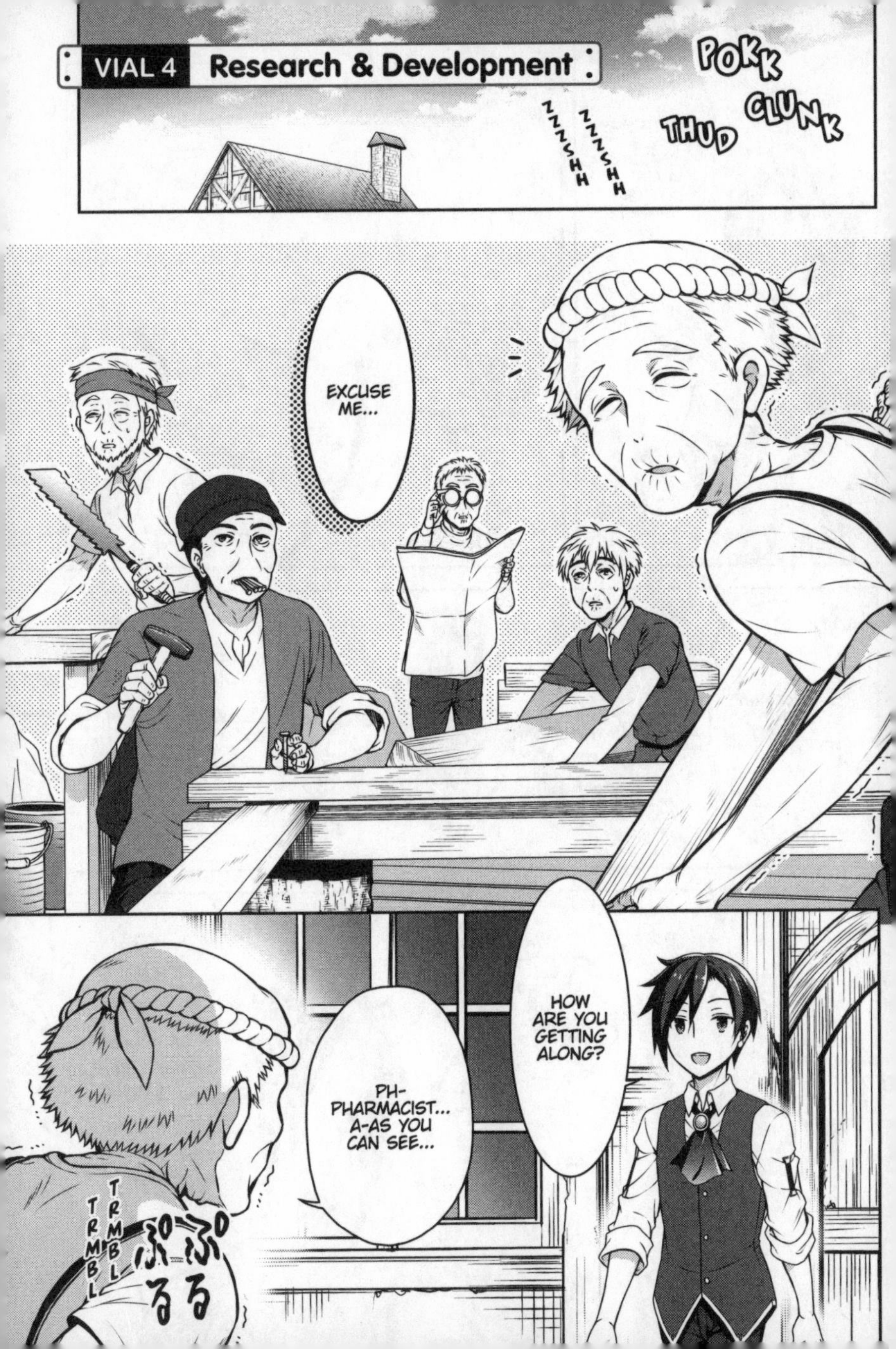
POKK
CLUNK
THUD
ZZZSHH
ZZZSHH
EXCUSE ME...
HOW ARE YOU GETTING ALONG?
PH-PHARMACIST... A-AS YOU CAN SEE...
TRMBL
TRMBL
ぷるぷる

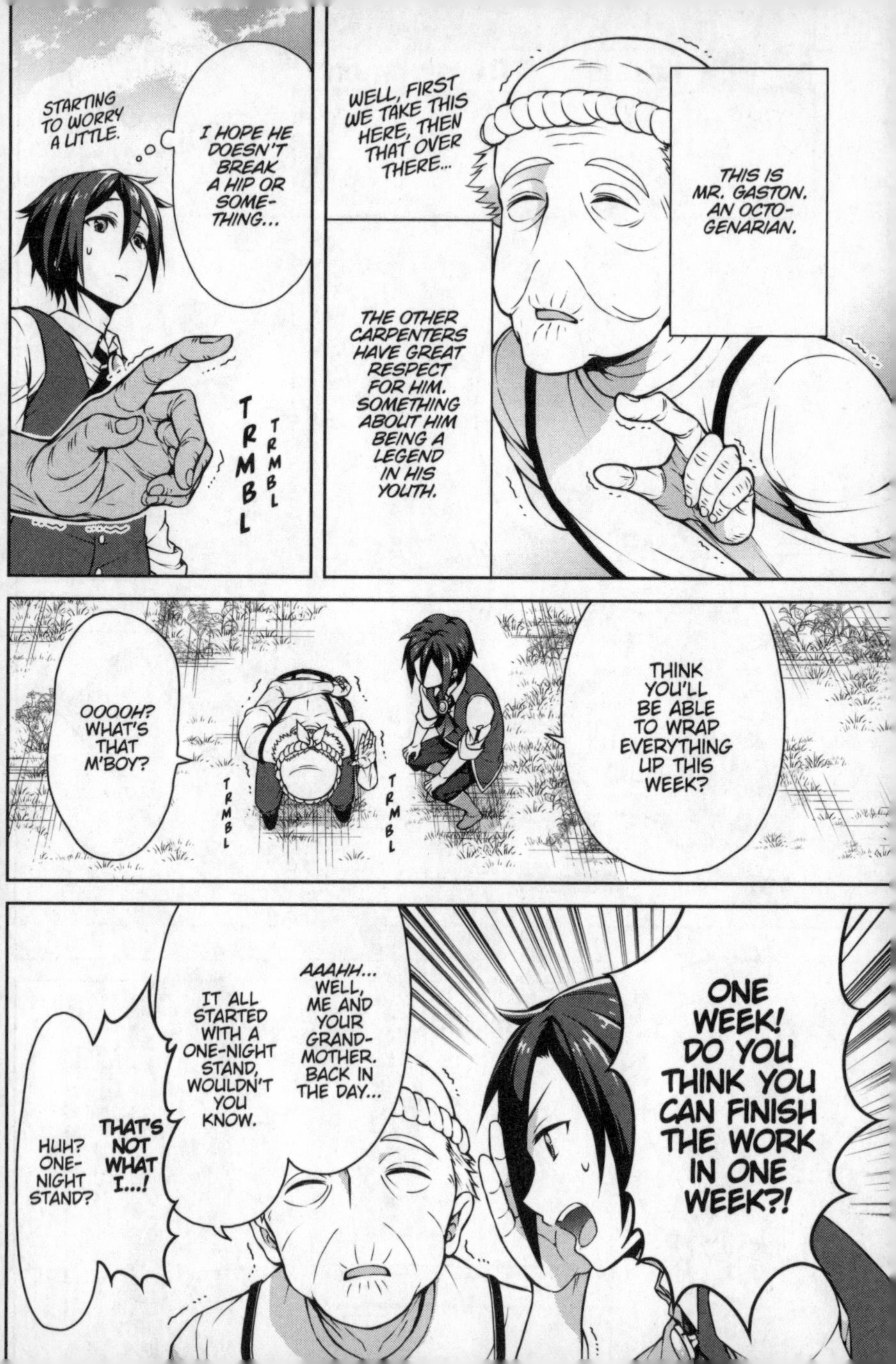
THIS IS MR. GASTON. AN OCTO-GENARIAN.
WELL, FIRST WE TAKE THIS HERE, THEN THAT OVER THERE...
THE OTHER CARPENTERS HAVE GREAT RESPECT FOR HIM. SOMETHING ABOUT HIM BEING A LEGEND IN HIS YOUTH.
I HOPE HE DOESN'T BREAK A HIP OR SOME-THING...
STARTING TO WORRY A LITTLE.
TRMBL
TRMBL
THINK YOU'LL BE ABLE TO WRAP EVERYTHING UP THIS WEEK?
TRMBL
TRMBL
OOOOH? WHAT'S THAT M'BOY?
ONE WEEK! DO YOU THINK YOU CAN FINISH THE WORK IN ONE WEEK?!
AAAHH... WELL, ME AND YOUR GRAND-MOTHER. BACK IN THE DAY...
IT ALL STARTED WITH A ONE-NIGHT STAND, WOULDN'T YOU KNOW.
THAT'S NOT WHAT I...!
HUH? ONE-NIGHT STAND?

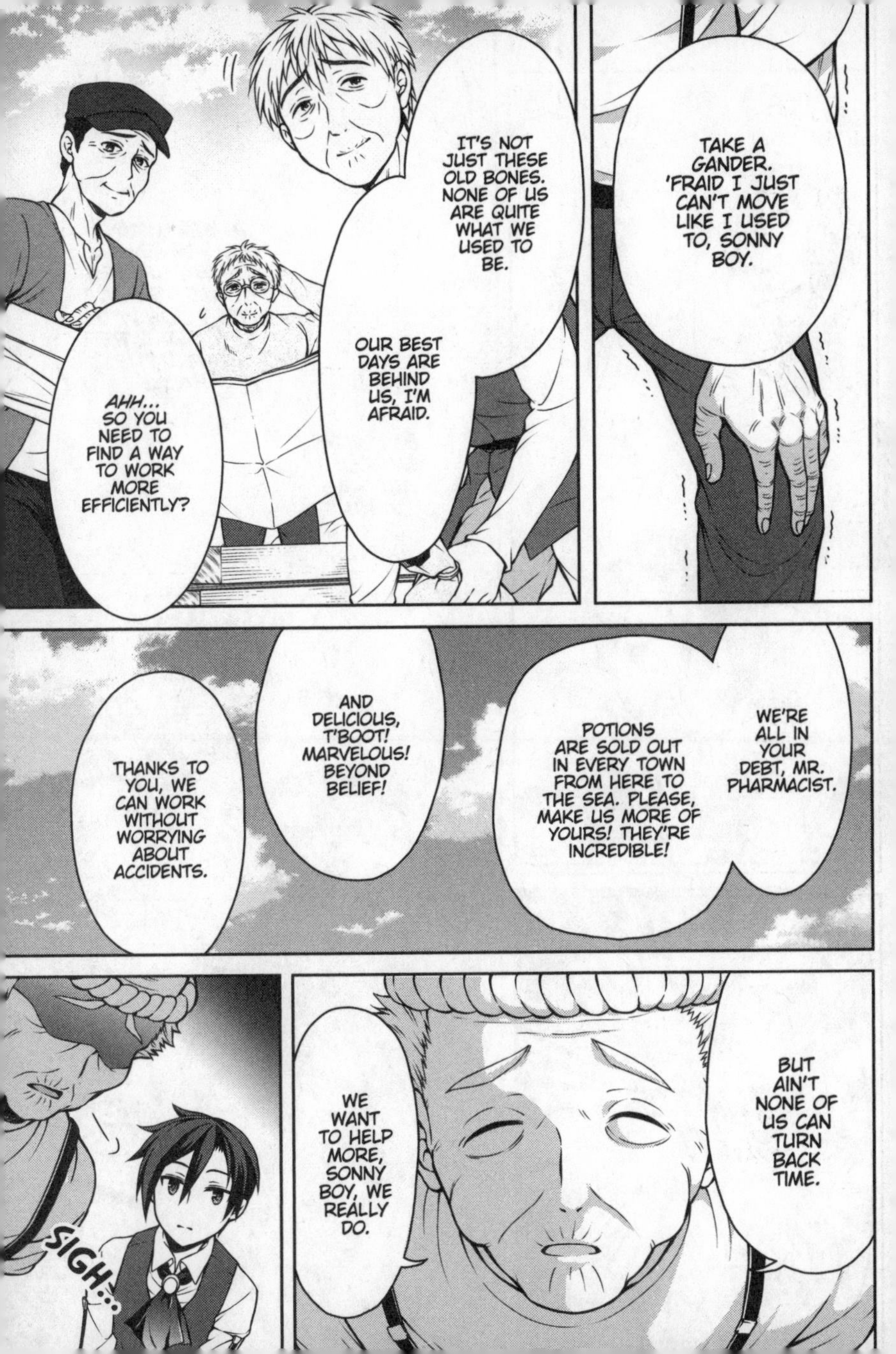
TAKE A GANDER. 'FRAID I JUST CAN'T MOVE LIKE I USED TO, SONNY BOY.
IT'S NOT JUST THESE OLD BONES. NONE OF US ARE QUITE WHAT WE USED TO BE.
OUR BEST DAYS ARE BEHIND US, I'M AFRAID.
AHH... SO YOU NEED TO FIND A WAY TO WORK MORE EFFICIENTLY?
WE'RE ALL IN YOUR DEBT, MR. PHARMACIST.
POTIONS ARE SOLD OUT IN EVERY TOWN FROM HERE TO THE SEA. PLEASE, MAKE US MORE OF YOURS! THEY'RE INCREDIBLE!
AND DELICIOUS, T'BOOT! MARVELOUS! BEYOND BELIEF!
THANKS TO YOU, WE CAN WORK WITHOUT WORRYING ABOUT ACCIDENTS.
BUT AIN'T NONE OF US CAN TURN BACK TIME.
WE WANT TO HELP MORE, SONNY BOY, WE REALLY DO.
SIGH...

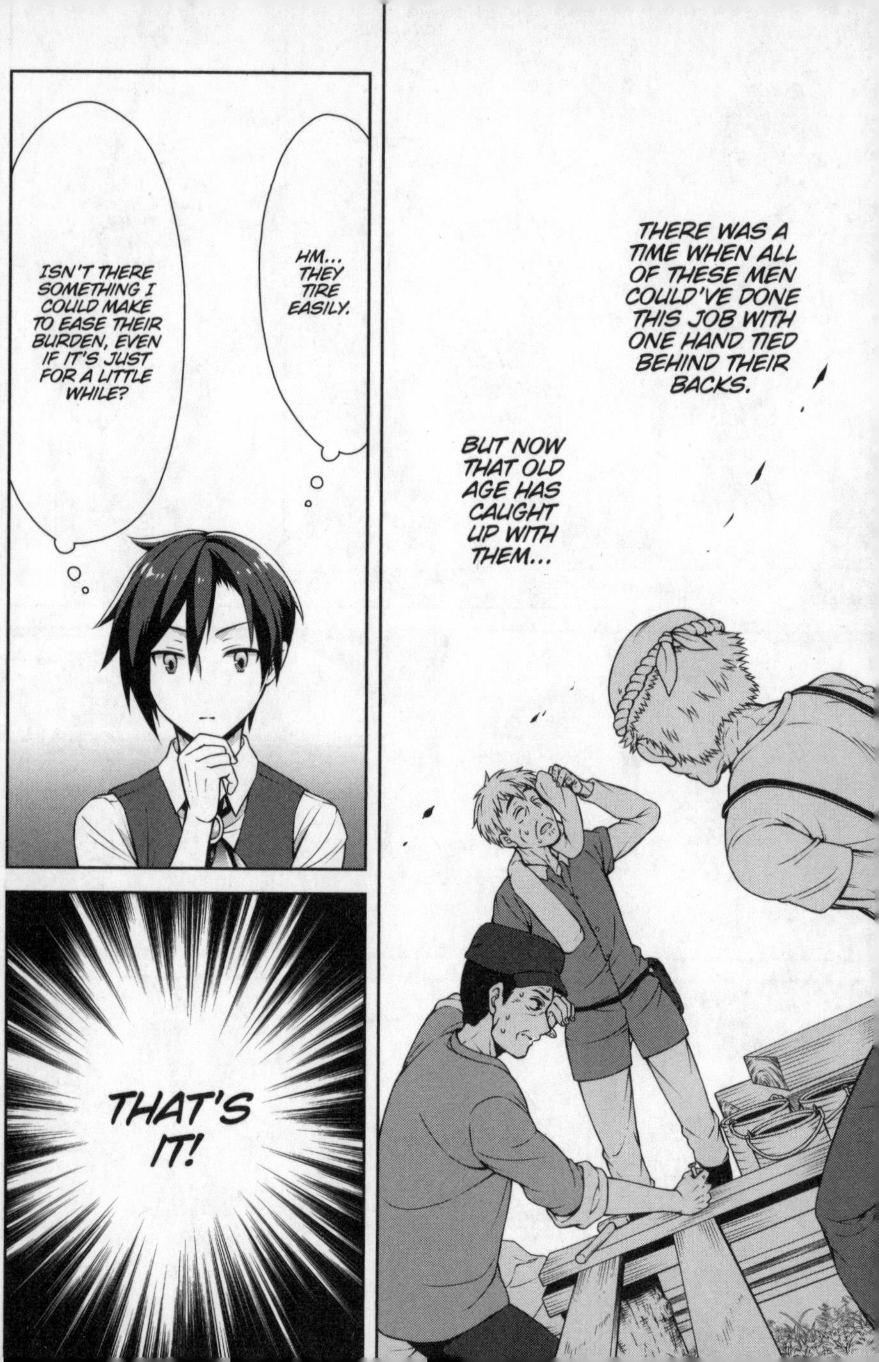
THERE WAS A TIME WHEN ALL OF THESE MEN COULD'VE DONE THIS JOB WITH ONE HAND TIED BEHIND THEIR BACKS.
BUT NOW THAT OLD AGE HAS CAUGHT UP WITH THEM...
HM... THEY TIRE EASILY.
ISN'T THERE SOMETHING I COULD MAKE TO EASE THEIR BURDEN, EVEN IF IT'S JUST FOR A LITTLE WHILE?
THAT'S IT!

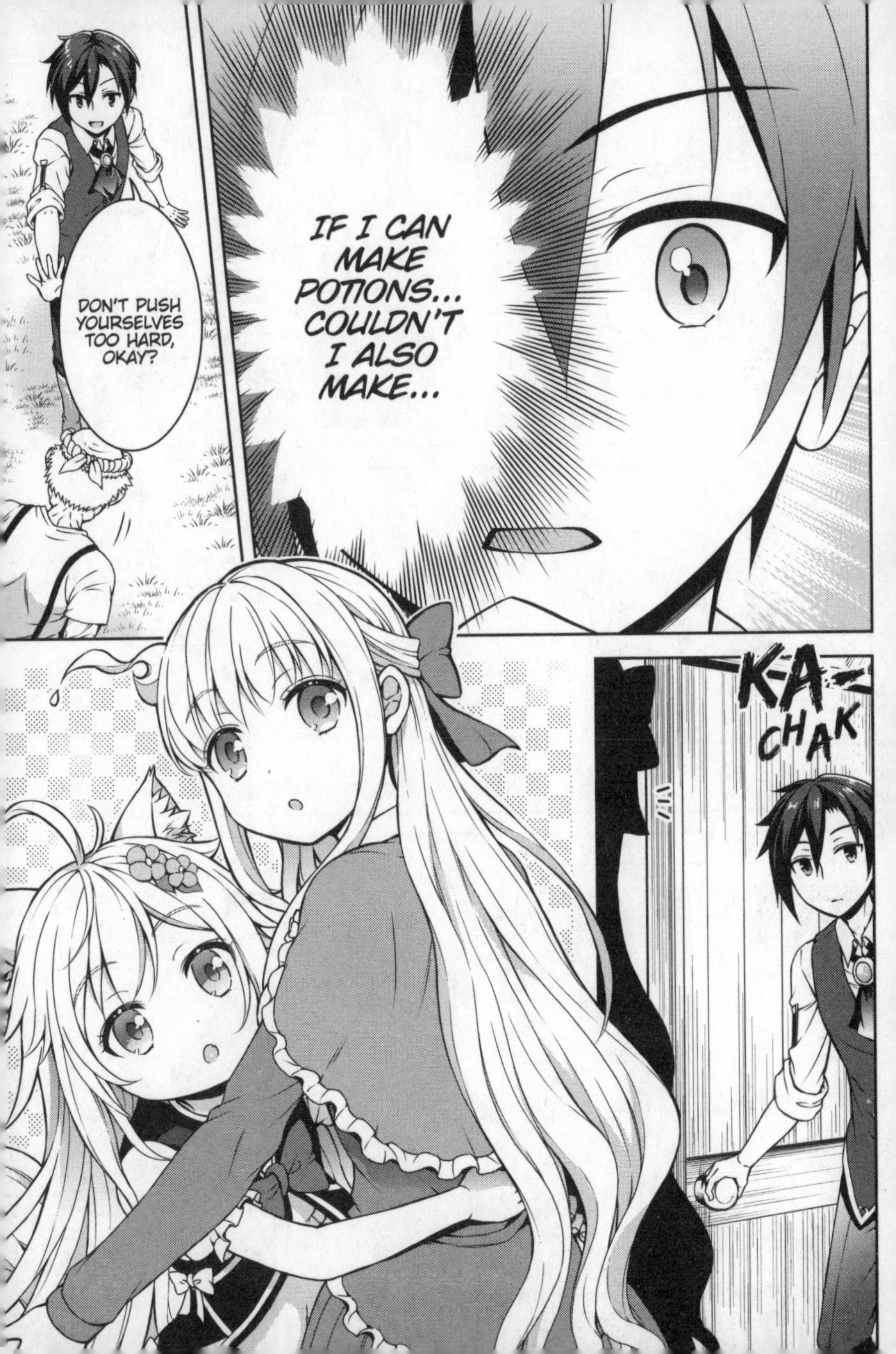
IF I CAN MAKE POTIONS... COULDN'T I ALSO MAKE...
DON'T PUSH YOURSELVES TOO HARD, OKAY?
KA-CHAK

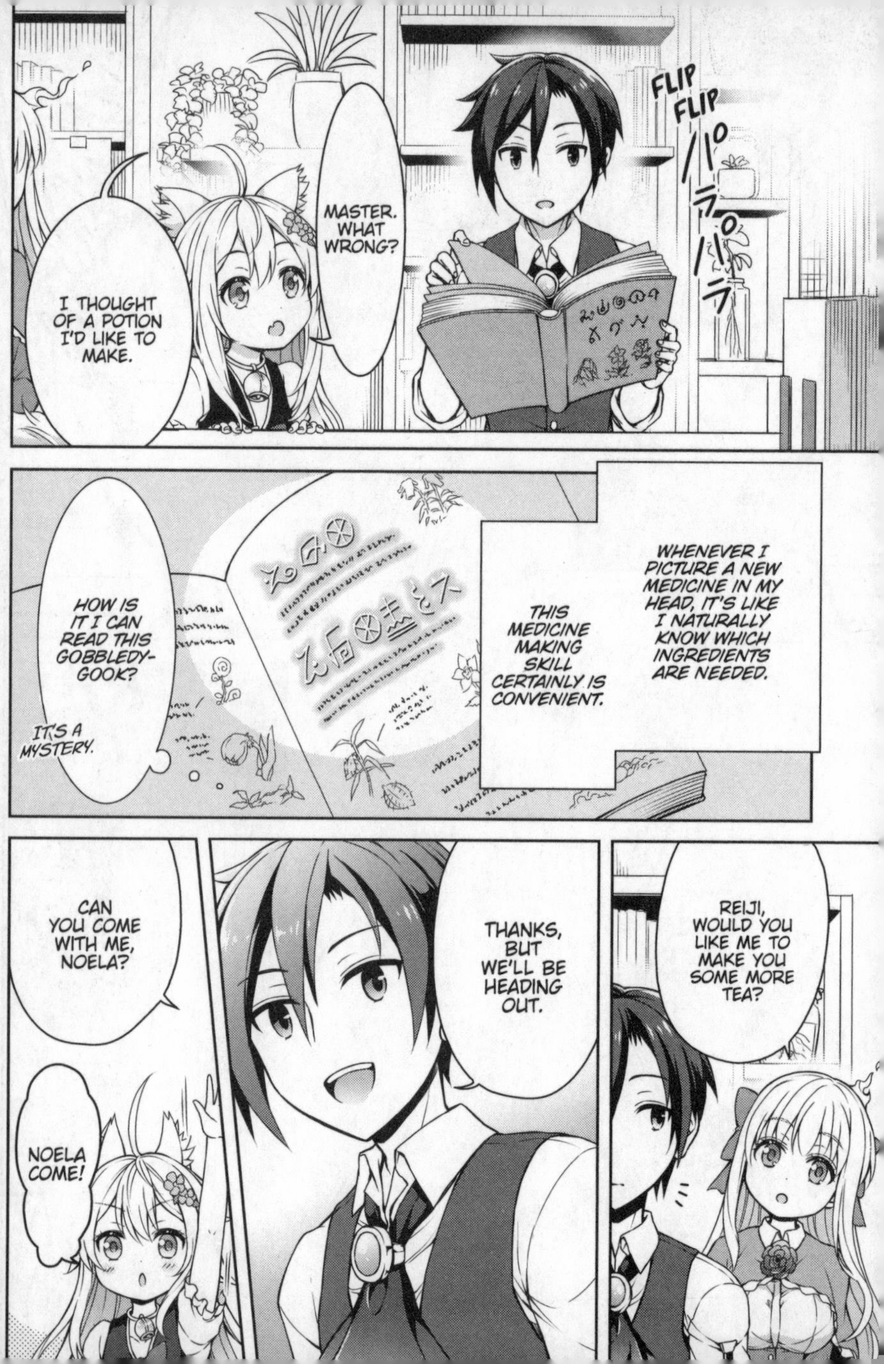
FLIP FLIP
パラパラ
MASTER. WHAT WRONG?
I THOUGHT OF A POTION I'D LIKE TO MAKE.
WHENEVER I PICTURE A NEW MEDICINE IN MY HEAD, IT'S LIKE I NATURALLY KNOW WHICH INGREDIENTS ARE NEEDED.
THIS MEDICINE MAKING SKILL CERTAINLY IS CONVENIENT.
HOW IS IT I CAN READ THIS GOBBLEDY-GOOK?
IT'S A MYSTERY.
REIJI, WOULD YOU LIKE ME TO MAKE YOU SOME MORE TEA?
THANKS, BUT WE'LL BE HEADING OUT.
CAN YOU COME WITH ME, NOELA?
NOELA COME!

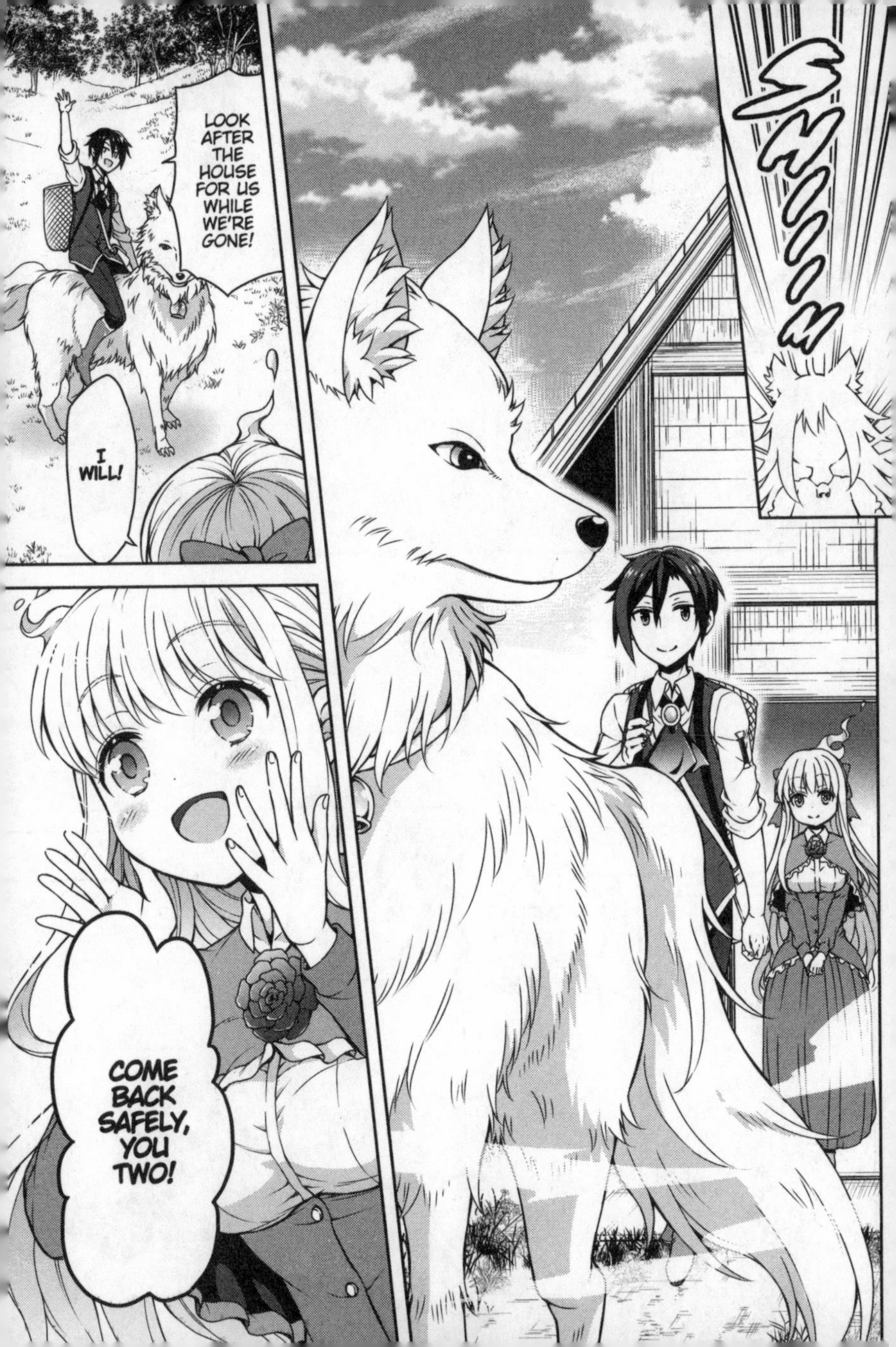
SWOOOM
LOOK AFTER THE HOUSE FOR US WHILE WE'RE GONE!
I WILL!
COME BACK SAFELY, YOU TWO!

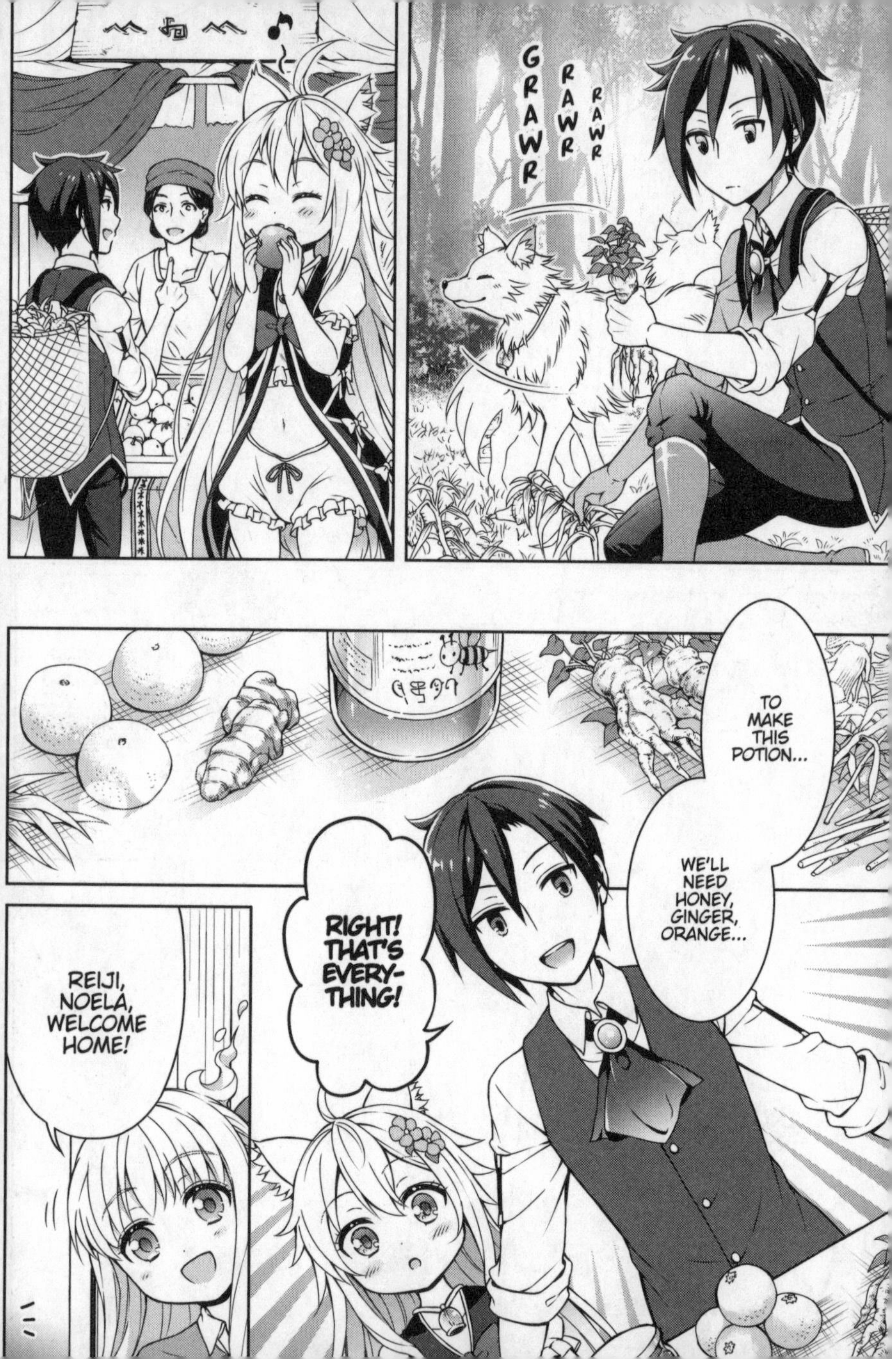
GRAWR
RAWR
RAWR
TO MAKE THIS POTION...
WE'LL NEED HONEY, GINGER, ORANGE...
RIGHT! THAT'S EVERY-THING!
REIJI, NOELA, WELCOME HOME!

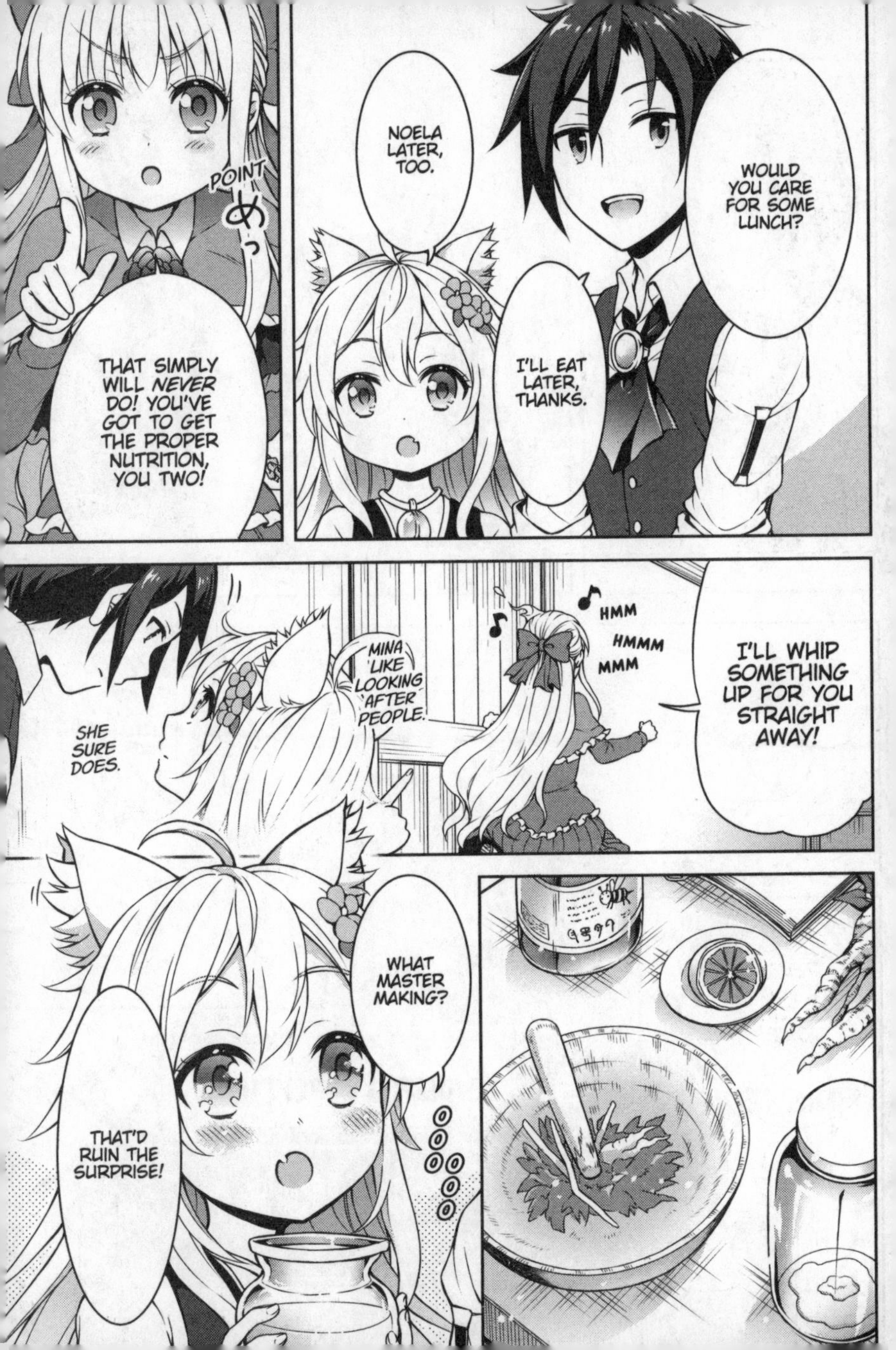

WOULD YOU CARE FOR SOME LUNCH?
I'LL EAT LATER, THANKS.
NOELA LATER, TOO.
POINT
めっ
THAT SIMPLY WILL *NEVER* DO! YOU'VE GOT TO GET THE PROPER NUTRITION, YOU TWO!
I'LL WHIP SOMETHING UP FOR YOU STRAIGHT AWAY!
HMM
HMMM
MMM
MINA LIKE LOOKING AFTER PEOPLE.
SHE SURE DOES.
WHAT MASTER MAKING?
THAT'D RUIN THE SURPRISE!

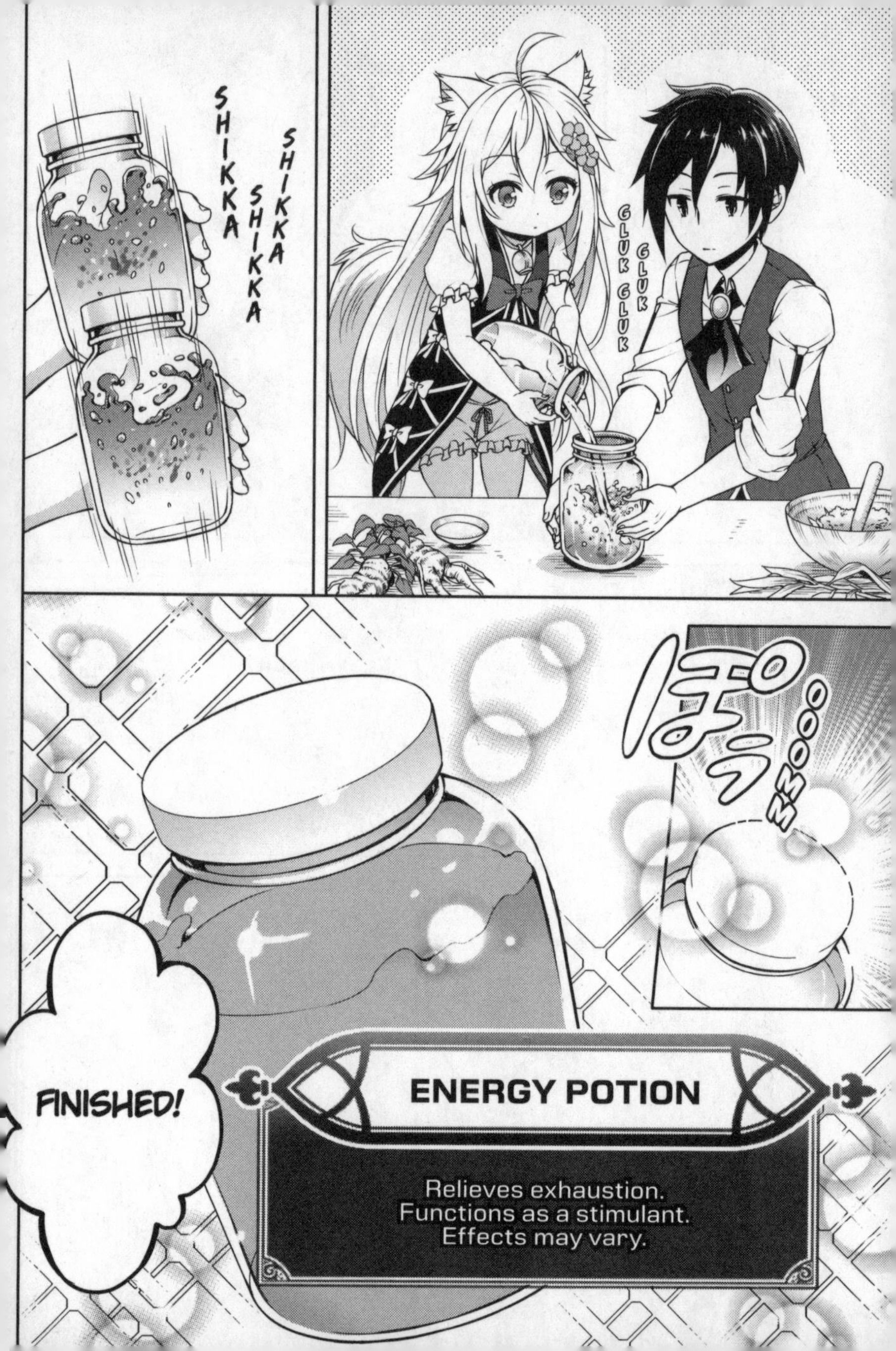
GLUK GLUK GLUK
SHIKKA SHIKKA SHIKKA
OOOOMM
FINISHED!
ENERGY POTION
Relieves exhaustion.
Functions as a stimulant.
Effects may vary.

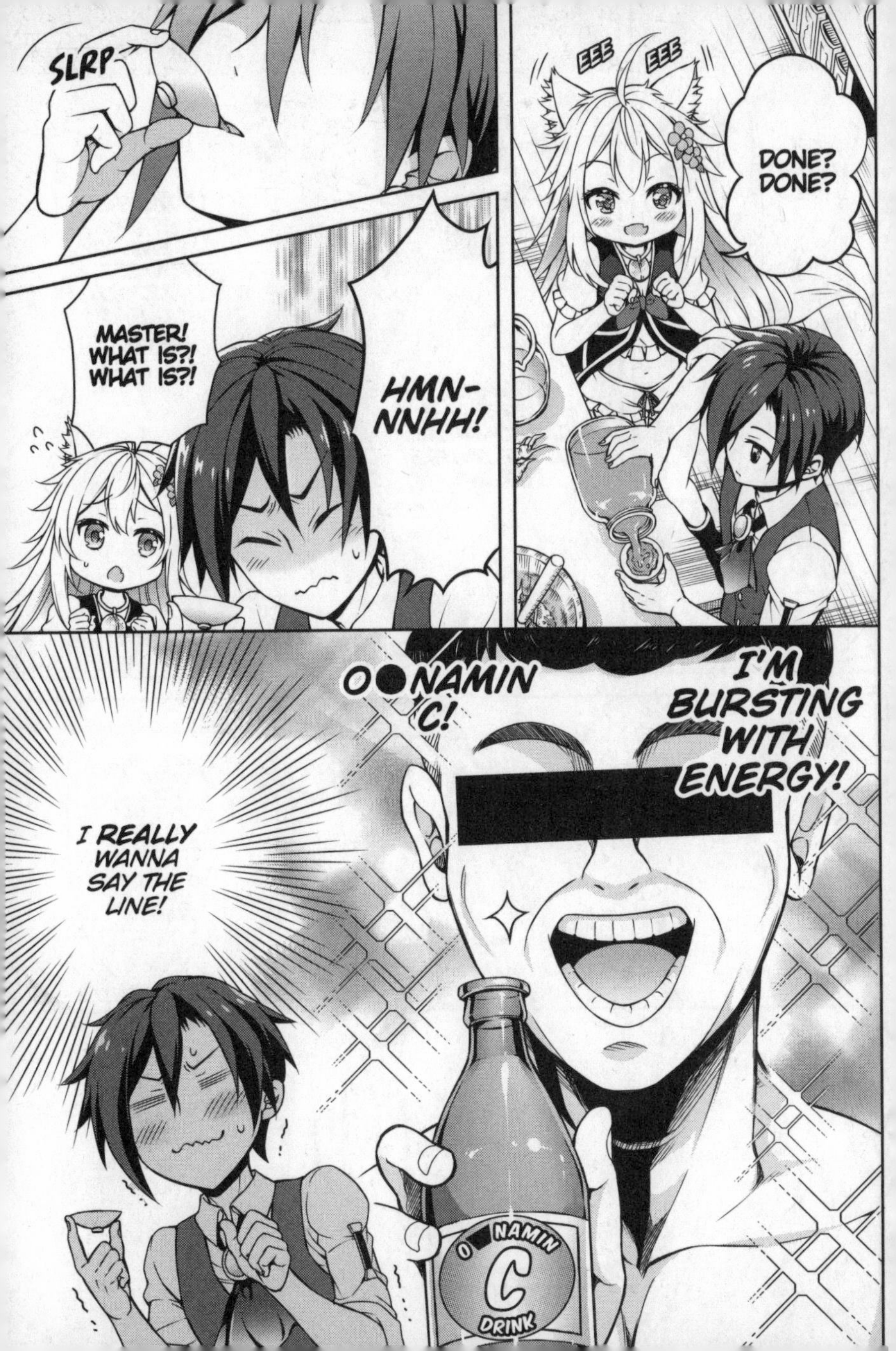
EEE
EEE
DONE? DONE?
SLRP
HMN-NNHH!
MASTER! WHAT IS?! WHAT IS?!
I'M BURSTING WITH ENERGY!
O●NAMIN C!
I REALLY WANNA SAY THE LINE!
O■NAMIN C DRINK

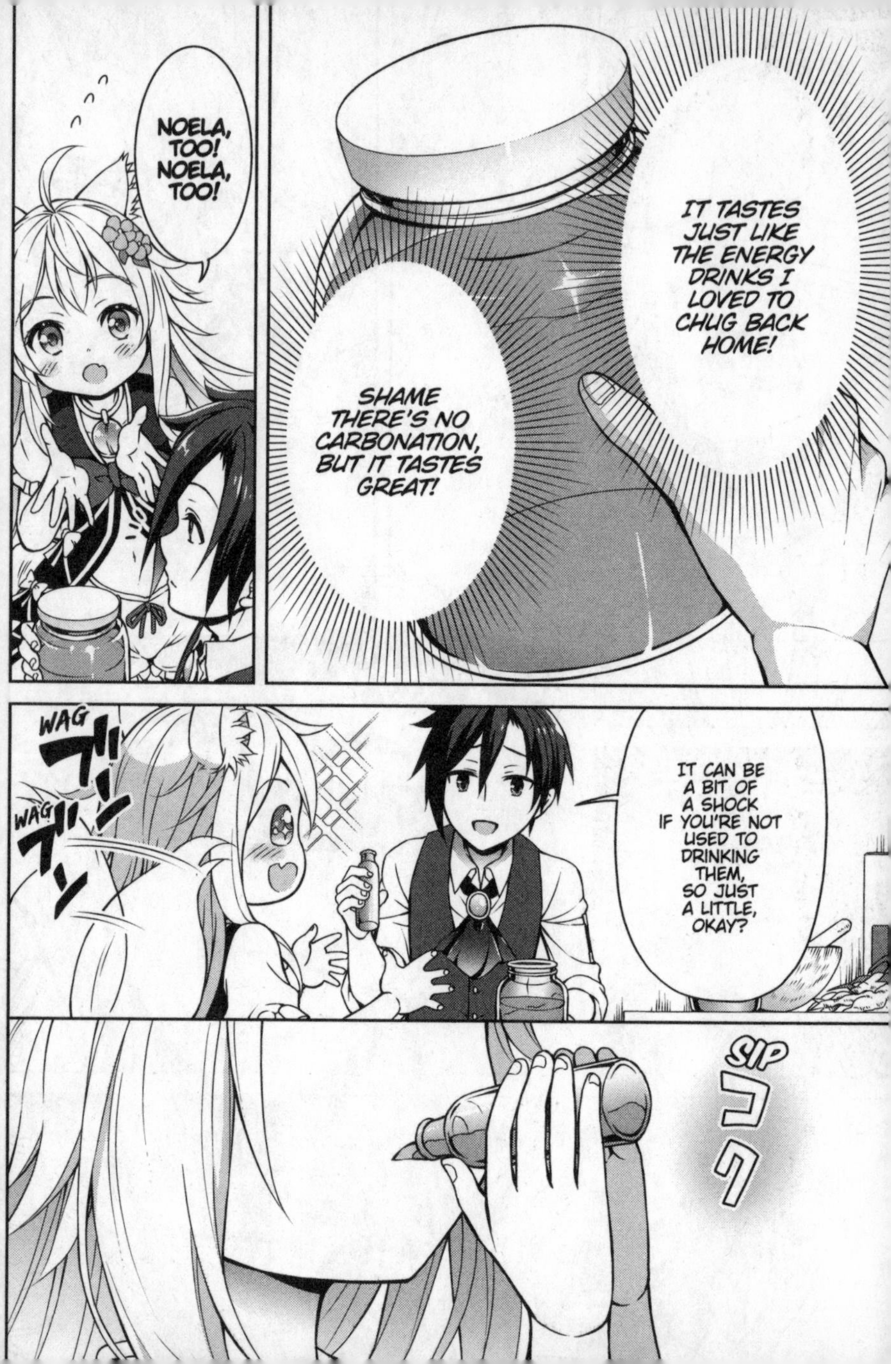
IT TASTES JUST LIKE THE ENERGY DRINKS I LOVED TO CHUG BACK HOME!
SHAME THERE'S NO CARBONATION, BUT IT TASTES GREAT!
NOELA, TOO! NOELA, TOO!
IT CAN BE A BIT OF A SHOCK IF YOU'RE NOT USED TO DRINKING THEM, SO JUST A LITTLE, OKAY?
WAG
WAG
SIP

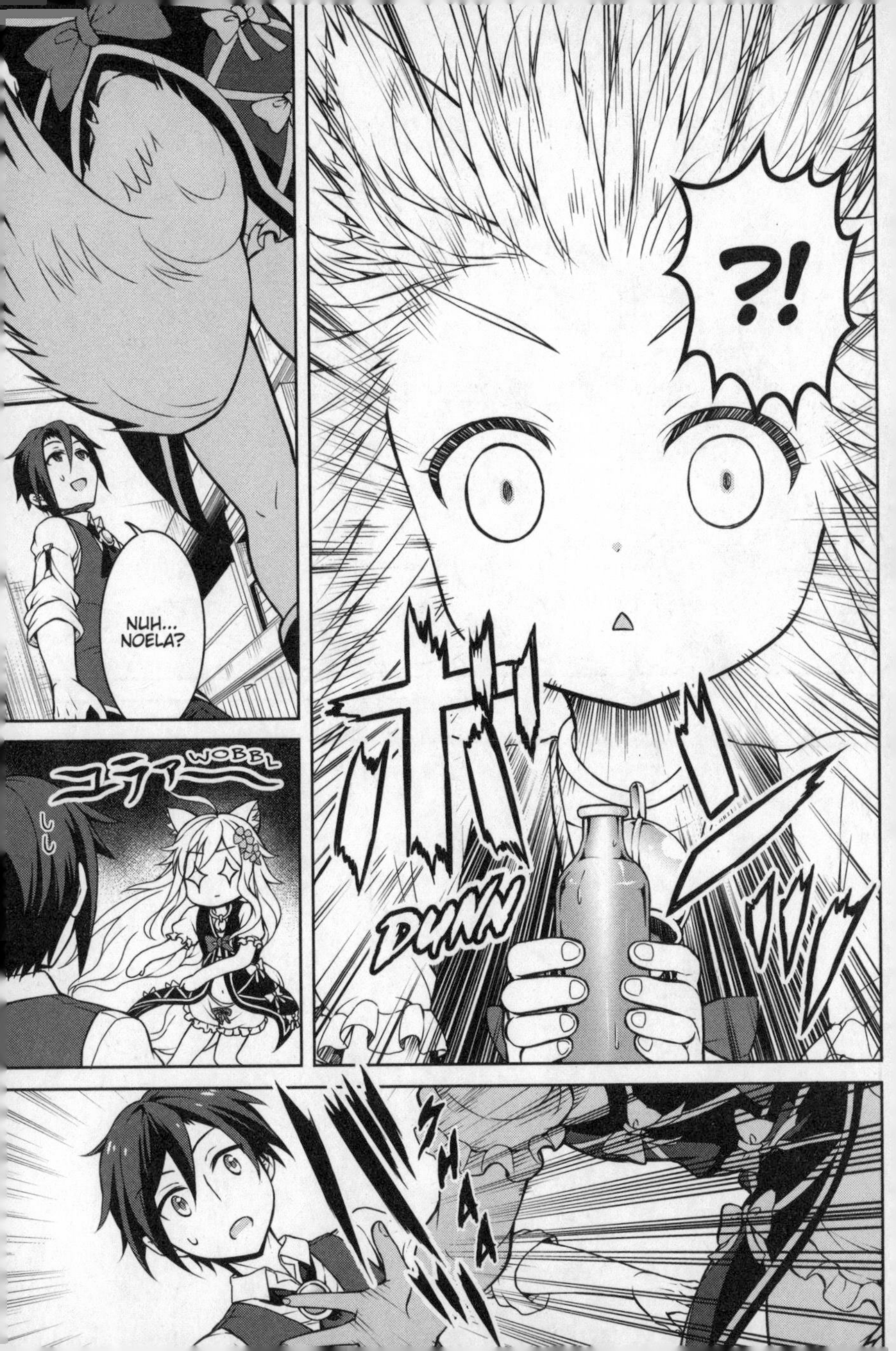
?!
DUNN
NUH... NOELA?
WOBBL
SHAA

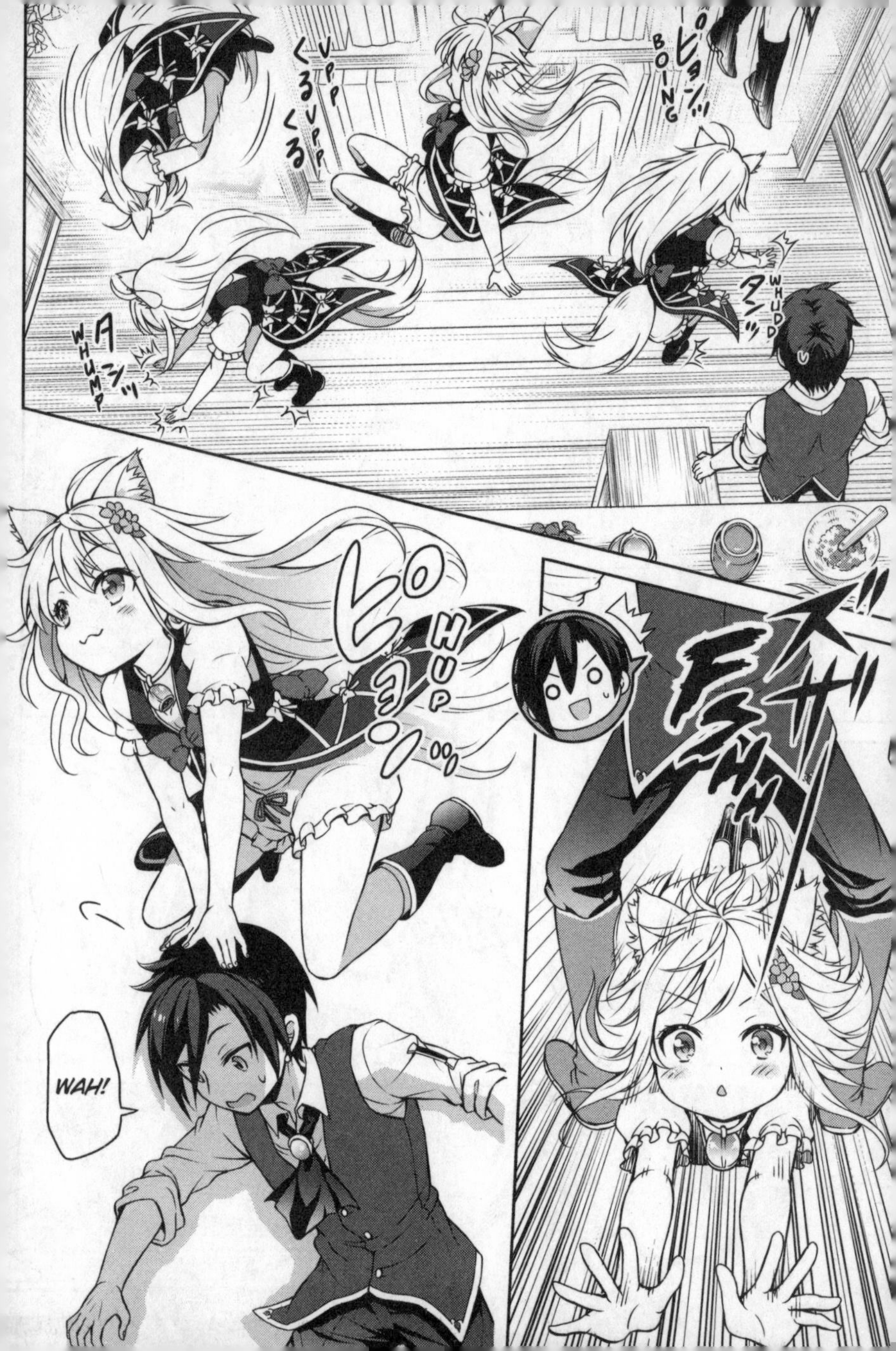
BOING
VPP VPP
くるくる
WHUD
WHUMP
ZMM
HUP
WAH!

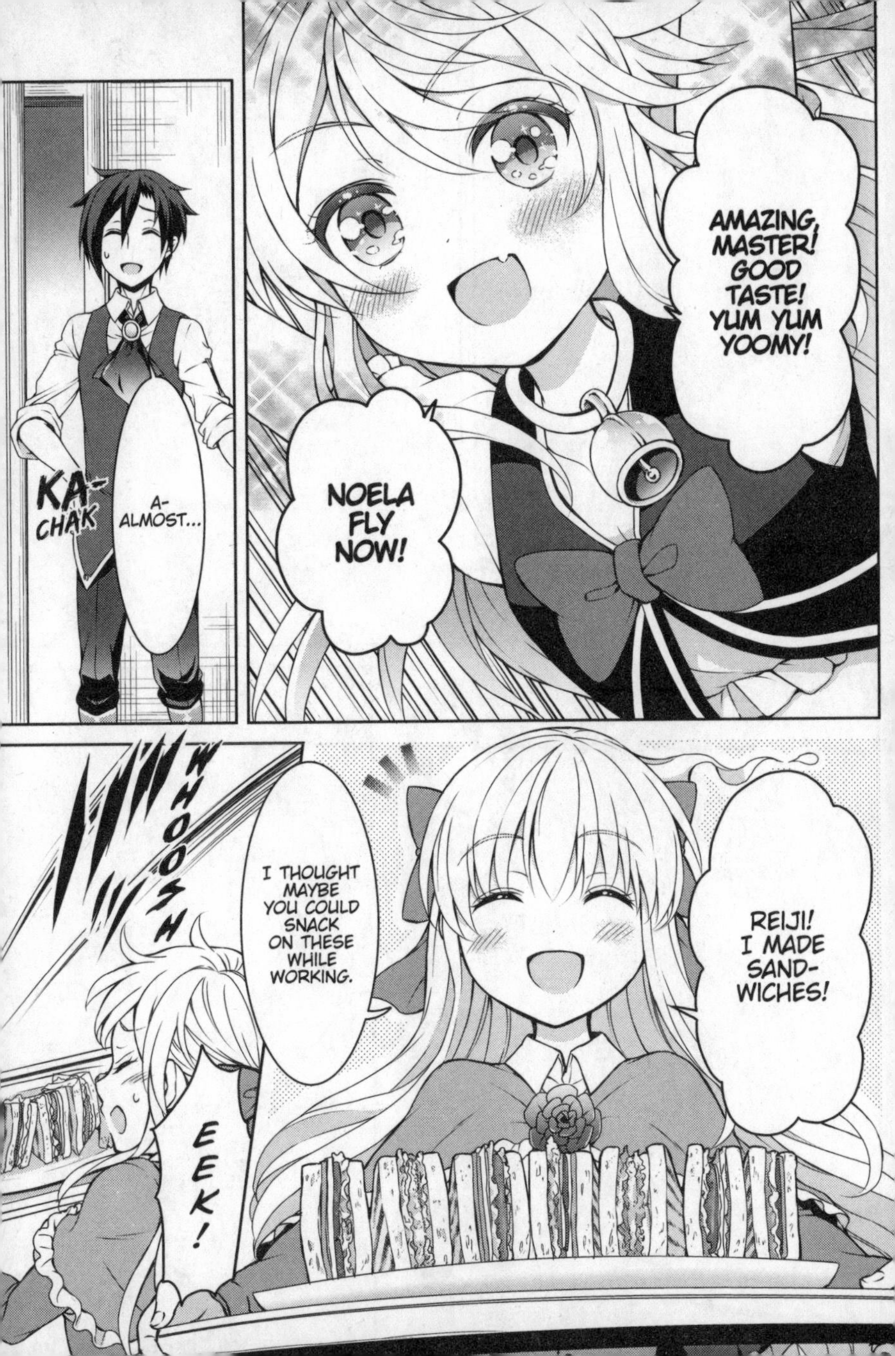
AMAZING, MASTER! GOOD TASTE! YUM YUM YOOMY!
NOELA FLY NOW!
KA-CHAK
A- ALMOST...
REIJI! I MADE SAND- WICHES!
I THOUGHT MAYBE YOU COULD SNACK ON THESE WHILE WORKING.
WHOOOSH
EEK!

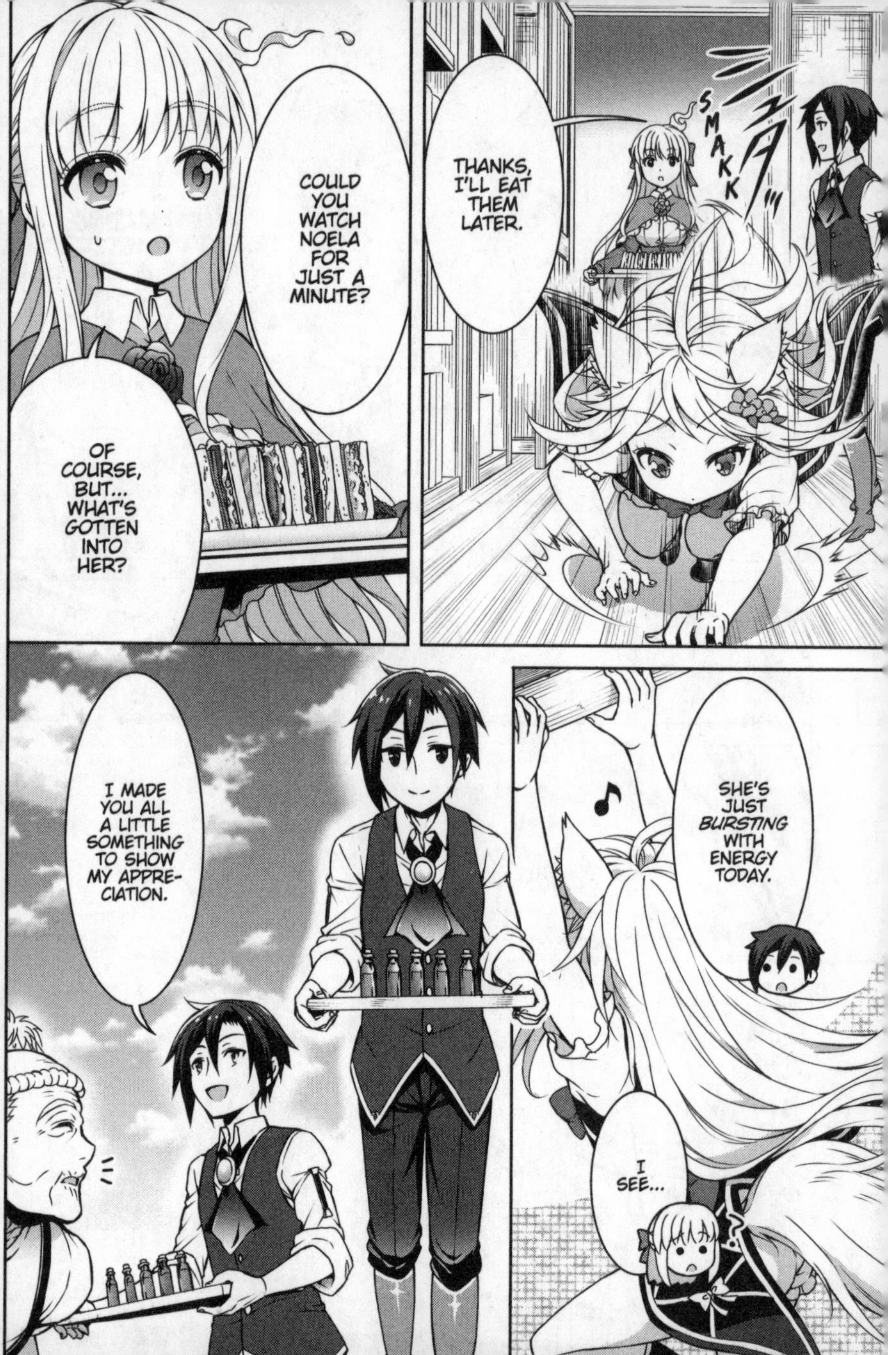

THANKS, I'LL EAT THEM LATER.
SMAKK
COULD YOU WATCH NOELA FOR JUST A MINUTE?
OF COURSE, BUT... WHAT'S GOTTEN INTO HER?
SHE'S JUST *BURSTING* WITH ENERGY TODAY.
I SEE...
I MADE YOU ALL A LITTLE SOMETHING TO SHOW MY APPRE-CIATION.

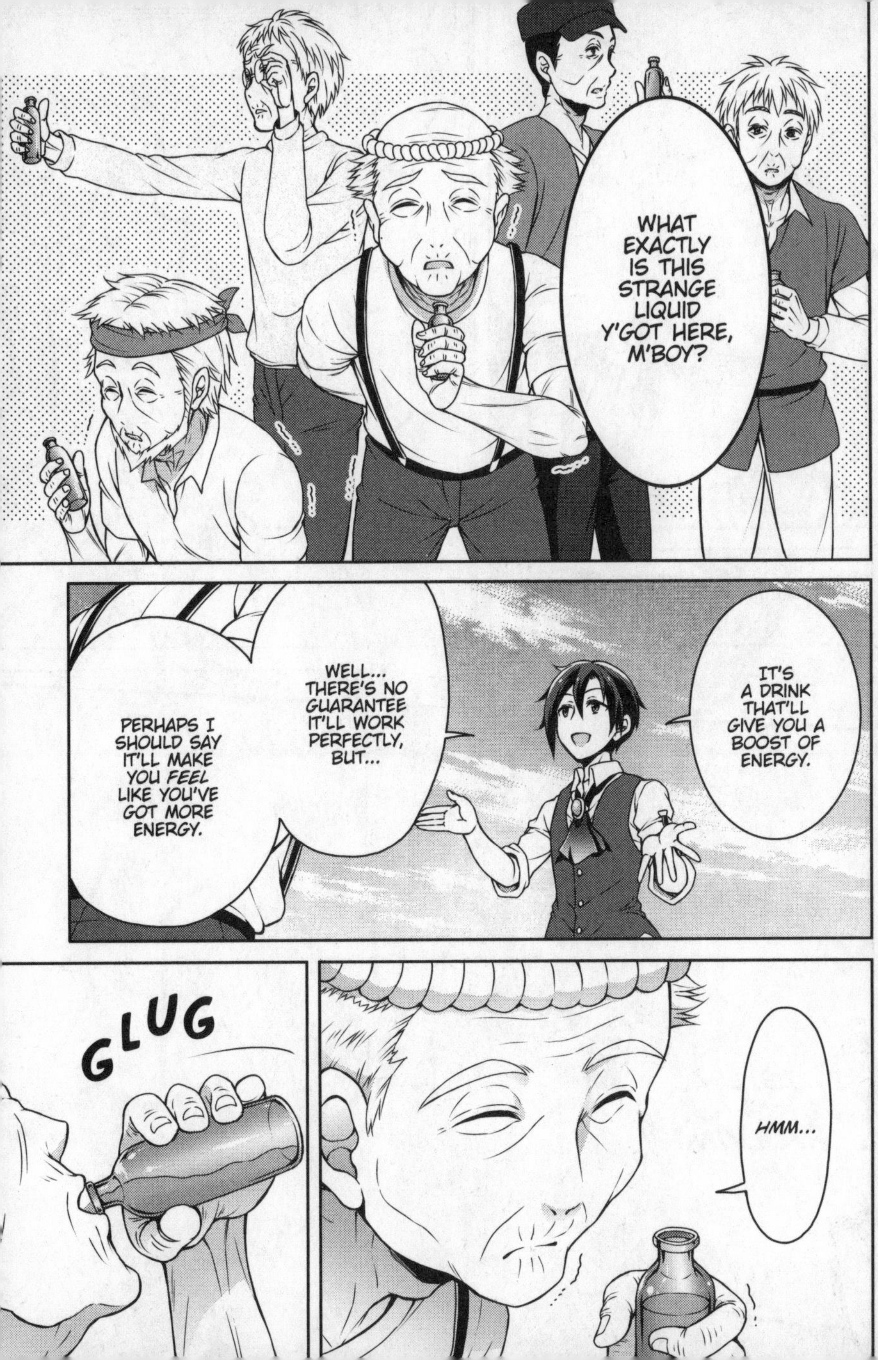
WHAT EXACTLY IS THIS STRANGE LIQUID Y'GOT HERE, M'BOY?
IT'S A DRINK THAT'LL GIVE YOU A BOOST OF ENERGY.
WELL... THERE'S NO GUARANTEE IT'LL WORK PERFECTLY, BUT...
PERHAPS I SHOULD SAY IT'LL MAKE YOU *FEEL* LIKE YOU'VE GOT MORE ENERGY.
HMM...
GLUG

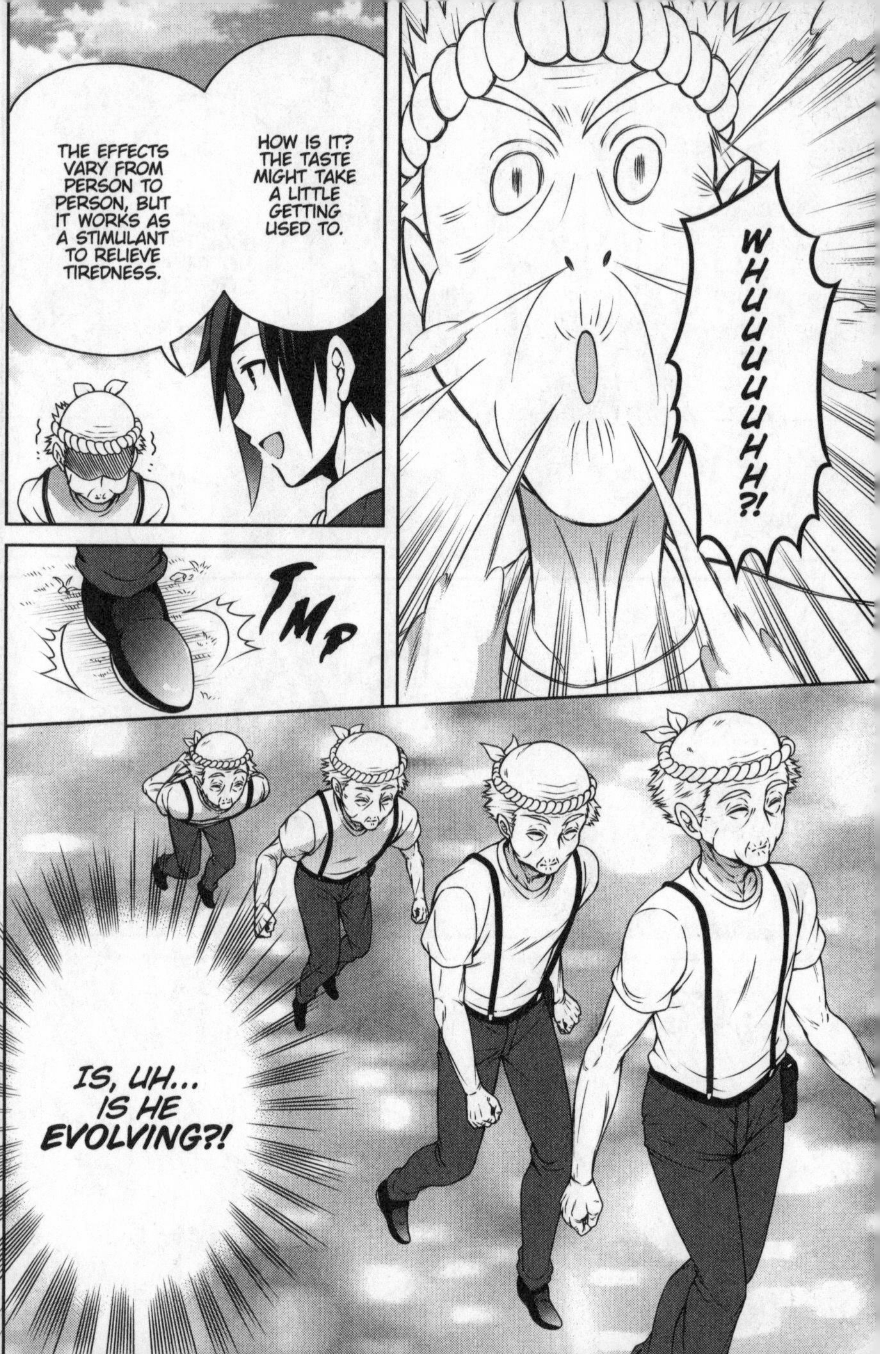
WHUUUUUUHH?!
HOW IS IT? THE TASTE MIGHT TAKE A LITTLE GETTING USED TO.
THE EFFECTS VARY FROM PERSON TO PERSON, BUT IT WORKS AS A STIMULANT TO RELIEVE TIREDNESS.
TMP
IS, UH... IS HE EVOLVING?!

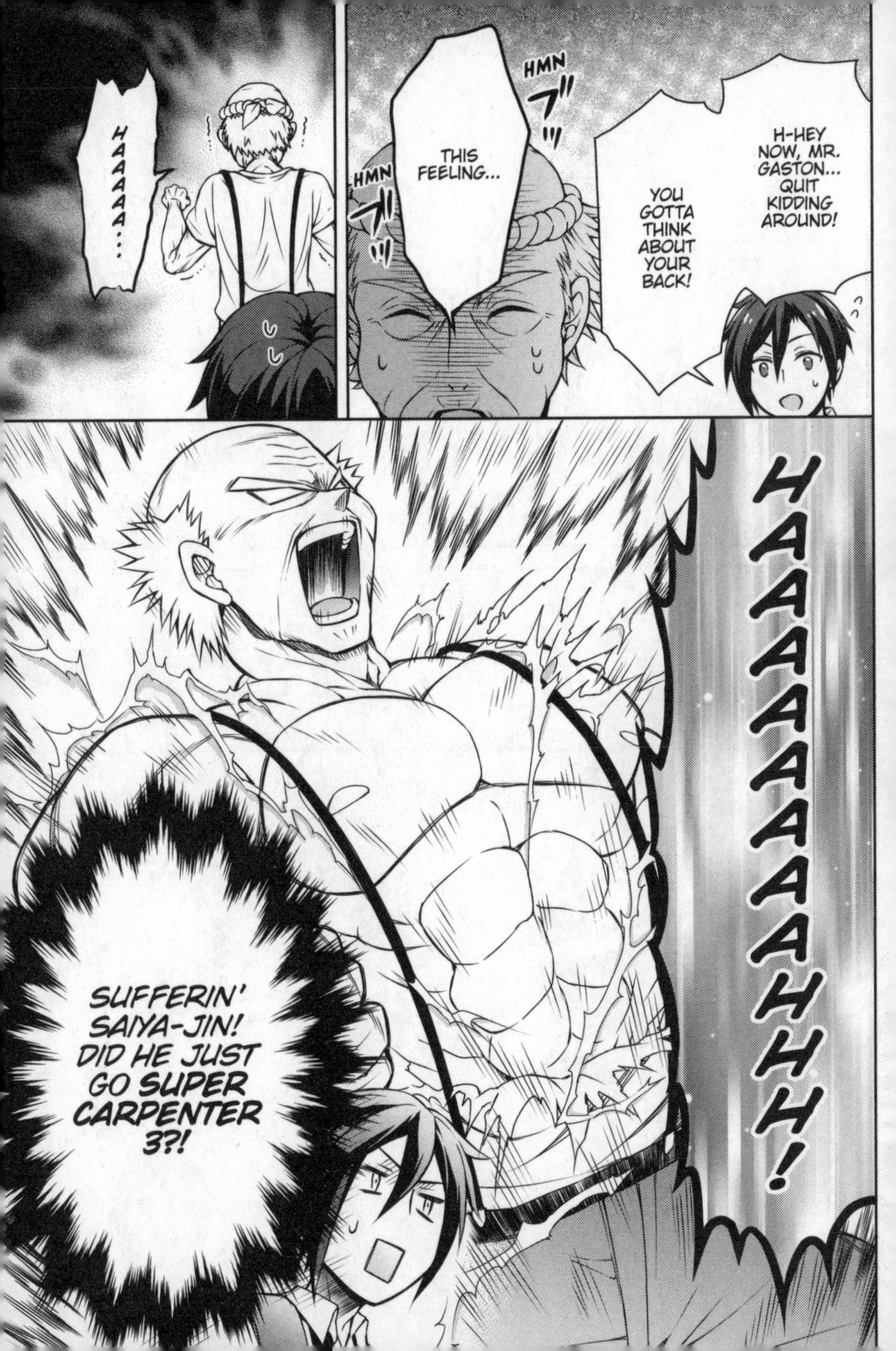
H-HEY NOW, MR. GASTON... QUIT KIDDING AROUND!
YOU GOTTA THINK ABOUT YOUR BACK!
HMN
THIS FEELING...
HMN
HAAAAAA...
HAAAAAAAAAHHH!
SUFFERIN' SAIYA-JIN! DID HE JUST GO SUPER CARPENTER 3?!

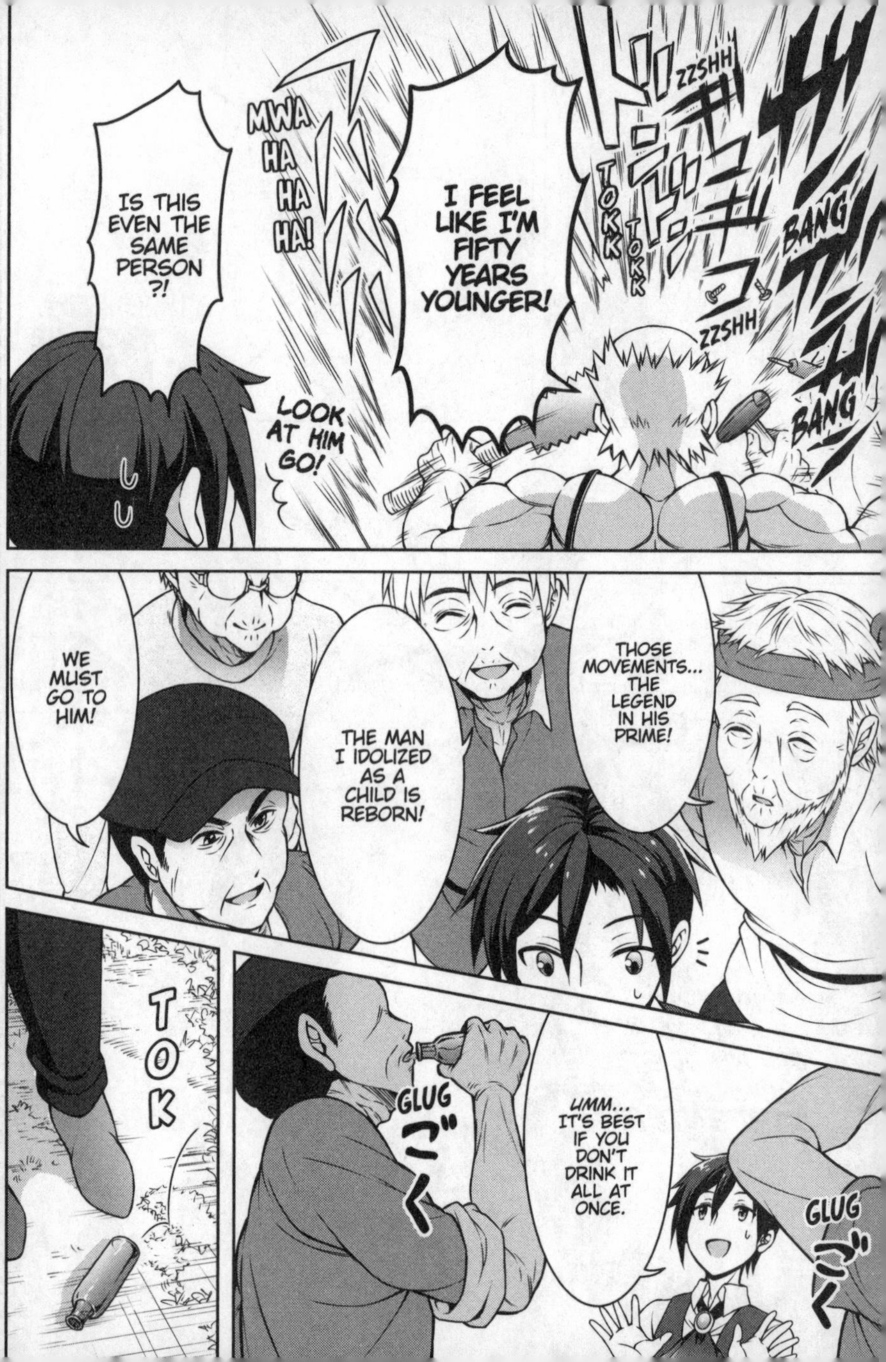

ZZSHH
TOKK TOKK
BANG
BANG
ZZSHH
I FEEL LIKE I'M FIFTY YEARS YOUNGER!
MWA HA HA HA HA!
LOOK AT HIM GO!
IS THIS EVEN THE SAME PERSON?!
THOSE MOVEMENTS... THE LEGEND IN HIS PRIME!
THE MAN I IDOLIZED AS A CHILD IS REBORN!
WE MUST GO TO HIM!
GLUG
ごく
UMM... IT'S BEST IF YOU DON'T DRINK IT ALL AT ONCE.
GLUG
ごく
TOK

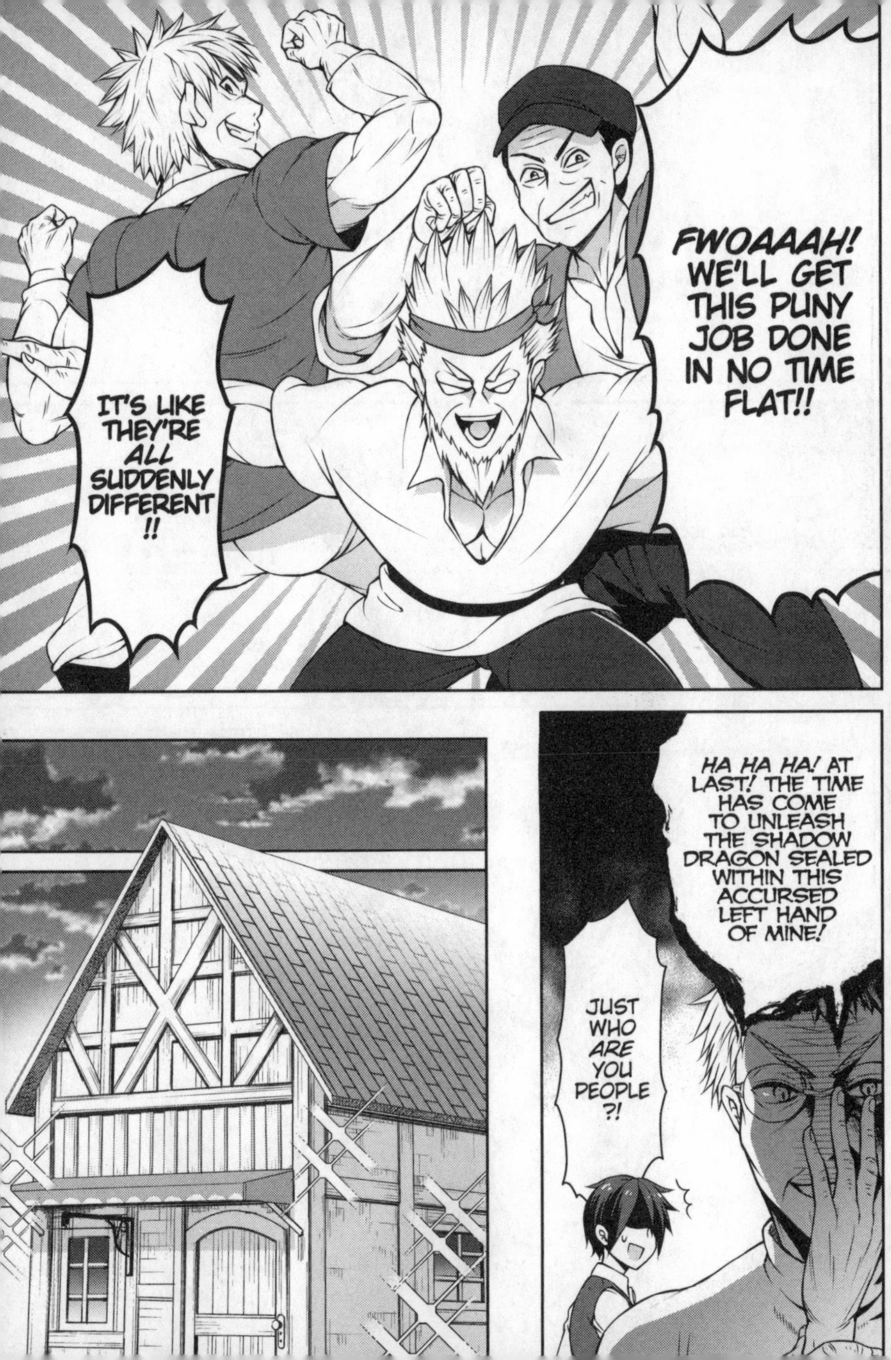
FWOAAAH! WE'LL GET THIS PUNY JOB DONE IN NO TIME FLAT!!
IT'S LIKE THEY'RE ALL SUDDENLY DIFFERENT!!
HA HA HA! AT LAST! THE TIME HAS COME TO UNLEASH THE SHADOW DRAGON SEALED WITHIN THIS ACCURSED LEFT HAND OF MINE!
JUST WHO ARE YOU PEOPLE?!

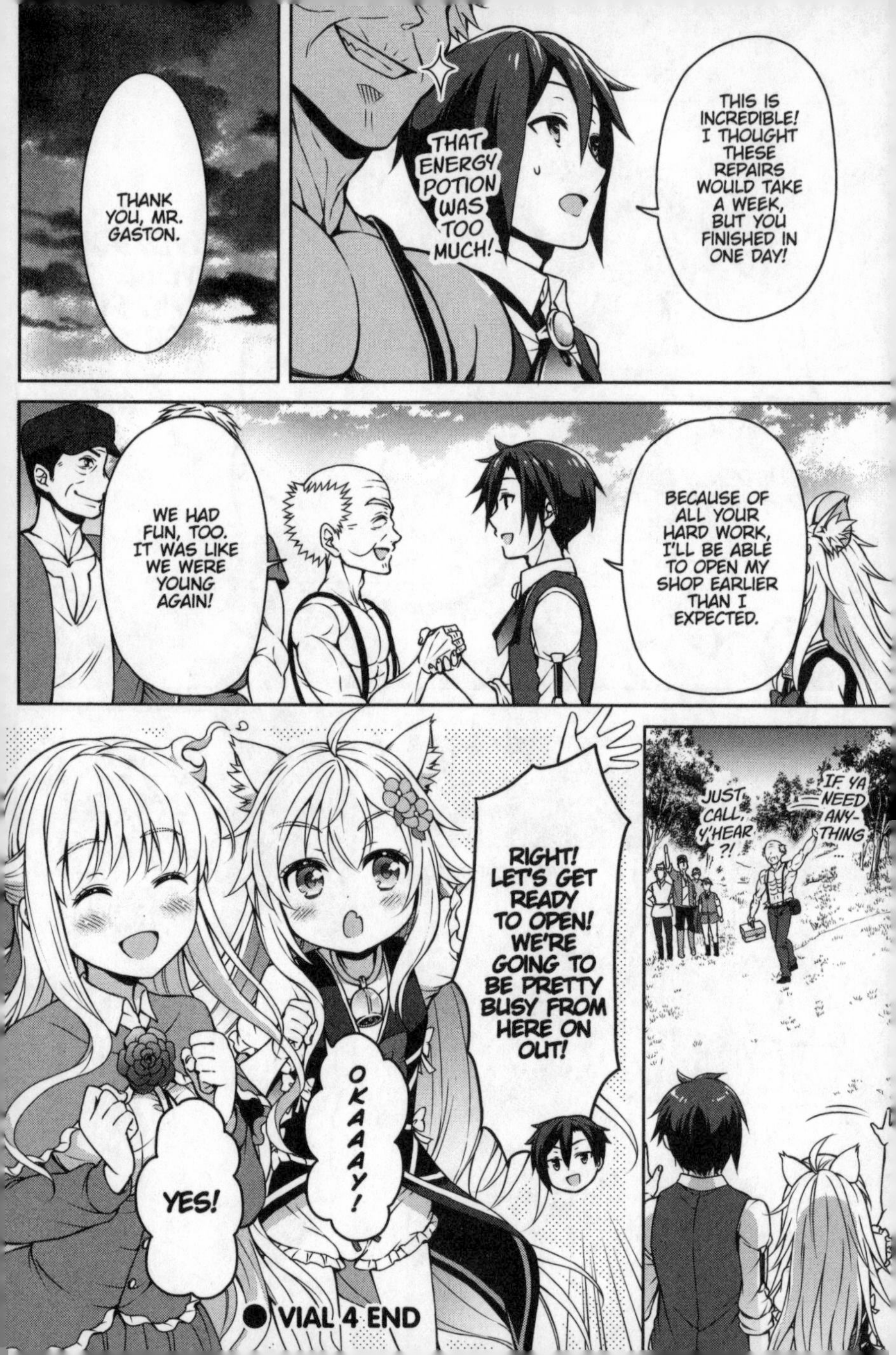
THIS IS INCREDIBLE! I THOUGHT THESE REPAIRS WOULD TAKE A WEEK, BUT YOU FINISHED IN ONE DAY!
THAT ENERGY POTION WAS TOO MUCH!
THANK YOU, MR. GASTON.
BECAUSE OF ALL YOUR HARD WORK, I'LL BE ABLE TO OPEN MY SHOP EARLIER THAN I EXPECTED.
WE HAD FUN, TOO. IT WAS LIKE WE WERE YOUNG AGAIN!
IF YA NEED ANYTHING...
JUST CALL, Y'HEAR?!
RIGHT! LET'S GET READY TO OPEN! WE'RE GOING TO BE PRETTY BUSY FROM HERE ON OUT!
OKAAAY!
YES!
VIAL 4 END

DRUGSTORE in Another World

~ The Slow Life of a ~
~ Cheat Pharmacist

DRUGSTORE
in AnOTHer WORLD

~ The Slow Life of a ~
Cheat Pharmacist

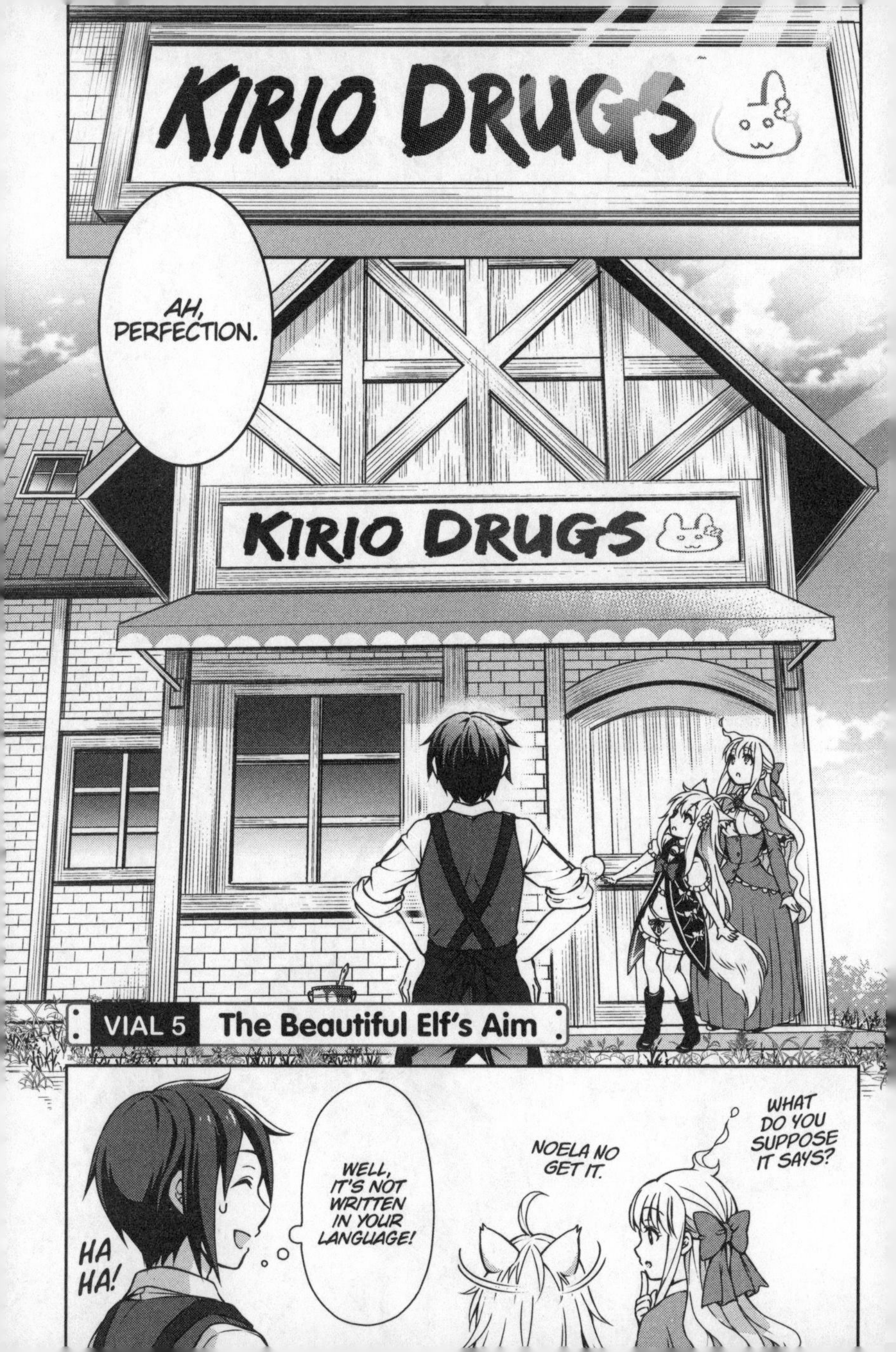
KIRIO DRUGS
AH, PERFECTION.
KIRIO DRUGS
VIAL 5 The Beautiful Elf's Aim
WHAT DO YOU SUPPOSE IT SAYS?
NOELA NO GET IT.
WELL, IT'S NOT WRITTEN IN YOUR LANGUAGE!
HA HA!

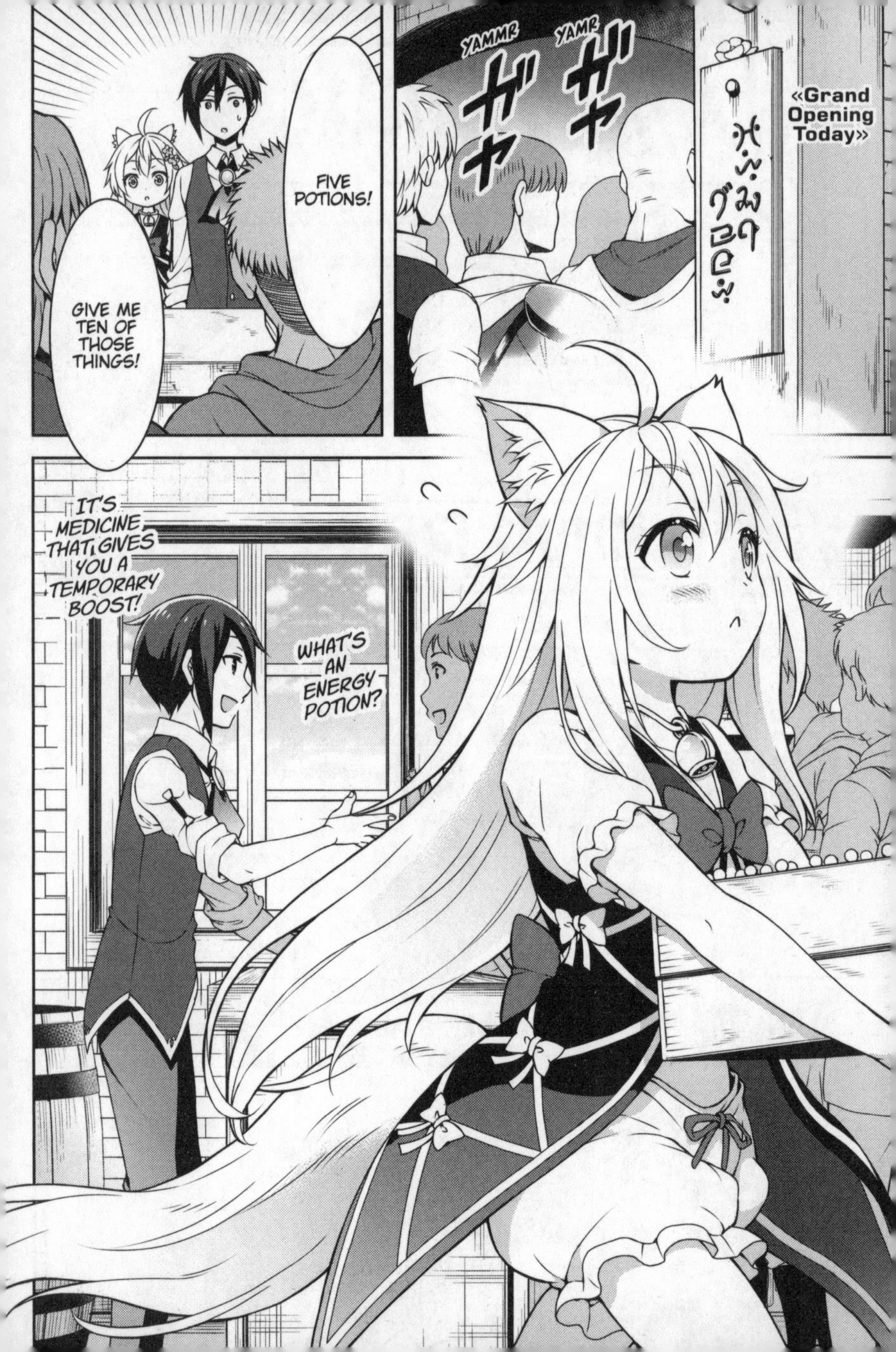
«Grand Opening Today»
YAMR
ガヤ
YAMMR
ガヤ
FIVE POTIONS!
GIVE ME TEN OF THOSE THINGS!
WHAT'S AN ENERGY POTION?
IT'S MEDICINE THAT GIVES YOU A TEMPORARY BOOST!

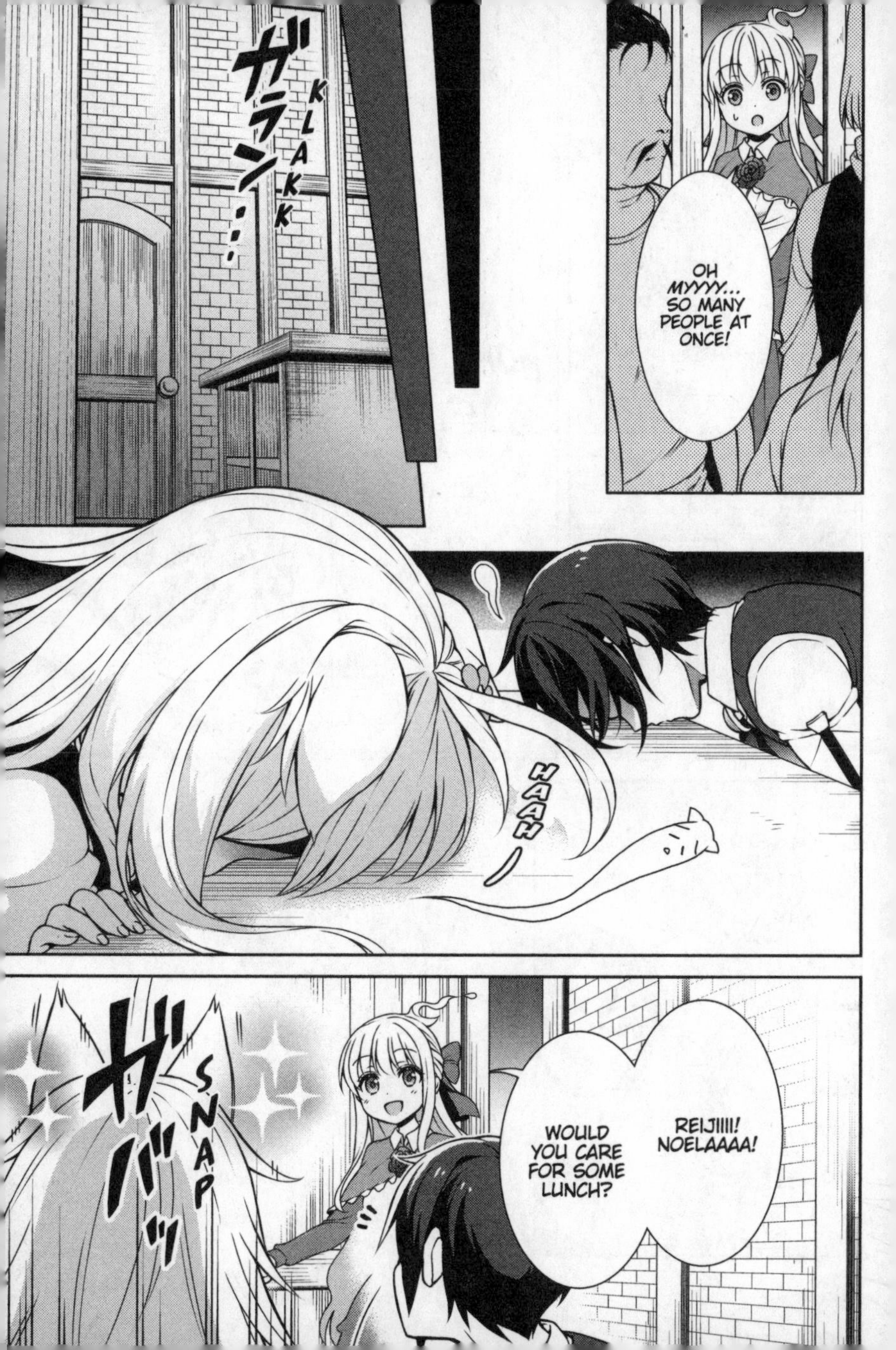
OH MYYYY... SO MANY PEOPLE AT ONCE!
ガラン…
KLAKK
HAAAH
REIJIIII! NOELAAAA!
WOULD YOU CARE FOR SOME LUNCH?
SNAP

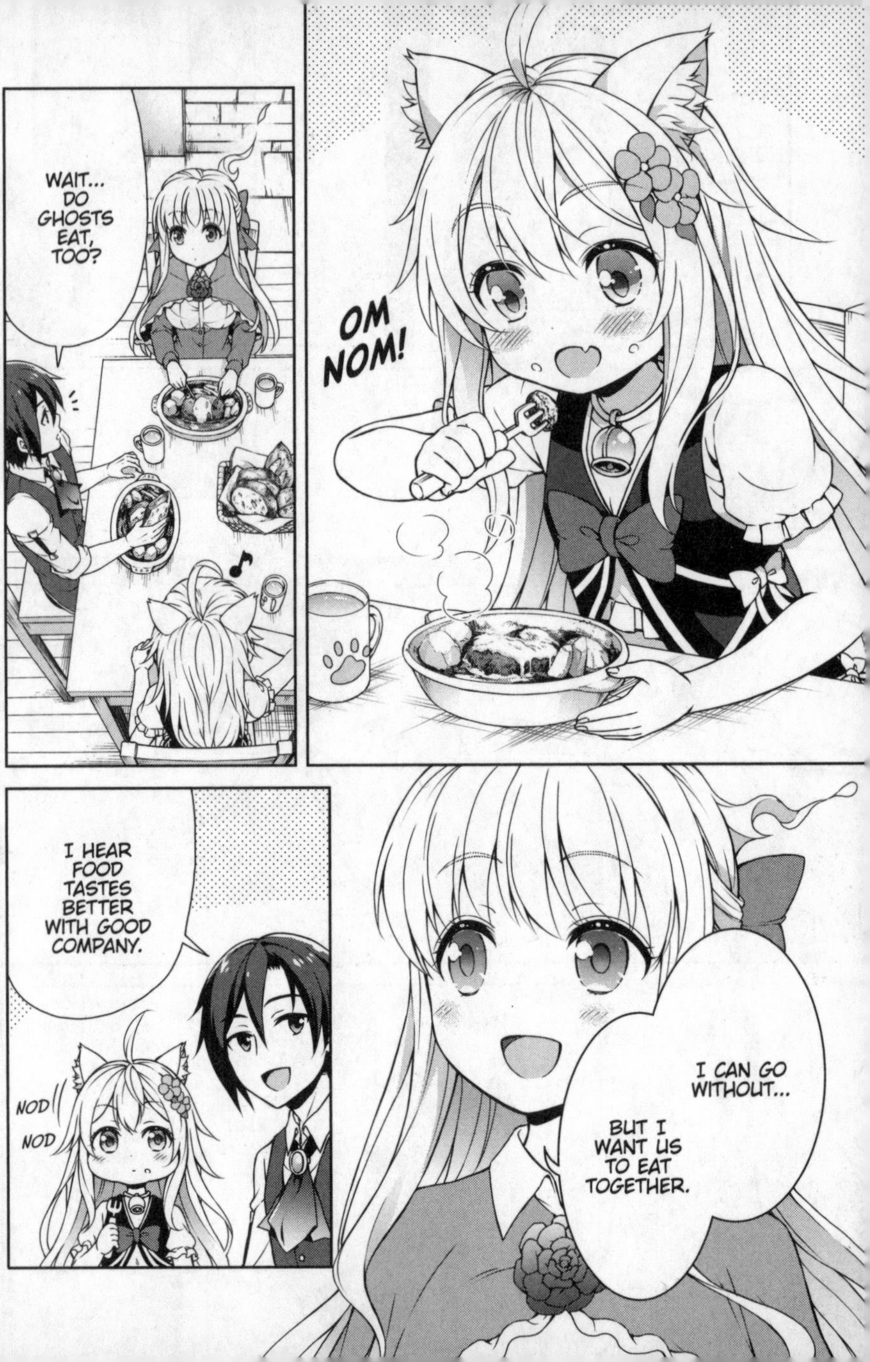
OM NOM!
WAIT... DO GHOSTS EAT, TOO?
I CAN GO WITHOUT...
BUT I WANT US TO EAT TOGETHER.
I HEAR FOOD TASTES BETTER WITH GOOD COMPANY.
NOD NOD

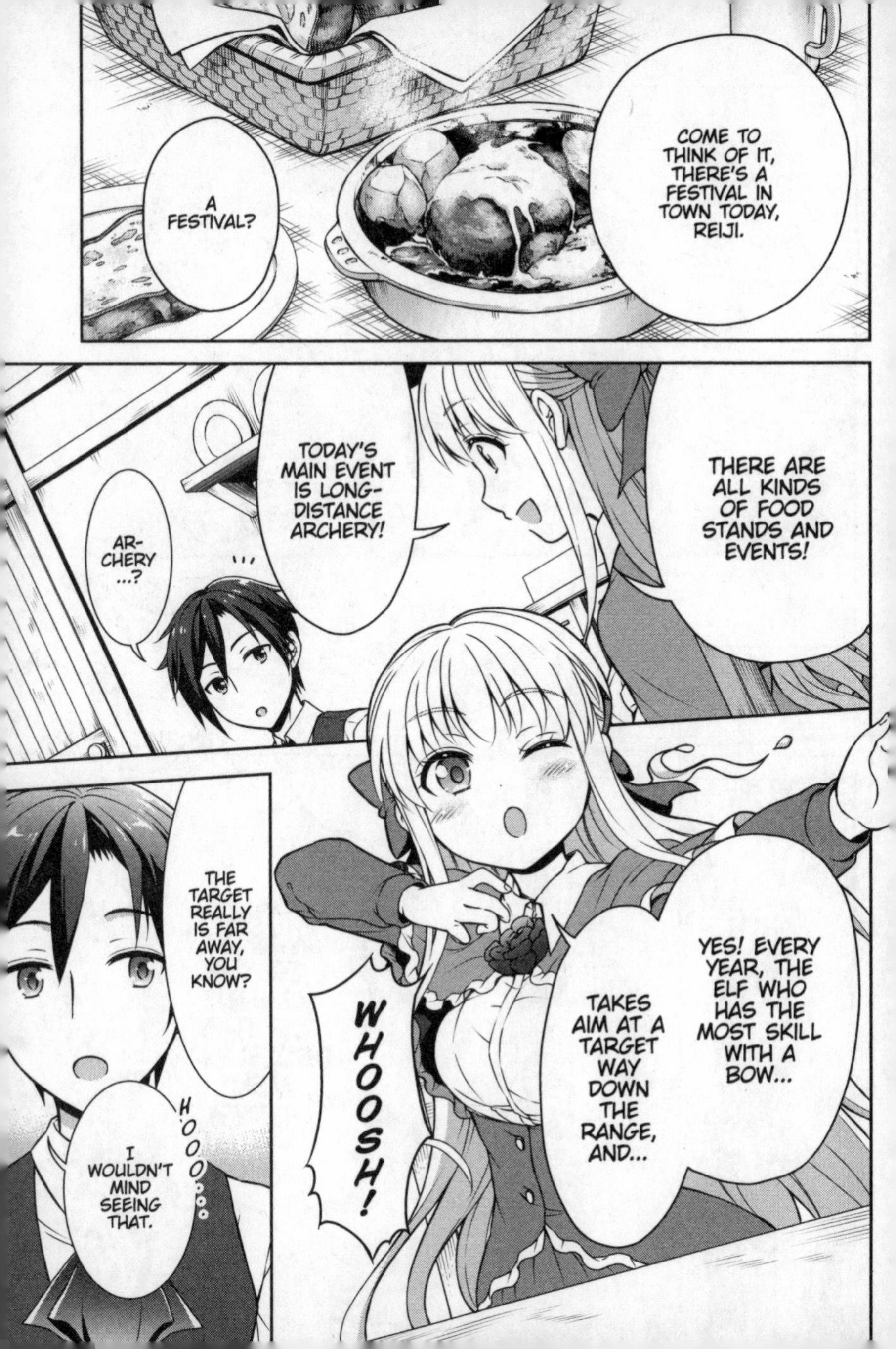
COME TO THINK OF IT, THERE'S A FESTIVAL IN TOWN TODAY, REIJI.
A FESTIVAL?
THERE ARE ALL KINDS OF FOOD STANDS AND EVENTS!
TODAY'S MAIN EVENT IS LONG-DISTANCE ARCHERY!
...
AR-CHERY ...?
YES! EVERY YEAR, THE ELF WHO HAS THE MOST SKILL WITH A BOW...
TAKES AIM AT A TARGET WAY DOWN THE RANGE, AND...
WHOOOSH!
THE TARGET REALLY IS FAR AWAY, YOU KNOW?
HOOOO...
I WOULDN'T MIND SEEING THAT.

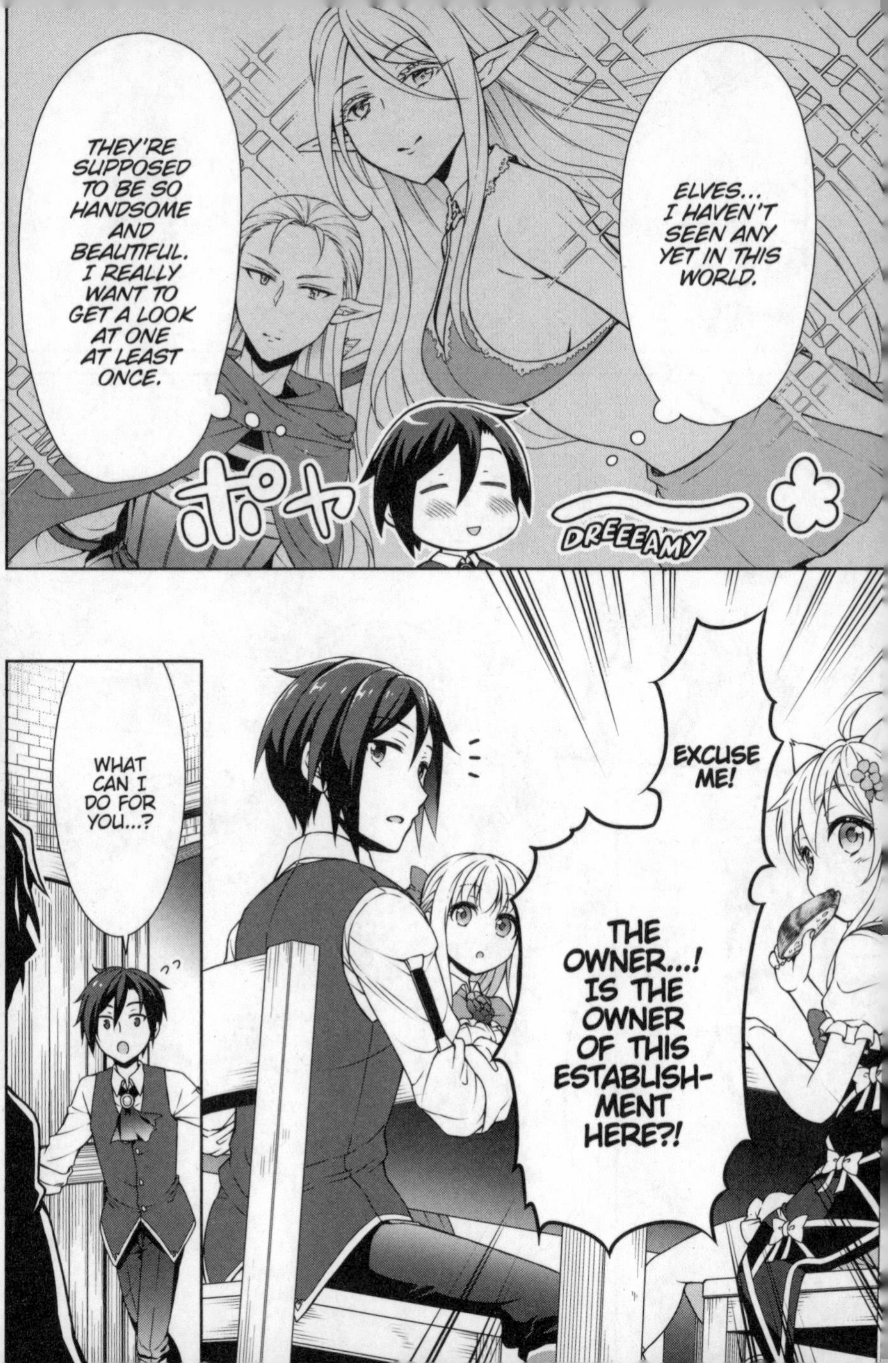
ELVES... I HAVEN'T SEEN ANY YET IN THIS WORLD.
THEY'RE SUPPOSED TO BE SO HANDSOME AND BEAUTIFUL. I REALLY WANT TO GET A LOOK AT ONE AT LEAST ONCE.
DREEEAMY
EXCUSE ME!
THE OWNER...! IS THE OWNER OF THIS ESTABLISH-MENT HERE?!
WHAT CAN I DO FOR YOU...?

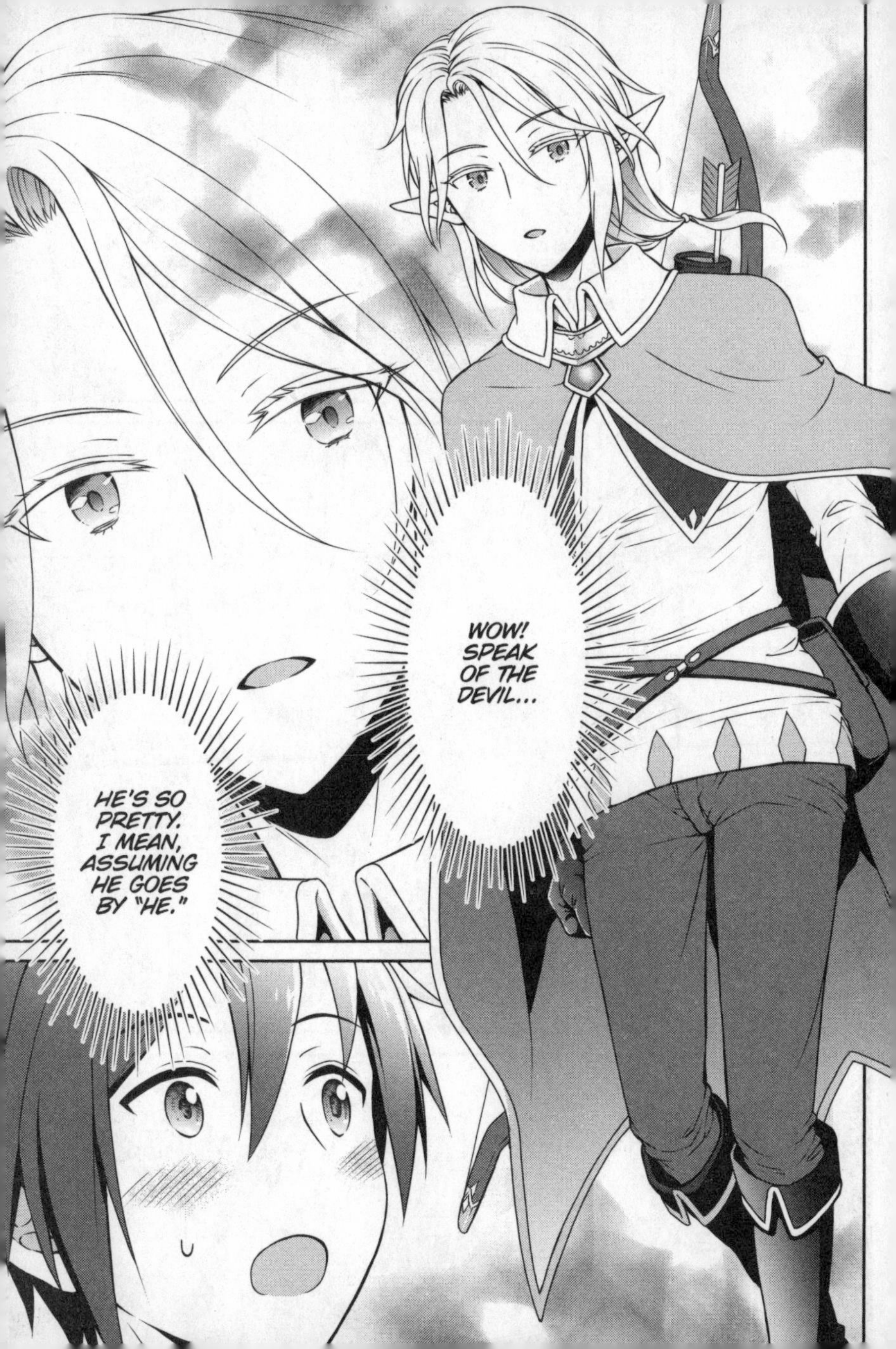
WOW! SPEAK OF THE DEVIL...
HE'S SO PRETTY. I MEAN, ASSUMING HE GOES BY "HE."

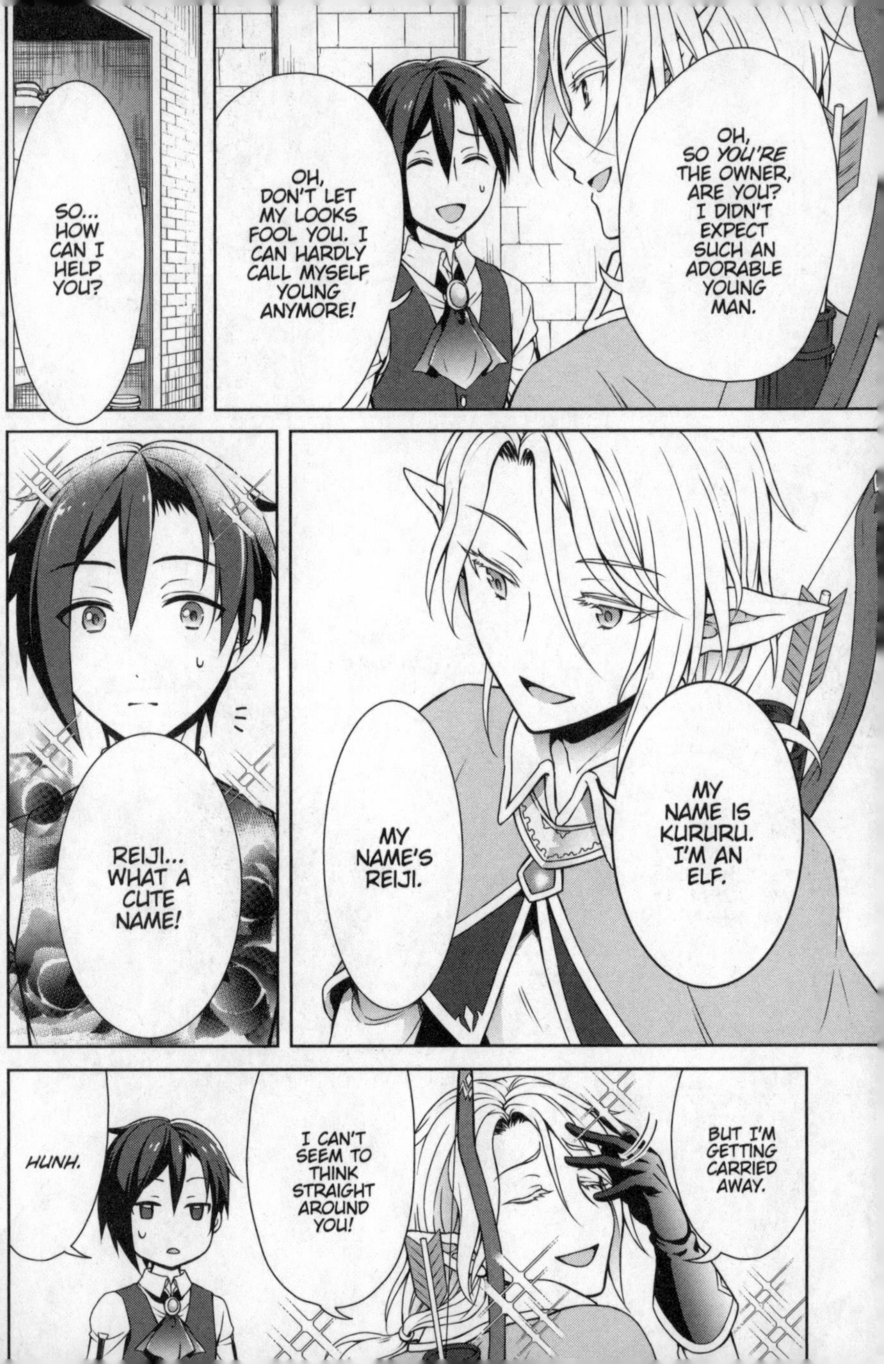
OH, SO YOU'RE THE OWNER, ARE YOU? I DIDN'T EXPECT SUCH AN ADORABLE YOUNG MAN.
OH, DON'T LET MY LOOKS FOOL YOU. I CAN HARDLY CALL MYSELF YOUNG ANYMORE!
SO... HOW CAN I HELP YOU?
MY NAME IS KURURU. I'M AN ELF.
MY NAME'S REIJI.
REIJI... WHAT A CUTE NAME!
BUT I'M GETTING CARRIED AWAY.
I CAN'T SEEM TO THINK STRAIGHT AROUND YOU!
HUNH.

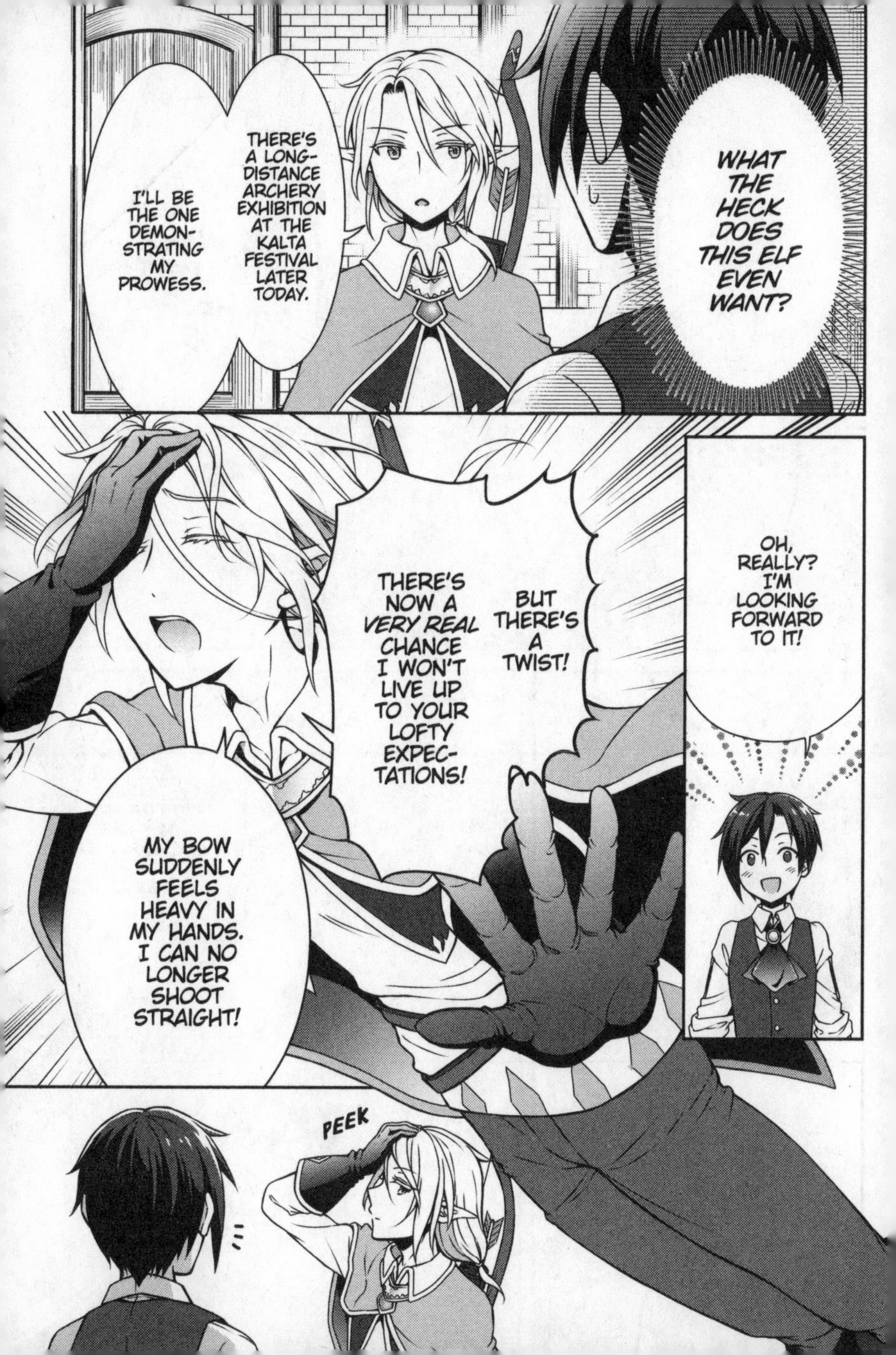
WHAT THE HECK DOES THIS ELF EVEN WANT?
THERE'S A LONG-DISTANCE ARCHERY EXHIBITION AT THE KALTA FESTIVAL LATER TODAY.
I'LL BE THE ONE DEMONSTRATING MY PROWESS.
OH, REALLY? I'M LOOKING FORWARD TO IT!
BUT THERE'S A TWIST!
THERE'S NOW A *VERY REAL* CHANCE I WON'T LIVE UP TO YOUR LOFTY EXPECTATIONS!
MY BOW SUDDENLY FEELS HEAVY IN MY HANDS. I CAN NO LONGER SHOOT STRAIGHT!
PEEK

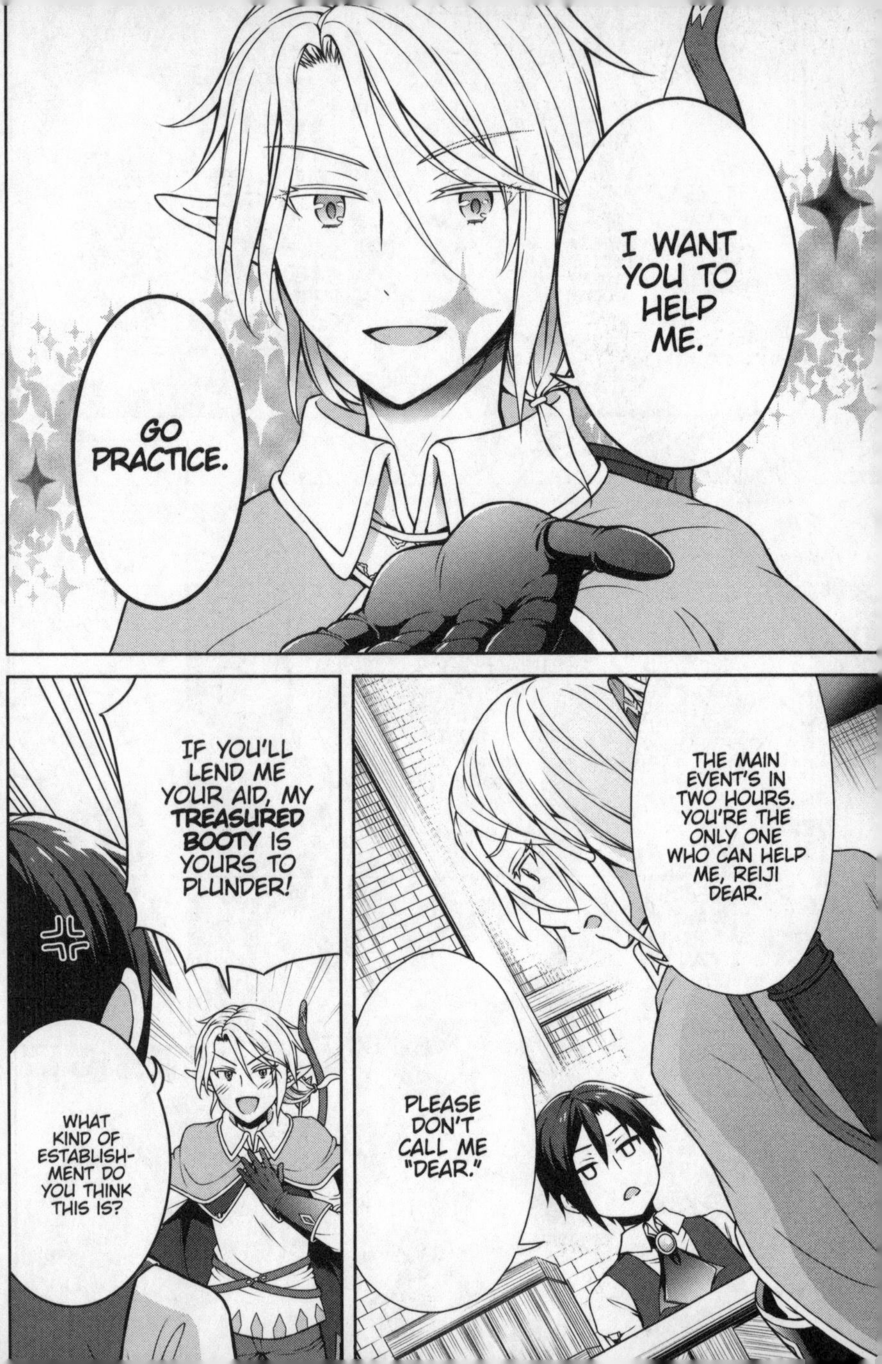
I WANT YOU TO HELP ME.
GO PRACTICE.
THE MAIN EVENT'S IN TWO HOURS. YOU'RE THE ONLY ONE WHO CAN HELP ME, REIJI DEAR.
PLEASE DON'T CALL ME "DEAR."
IF YOU'LL LEND ME YOUR AID, MY **TREASURED BOOTY** IS YOURS TO PLUNDER!
WHAT KIND OF ESTABLISHMENT DO YOU THINK THIS IS?

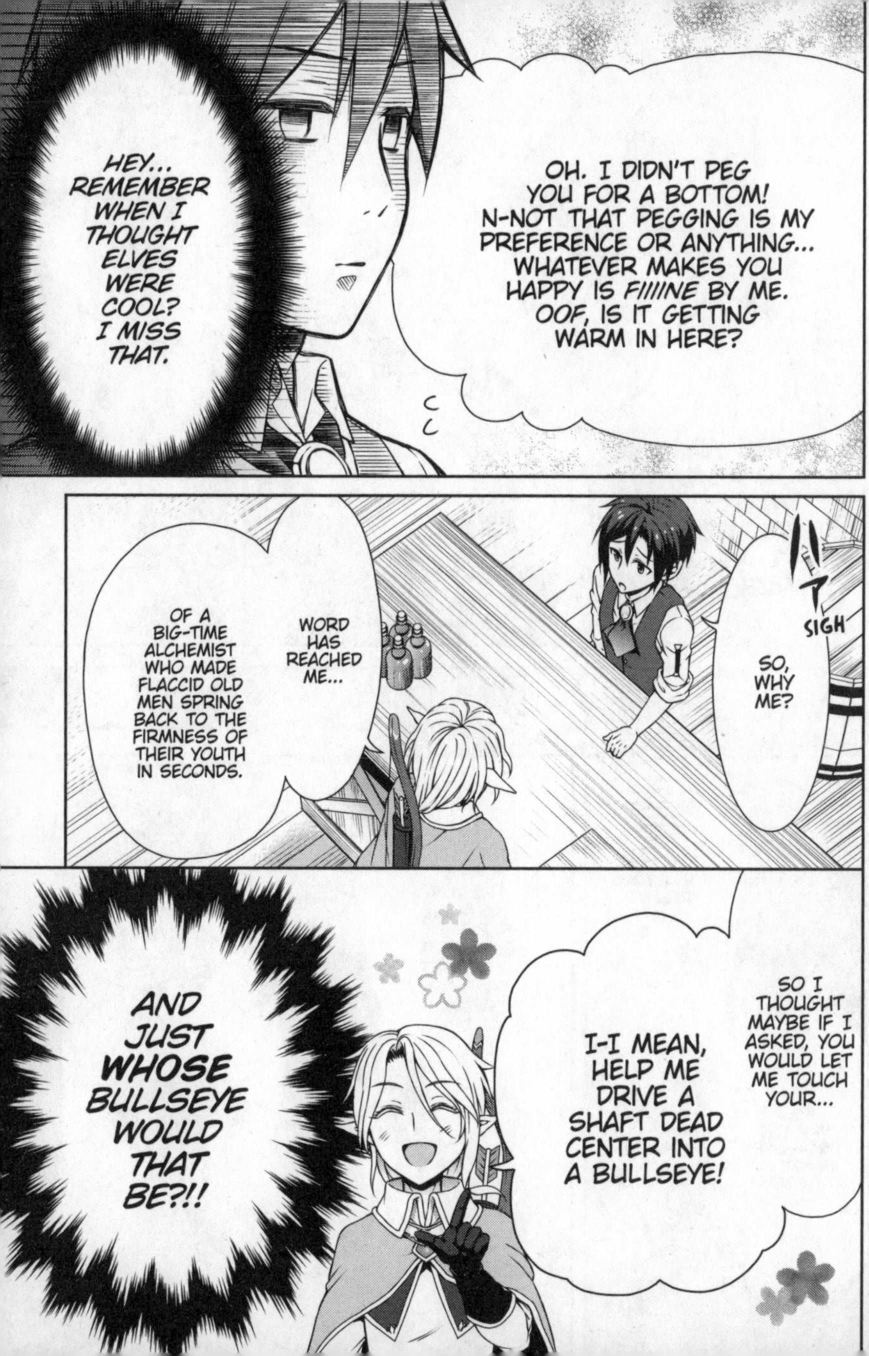
OH. I DIDN'T PEG YOU FOR A BOTTOM! N-NOT THAT PEGGING IS MY PREFERENCE OR ANYTHING... WHATEVER MAKES YOU HAPPY IS *FIIIINE* BY ME. *OOF*, IS IT GETTING WARM IN HERE?
HEY... REMEMBER WHEN I THOUGHT ELVES WERE COOL? I MISS THAT.
SIGH
SO, WHY ME?
WORD HAS REACHED ME...
OF A BIG-TIME ALCHEMIST WHO MADE FLACCID OLD MEN SPRING BACK TO THE FIRMNESS OF THEIR YOUTH IN SECONDS.
SO I THOUGHT MAYBE IF I ASKED, YOU WOULD LET ME TOUCH YOUR...
I-I MEAN, HELP ME DRIVE A SHAFT DEAD CENTER INTO A BULLSEYE!
AND JUST WHOSE BULLSEYE WOULD THAT BE?!!

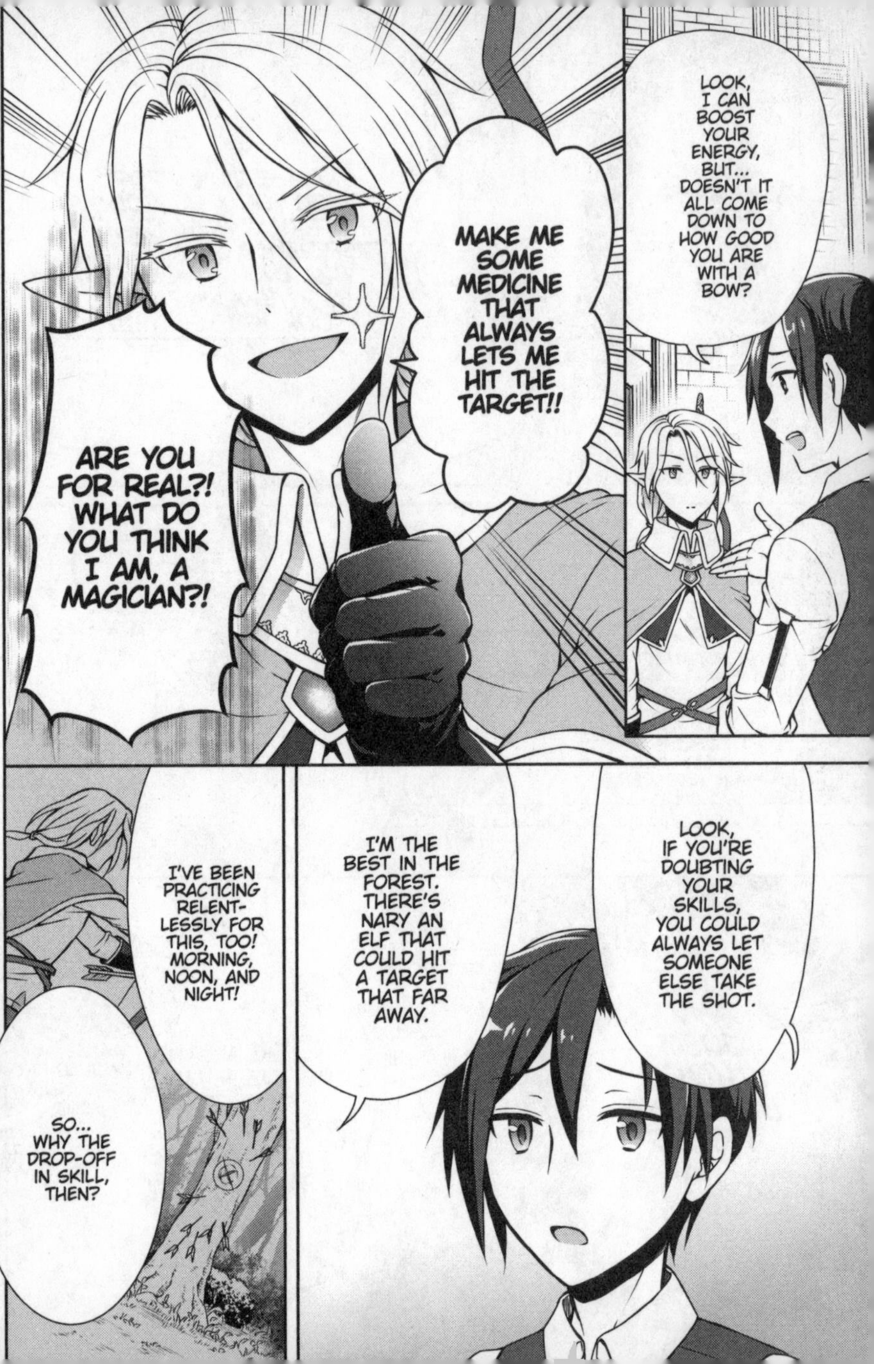
LOOK, I CAN BOOST YOUR ENERGY, BUT... DOESN'T IT ALL COME DOWN TO HOW GOOD YOU ARE WITH A BOW?
MAKE ME SOME MEDICINE THAT ALWAYS LETS ME HIT THE TARGET!!
ARE YOU FOR REAL?! WHAT DO YOU THINK I AM, A MAGICIAN?!
LOOK, IF YOU'RE DOUBTING YOUR SKILLS, YOU COULD ALWAYS LET SOMEONE ELSE TAKE THE SHOT.
I'M THE BEST IN THE FOREST. THERE'S NARY AN ELF THAT COULD HIT A TARGET THAT FAR AWAY.
I'VE BEEN PRACTICING RELENT-LESSLY FOR THIS, TOO! MORNING, NOON, AND NIGHT!
SO... WHY THE DROP-OFF IN SKILL, THEN?

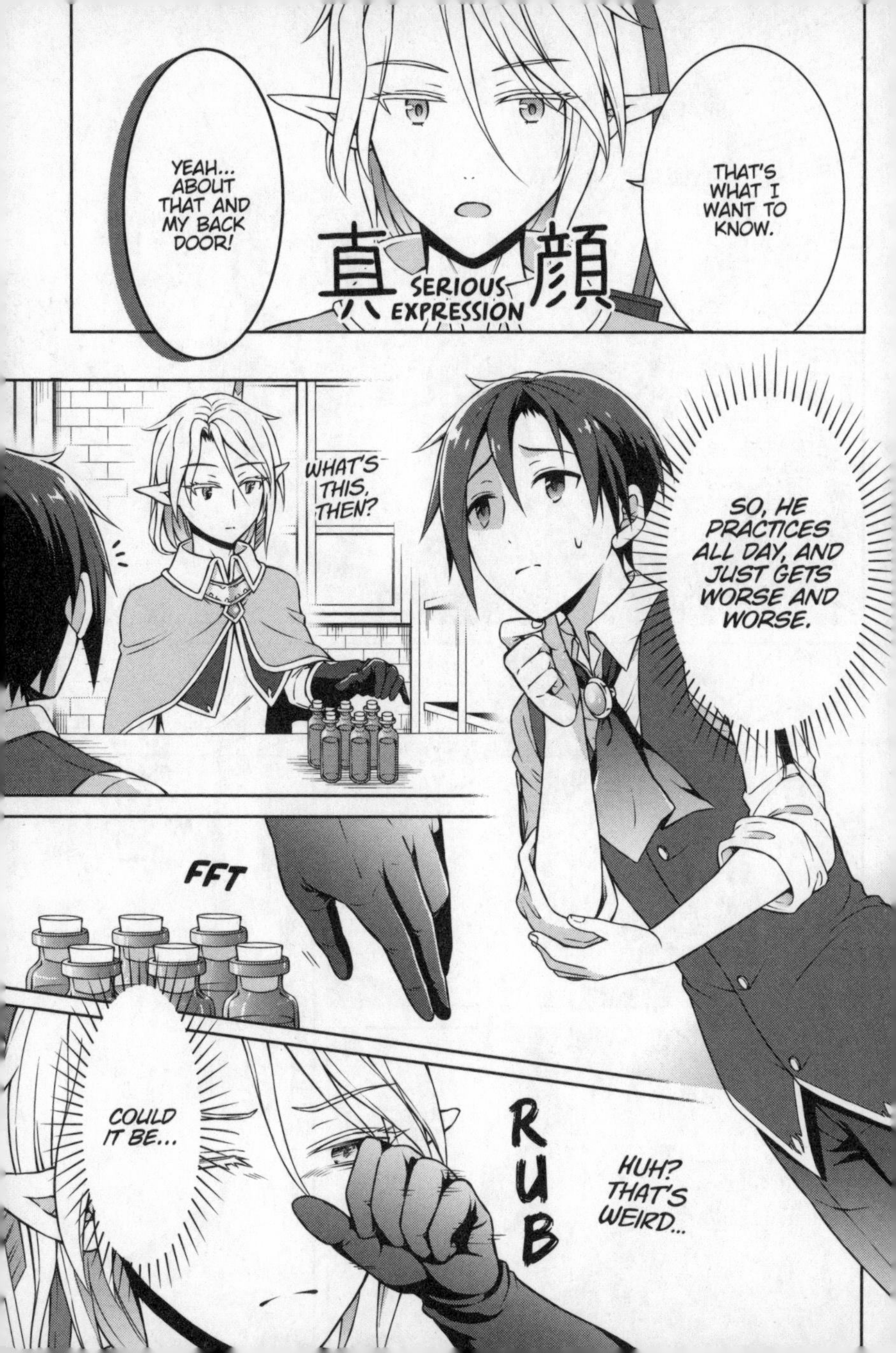
THAT'S WHAT I WANT TO KNOW.
YEAH... ABOUT THAT AND MY BACK DOOR!
真顔
SERIOUS EXPRESSION
SO, HE PRACTICES ALL DAY, AND JUST GETS WORSE AND WORSE.
WHAT'S THIS, THEN?
FFT
HUH? THAT'S WEIRD...
RUB
COULD IT BE...

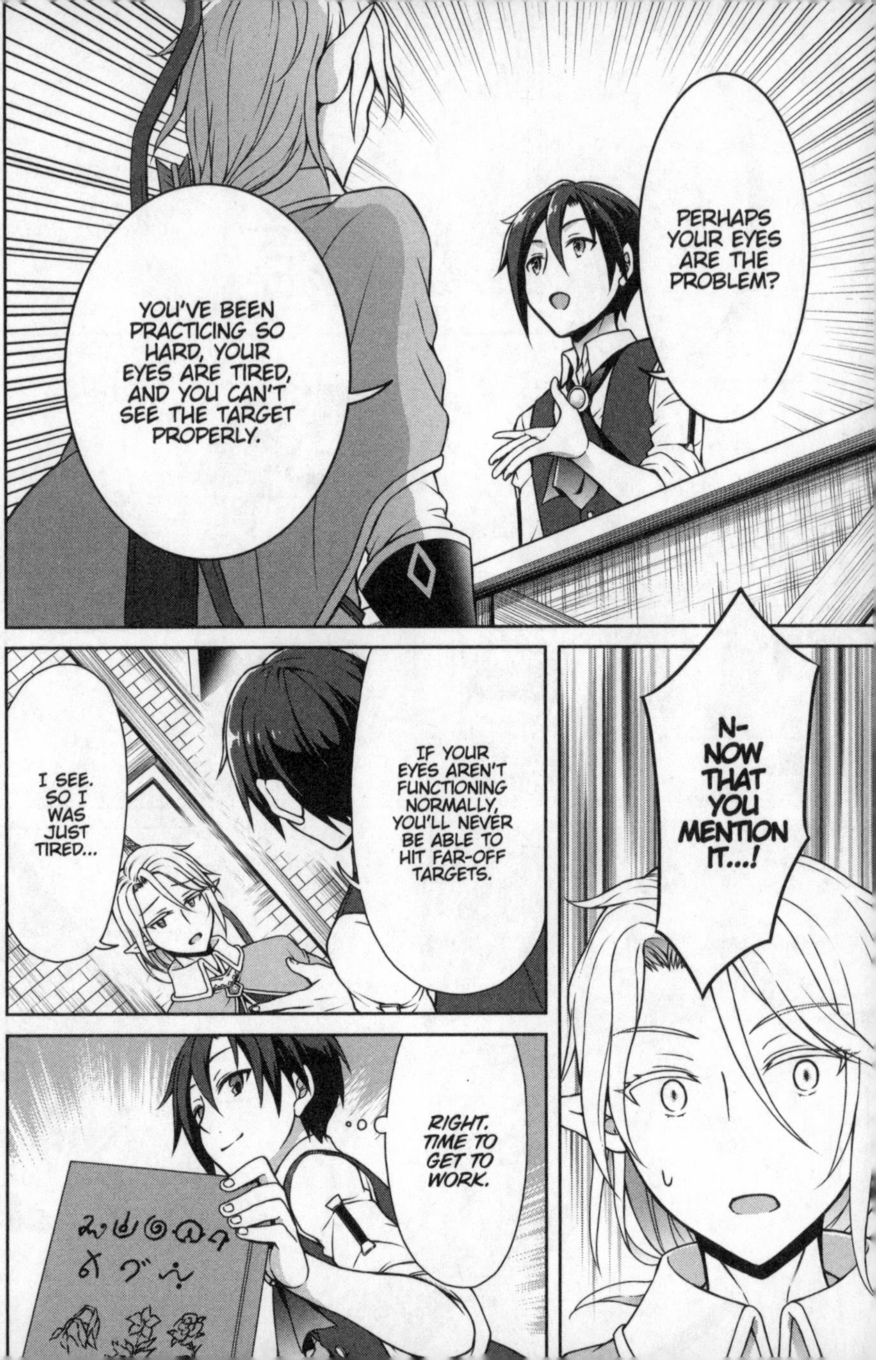
PERHAPS YOUR EYES ARE THE PROBLEM?
YOU'VE BEEN PRACTICING SO HARD, YOUR EYES ARE TIRED, AND YOU CAN'T SEE THE TARGET PROPERLY.
N- NOW THAT YOU MENTION IT...!
IF YOUR EYES AREN'T FUNCTIONING NORMALLY, YOU'LL NEVER BE ABLE TO HIT FAR-OFF TARGETS.
I SEE. SO I WAS JUST TIRED...
RIGHT. TIME TO GET TO WORK.

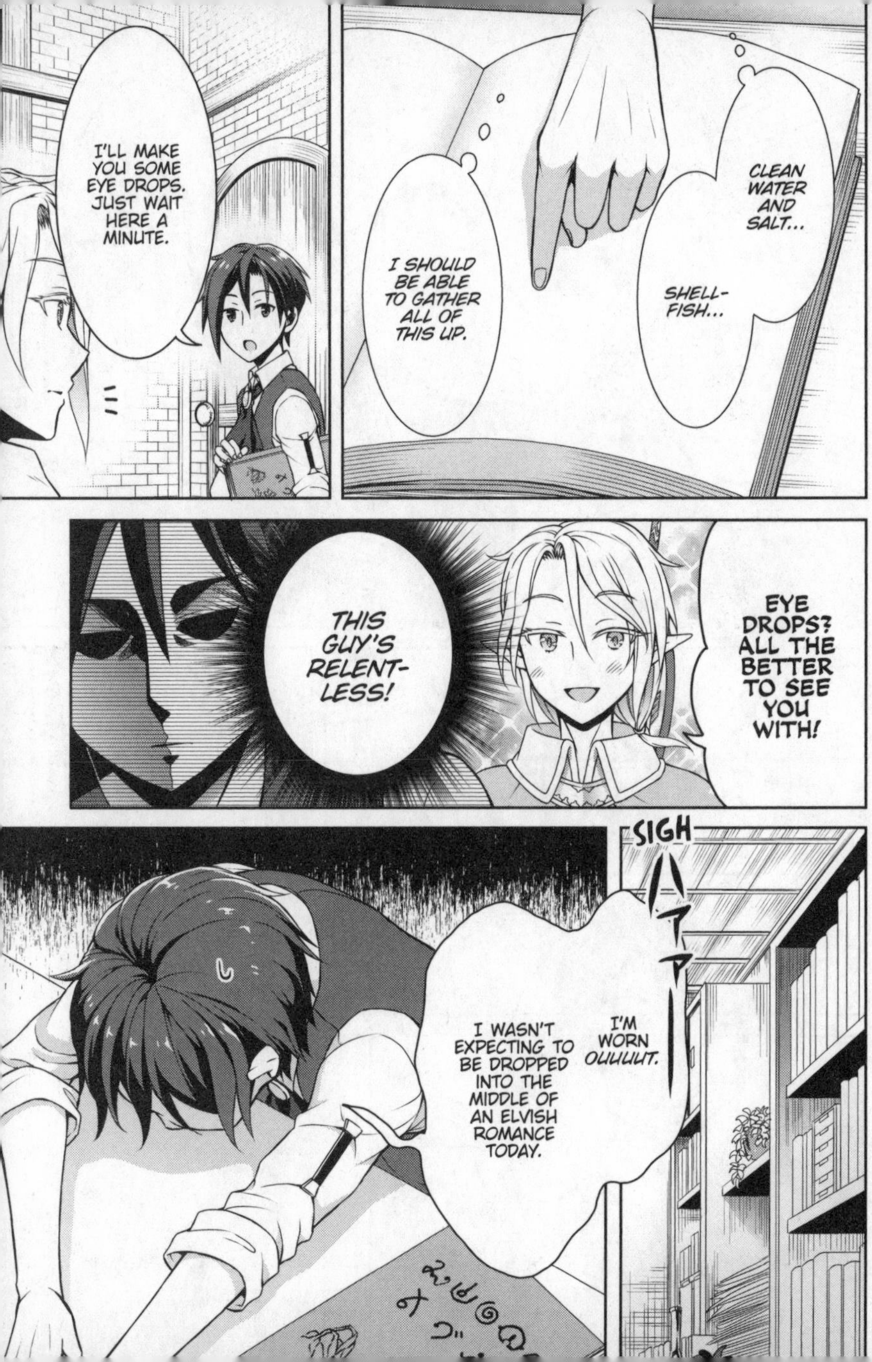
CLEAN WATER AND SALT...
SHELL-FISH...
I SHOULD BE ABLE TO GATHER ALL OF THIS UP.
I'LL MAKE YOU SOME EYE DROPS. JUST WAIT HERE A MINUTE.
EYE DROPS? ALL THE BETTER TO SEE YOU WITH!
THIS GUY'S RELENT-LESS!
SIGH
I'M WORN OUUUUT.
I WASN'T EXPECTING TO BE DROPPED INTO THE MIDDLE OF AN ELVISH ROMANCE TODAY.

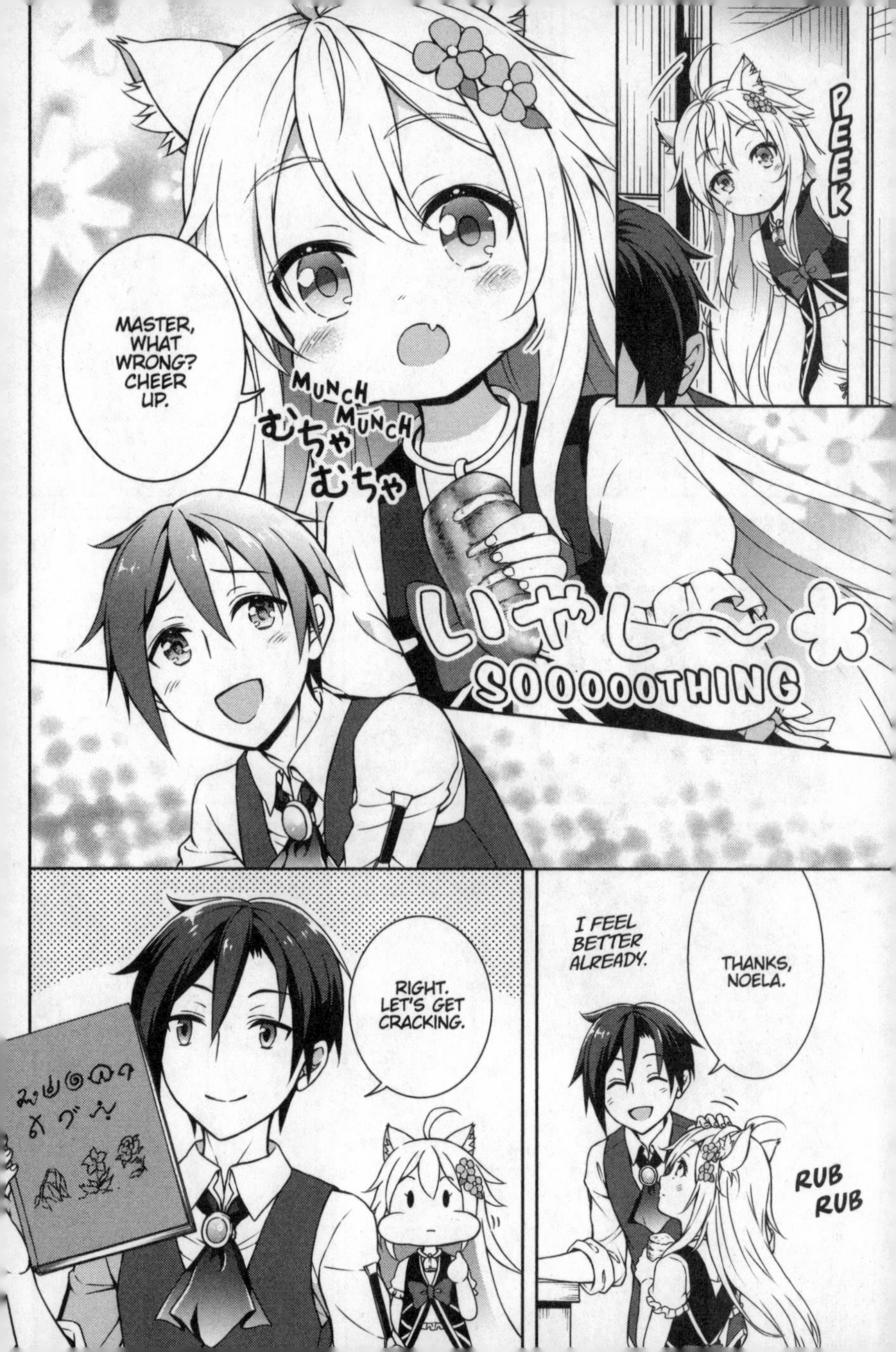
PEEK
MASTER, WHAT WRONG? CHEER UP.
MUNCH MUNCH
むちゃむちゃ
いやし〜
SOOOOOOTHING
THANKS, NOELA.
I FEEL BETTER ALREADY.
RUB RUB
RIGHT. LET'S GET CRACKING.

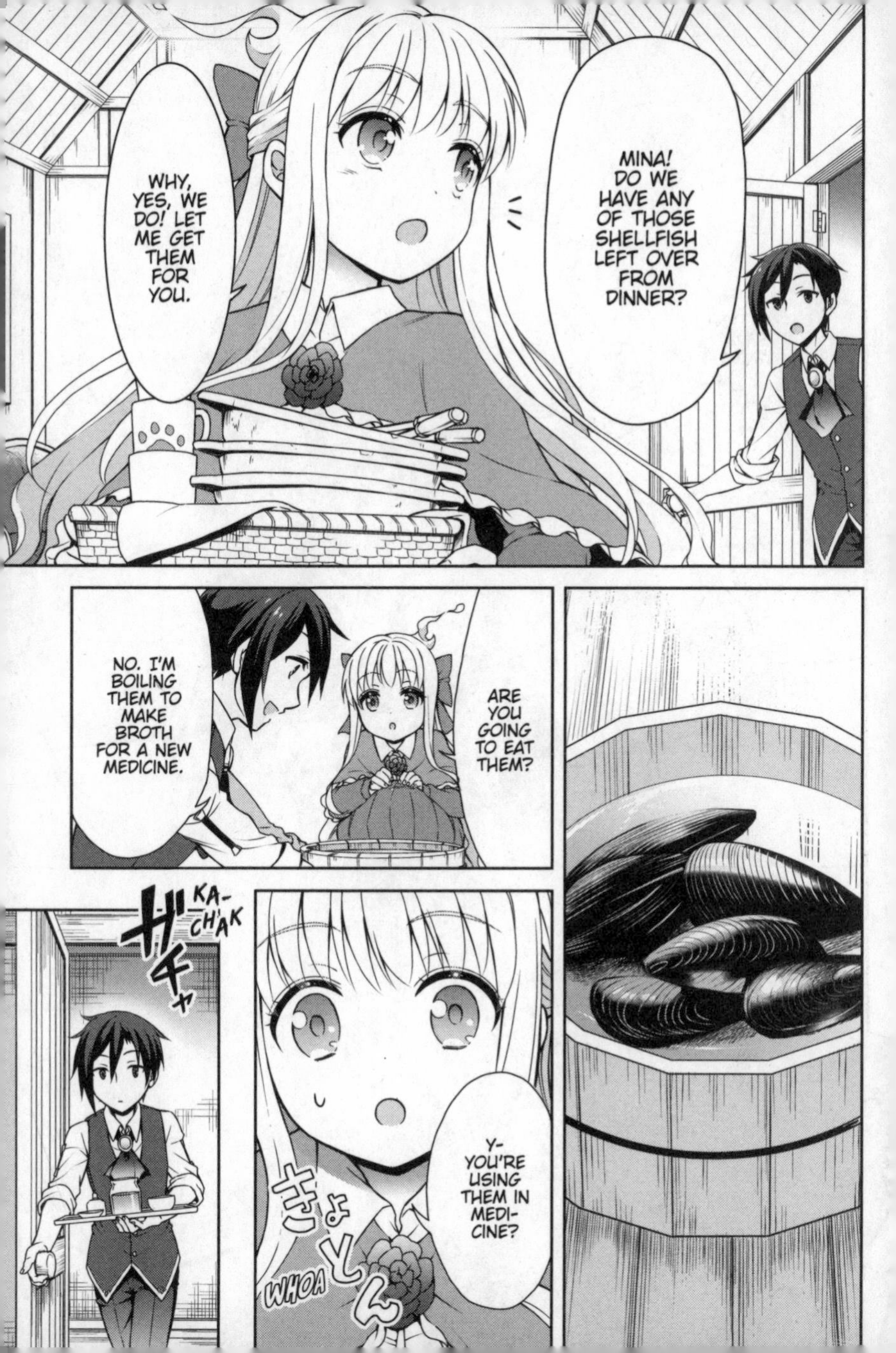
MINA! DO WE HAVE ANY OF THOSE SHELLFISH LEFT OVER FROM DINNER?
WHY, YES, WE DO! LET ME GET THEM FOR YOU.
ARE YOU GOING TO EAT THEM?
NO. I'M BOILING THEM TO MAKE BROTH FOR A NEW MEDICINE.
Y- YOU'RE USING THEM IN MEDI-CINE?
きょとん
WHOA
ガチャ
KA-CHAK

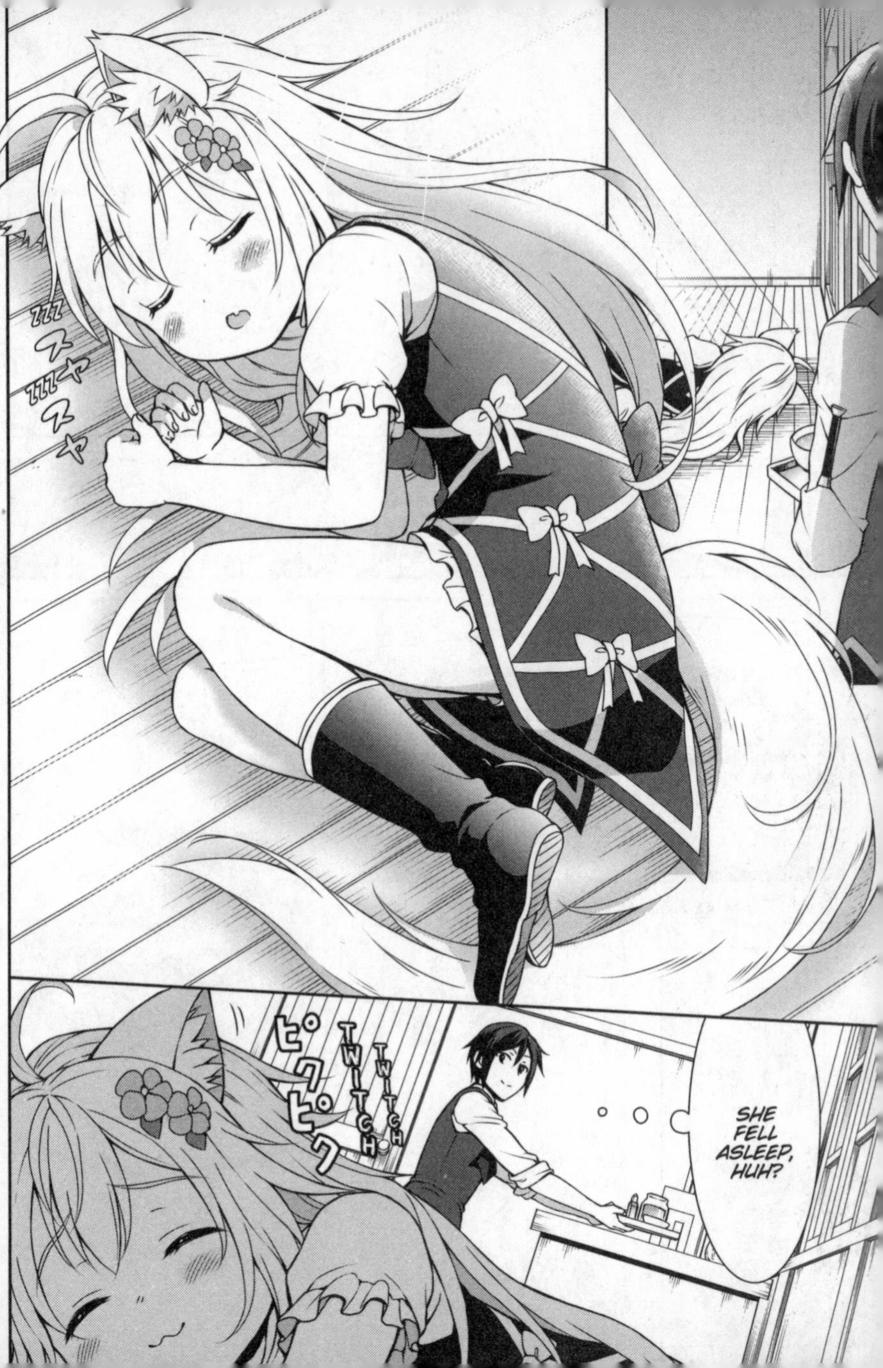
ZZZ スヤ
ZZZ スヤ
SHE FELL ASLEEP, HUH?
ピクピク
TWITCH TWITCH

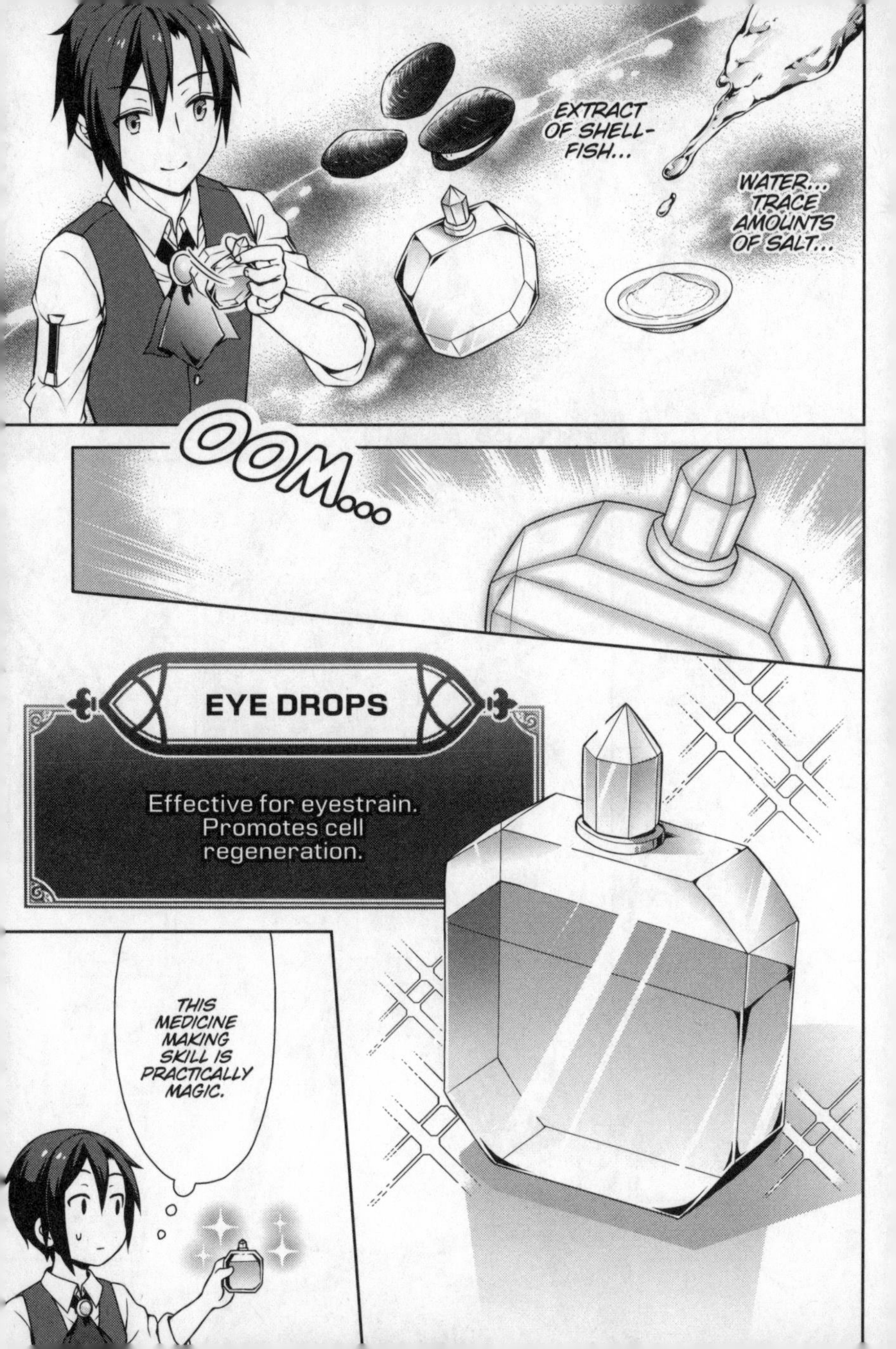
EXTRACT OF SHELL-FISH...
WATER... TRACE AMOUNTS OF SALT...
OOM...
EYE DROPS
Effective for eyestrain. Promotes cell regeneration.
THIS MEDICINE MAKING SKILL IS PRACTICALLY MAGIC.

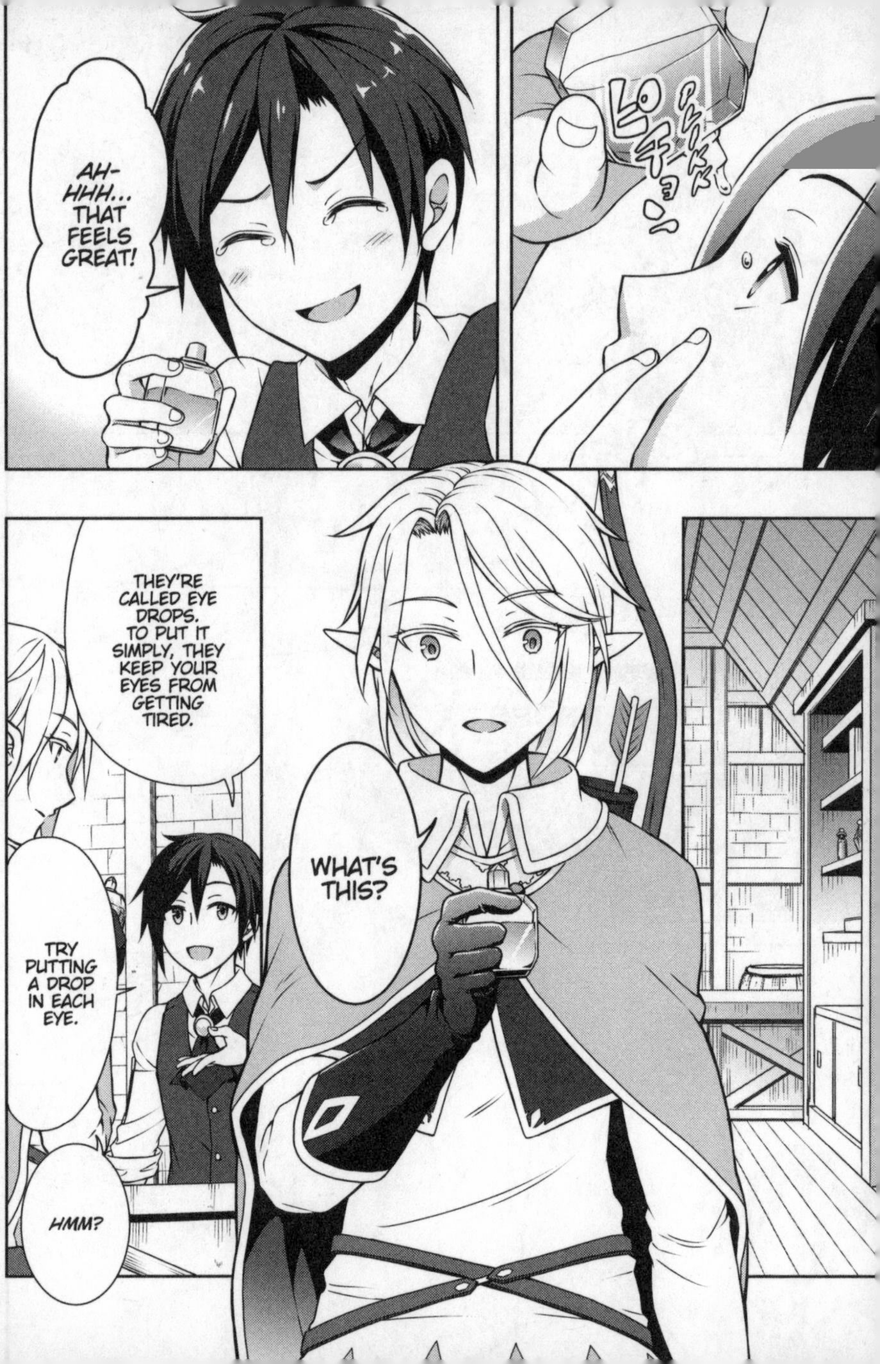

ピチョン
AH-HHH... THAT FEELS GREAT!
WHAT'S THIS?
THEY'RE CALLED EYE DROPS. TO PUT IT SIMPLY, THEY KEEP YOUR EYES FROM GETTING TIRED.
TRY PUTTING A DROP IN EACH EYE.
HMM?

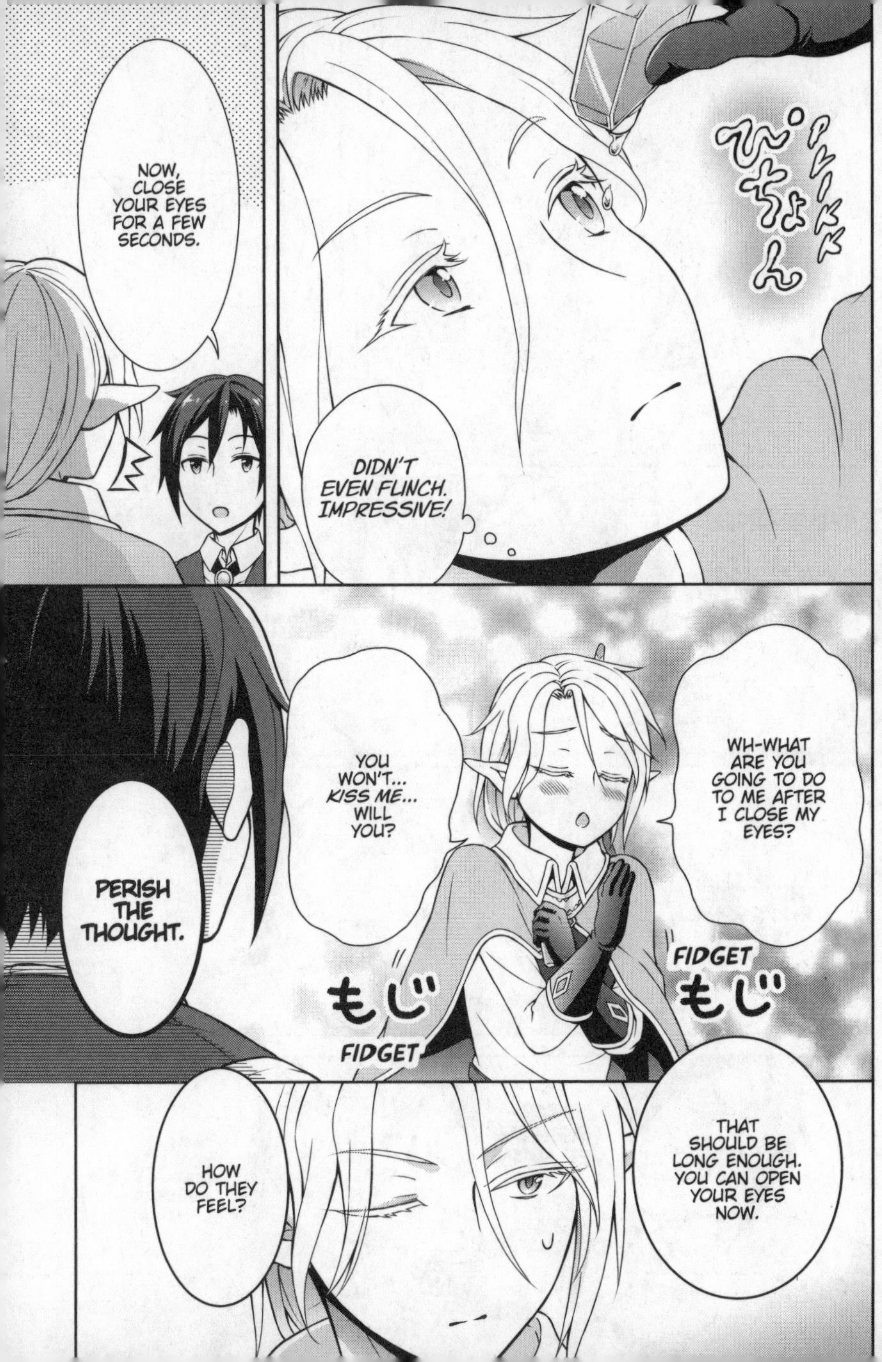
ぴちょん
DIDN'T EVEN FLINCH. IMPRESSIVE!
NOW, CLOSE YOUR EYES FOR A FEW SECONDS.
WH-WHAT ARE YOU GOING TO DO TO ME AFTER I CLOSE MY EYES?
YOU WON'T... KISS ME... WILL YOU?
もじ FIDGET
もじ FIDGET
PERISH THE THOUGHT.
THAT SHOULD BE LONG ENOUGH. YOU CAN OPEN YOUR EYES NOW.
HOW DO THEY FEEL?

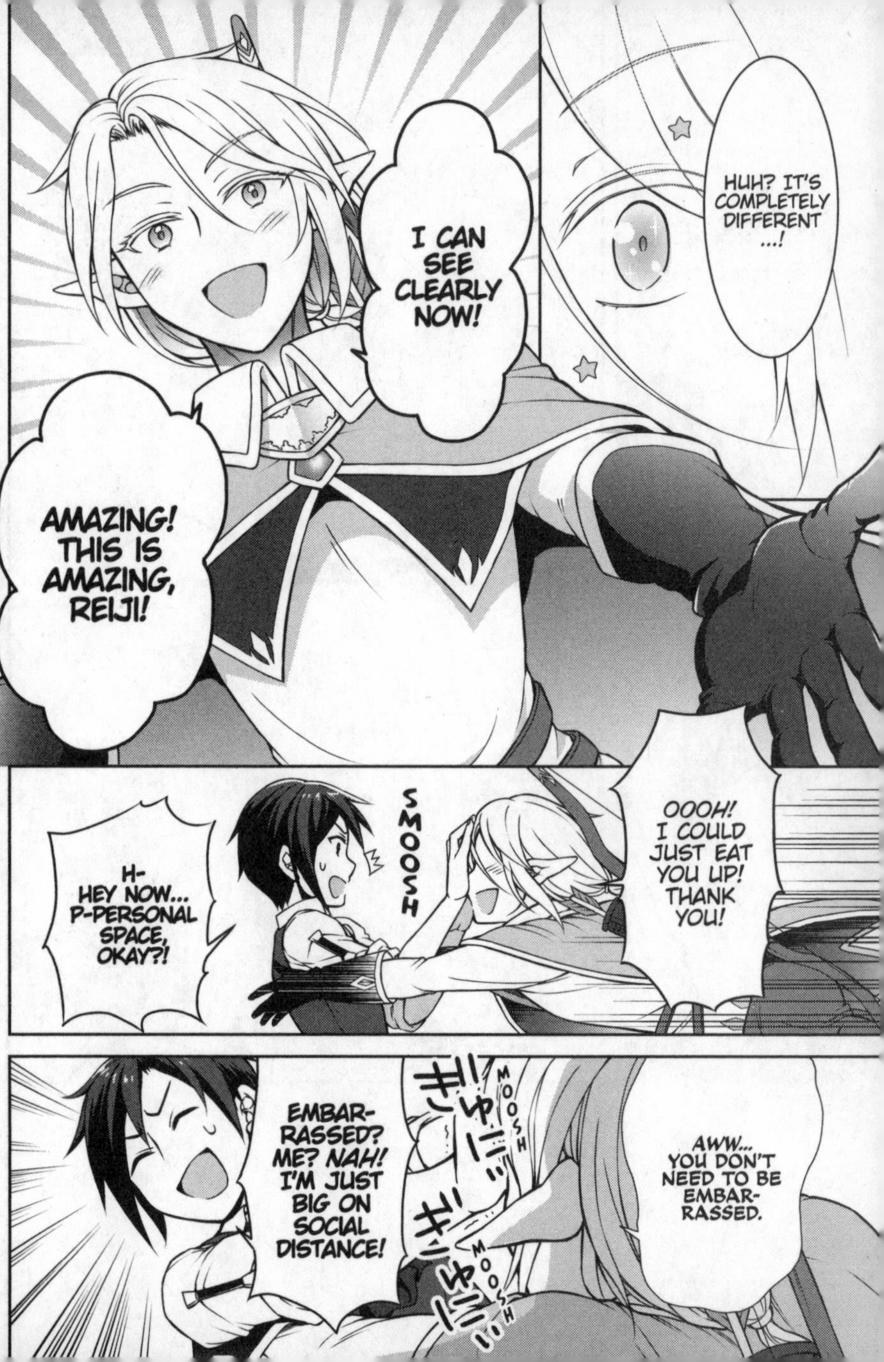
HUH? IT'S COMPLETELY DIFFERENT ...!
I CAN SEE CLEARLY NOW!
AMAZING! THIS IS AMAZING, REIJI!
OOOH! I COULD JUST EAT YOU UP! THANK YOU!
SMOOSH
H- HEY NOW... P-PERSONAL SPACE, OKAY?!
AWW... YOU DON'T NEED TO BE EMBARRASSED.
MOOSH
MOOSH
EMBARRASSED? ME? NAH! I'M JUST BIG ON SOCIAL DISTANCE!

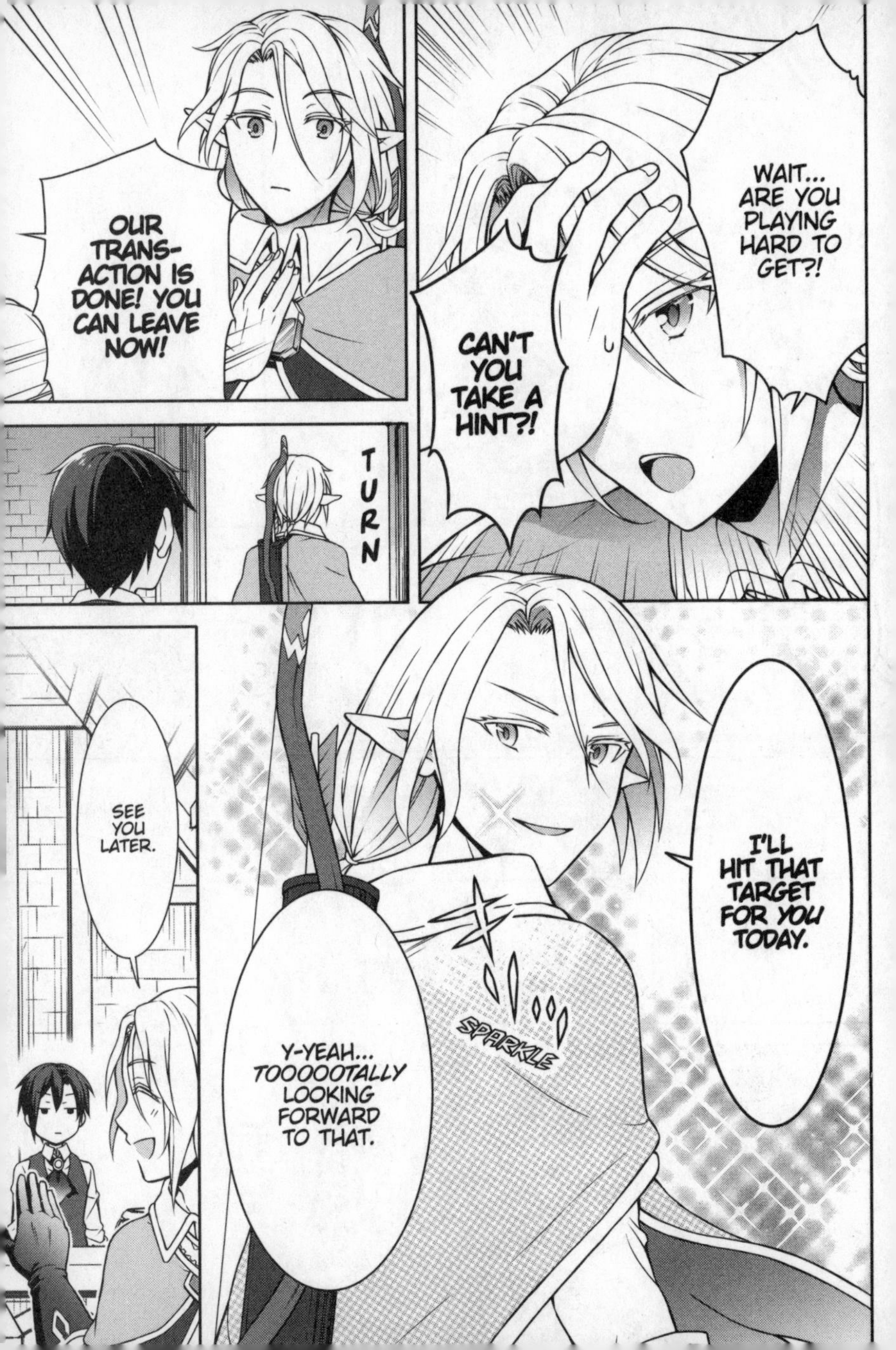
WAIT... ARE YOU PLAYING HARD TO GET?!
CAN'T YOU TAKE A HINT?!
OUR TRANS-ACTION IS DONE! YOU CAN LEAVE NOW!
TURN
I'LL HIT THAT TARGET FOR YOU TODAY.
SPARKLE
Y-YEAH... *TOOOOOTALLY* LOOKING FORWARD TO THAT.
SEE YOU LATER.

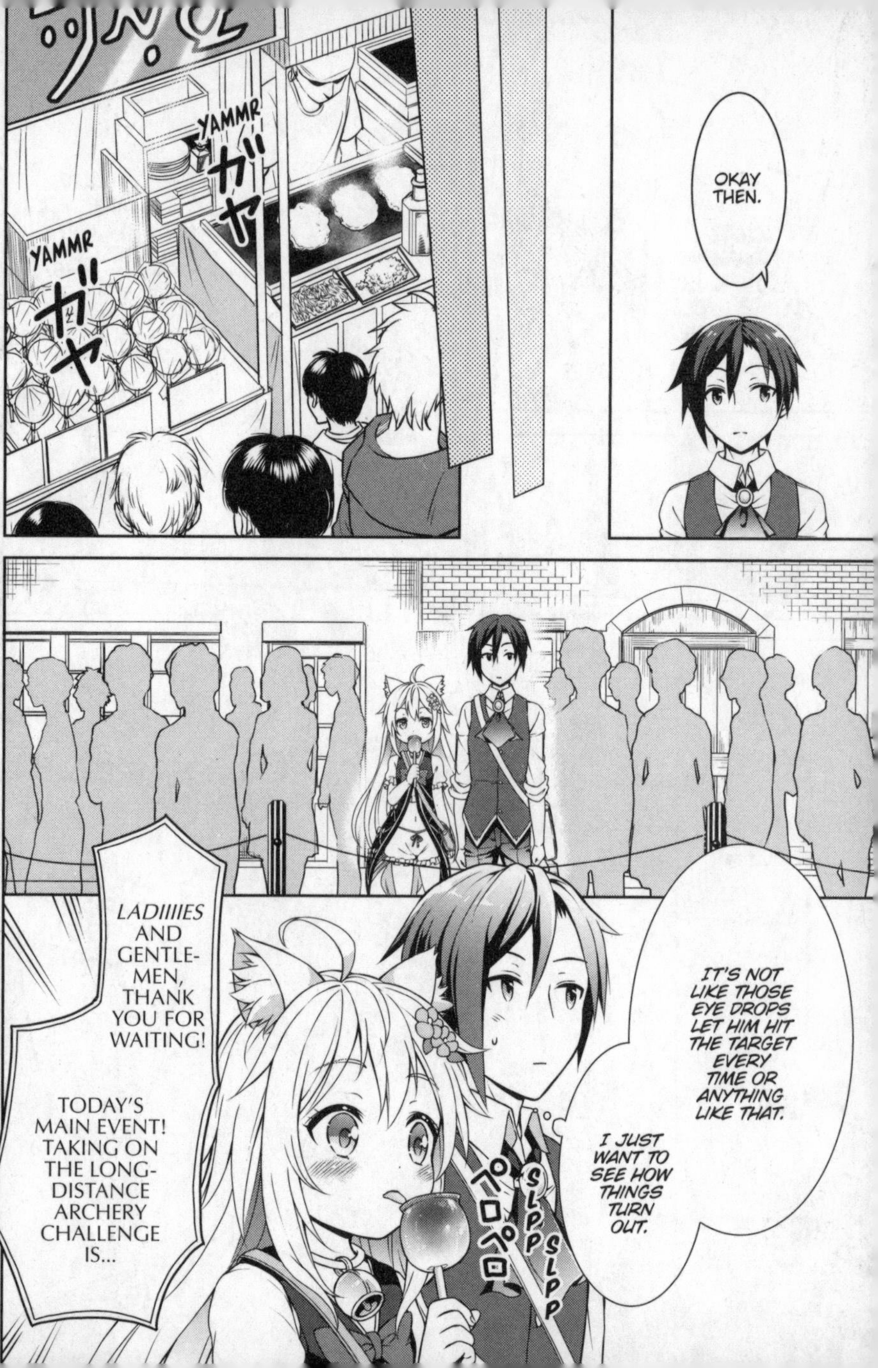
OKAY THEN.
YAMMR
ガヤ
YAMMR
ガヤ
IT'S NOT LIKE THOSE EYE DROPS LET HIM HIT THE TARGET EVERY TIME OR ANYTHING LIKE THAT.
I JUST WANT TO SEE HOW THINGS TURN OUT.
SLPP SLPP
ペロペロ
LADIIIIES AND GENTLEMEN, THANK YOU FOR WAITING!
TODAY'S MAIN EVENT! TAKING ON THE LONG-DISTANCE ARCHERY CHALLENGE IS...

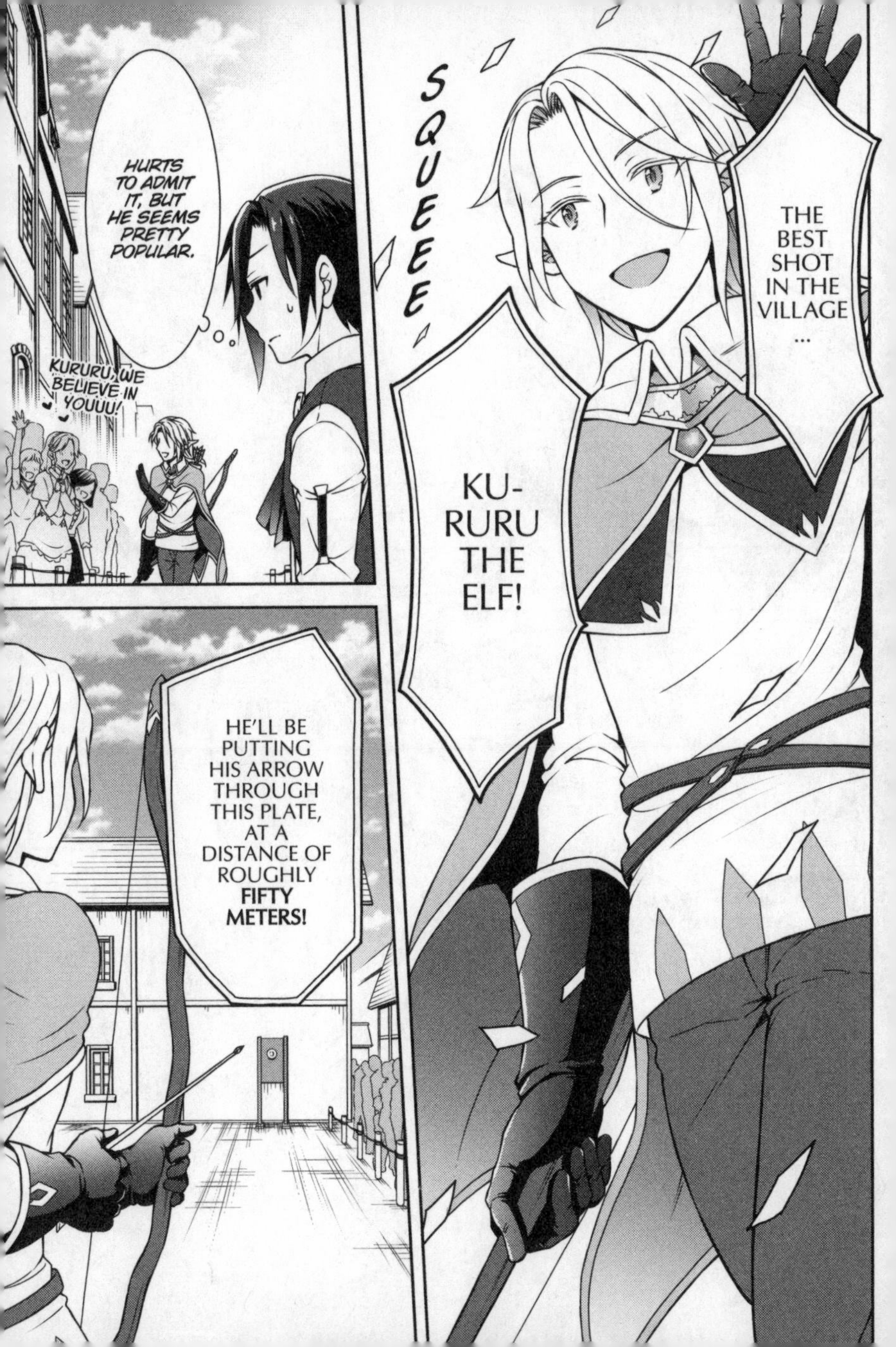
THE BEST SHOT IN THE VILLAGE ...
SQUEEE
KU-RURU THE ELF!
HURTS TO ADMIT IT, BUT HE SEEMS PRETTY POPULAR.
KURURU, WE BELIEVE IN YOUUU!
HE'LL BE PUTTING HIS ARROW THROUGH THIS PLATE, AT A DISTANCE OF ROUGHLY **FIFTY METERS!**

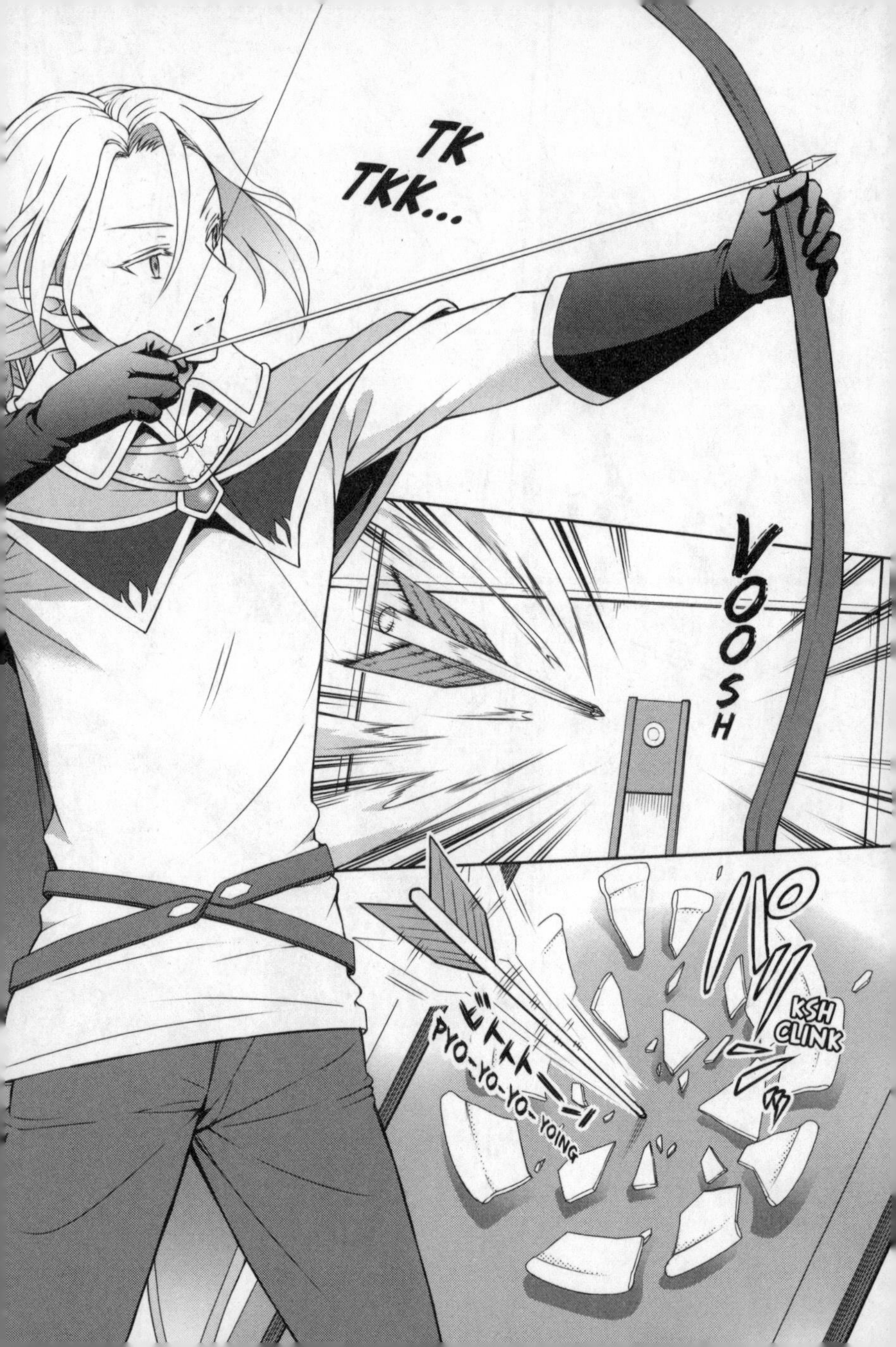
TK TKK...
VOOSH
KSH CLINK
PYO-YO-YO-YOING

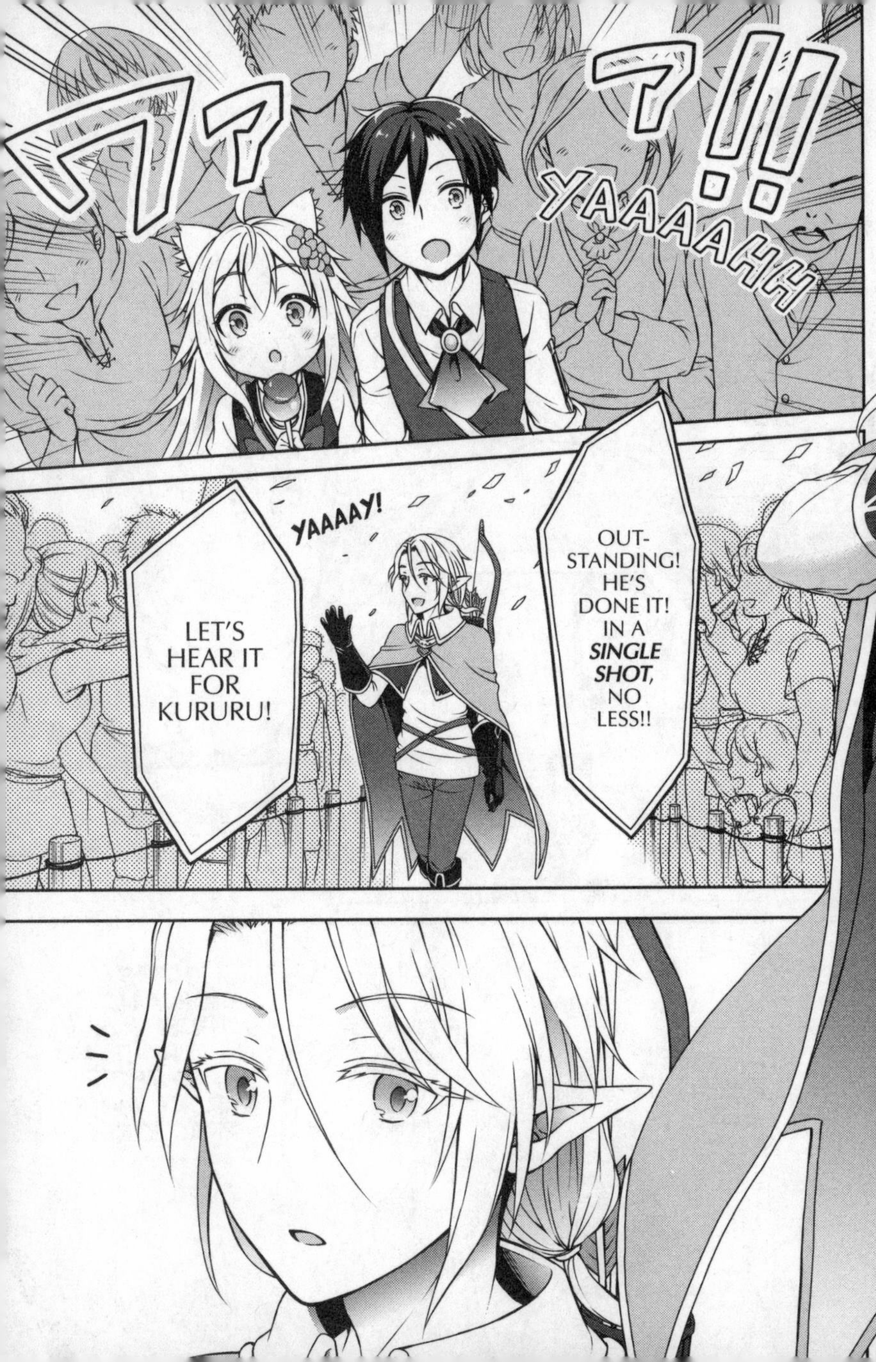
ワァ
ア!!
YAAAAAHH
OUT-STANDING! HE'S DONE IT! IN A *SINGLE SHOT,* NO LESS!!
YAAAAY!
LET'S HEAR IT FOR KURURU!

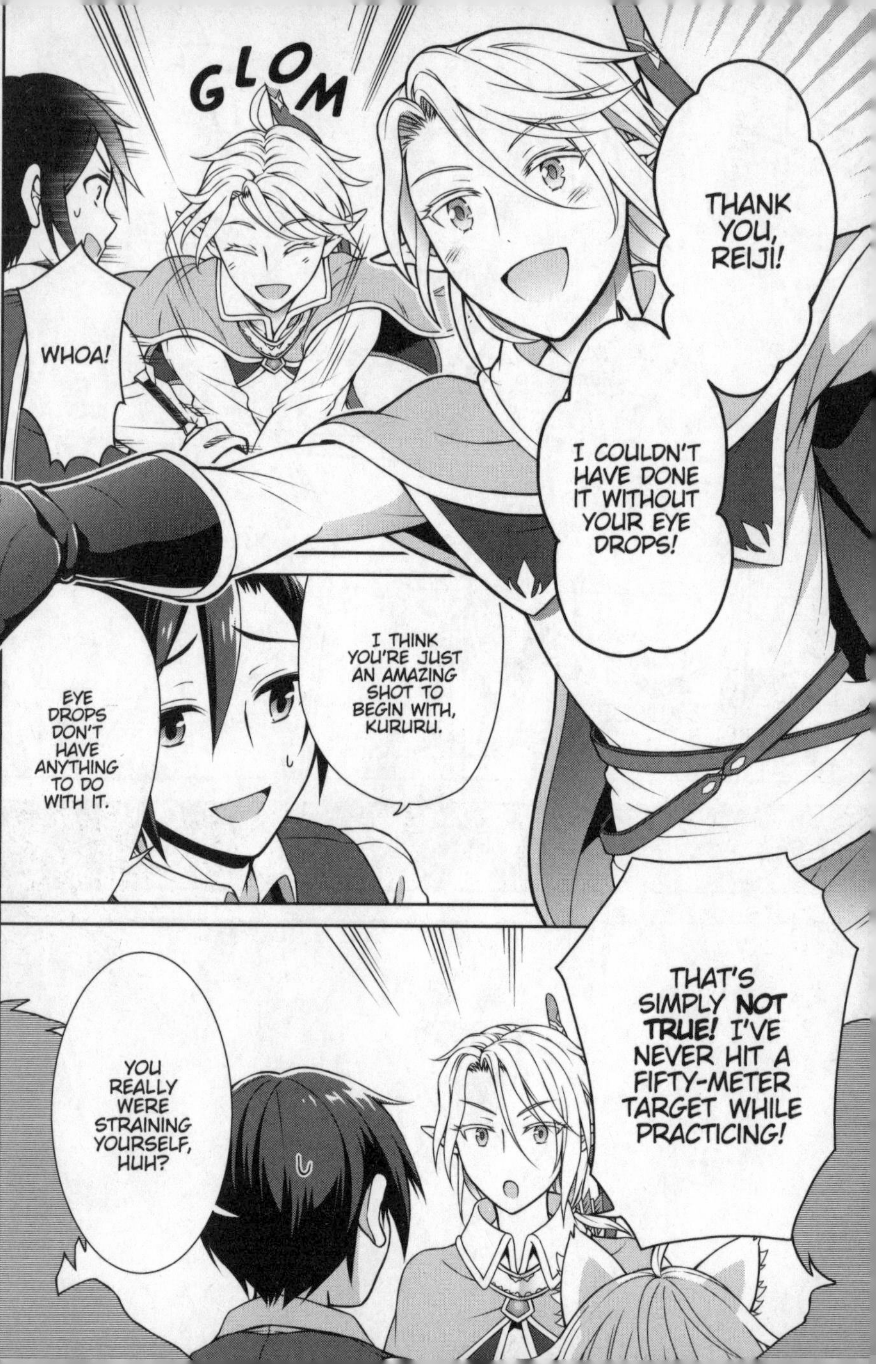
THANK YOU, REIJI!
GLOM
WHOA!
I COULDN'T HAVE DONE IT WITHOUT YOUR EYE DROPS!
I THINK YOU'RE JUST AN AMAZING SHOT TO BEGIN WITH, KURURU.
EYE DROPS DON'T HAVE ANYTHING TO DO WITH IT.
THAT'S SIMPLY NOT TRUE! I'VE NEVER HIT A FIFTY-METER TARGET WHILE PRACTICING!
YOU REALLY WERE STRAINING YOURSELF, HUH?

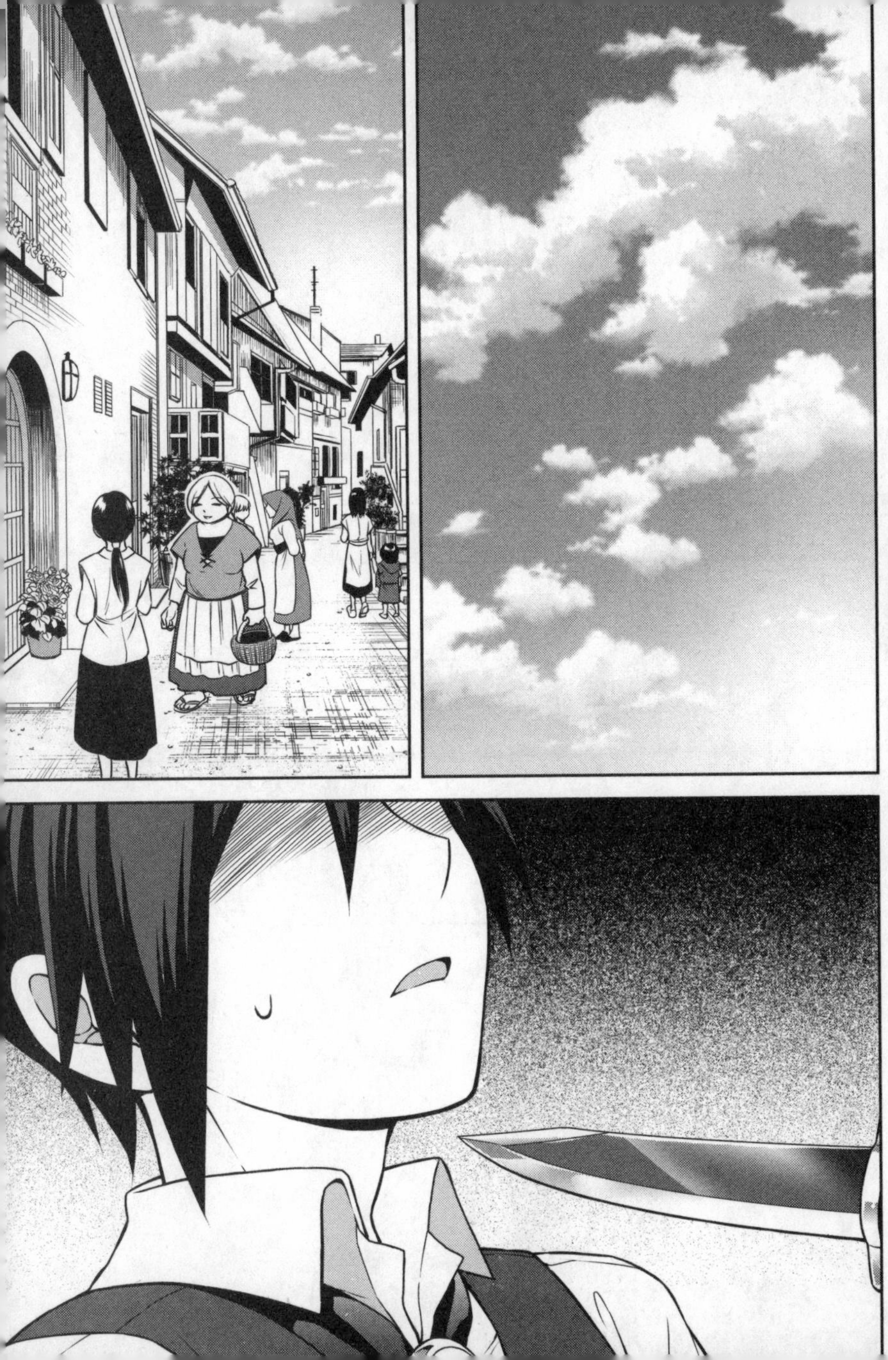

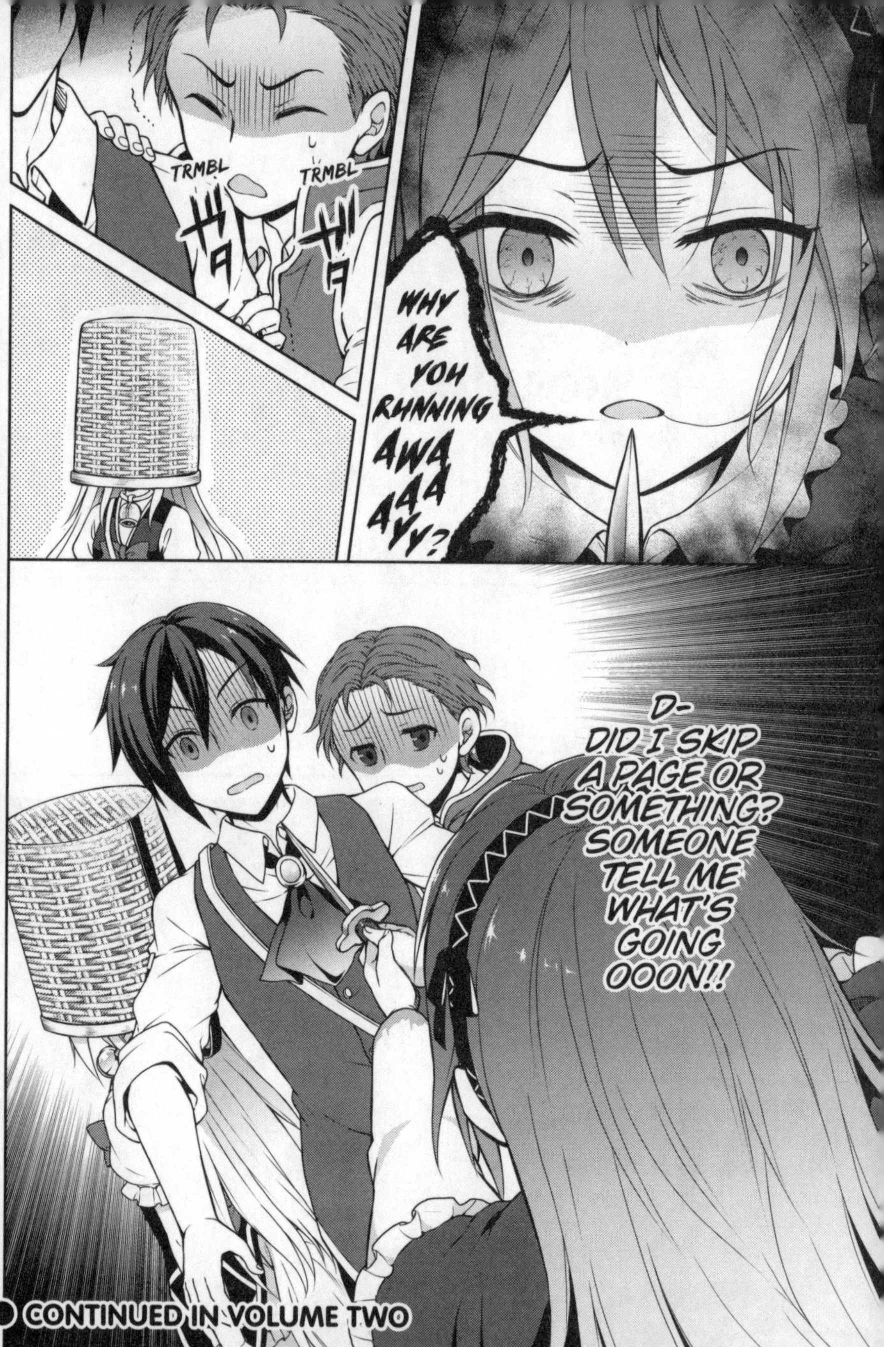
WHY ARE YOU RUNNING AWAAAAYY?
TRMBL
TRMBL
D- DID I SKIP A PAGE OR SOMETHING? SOMEONE TELL ME WHAT'S GOING OOON!!

CONTINUED IN VOLUME TWO

DRUGSTORE in Another World

The Slow Life of a ~ Cheat Pharmacist

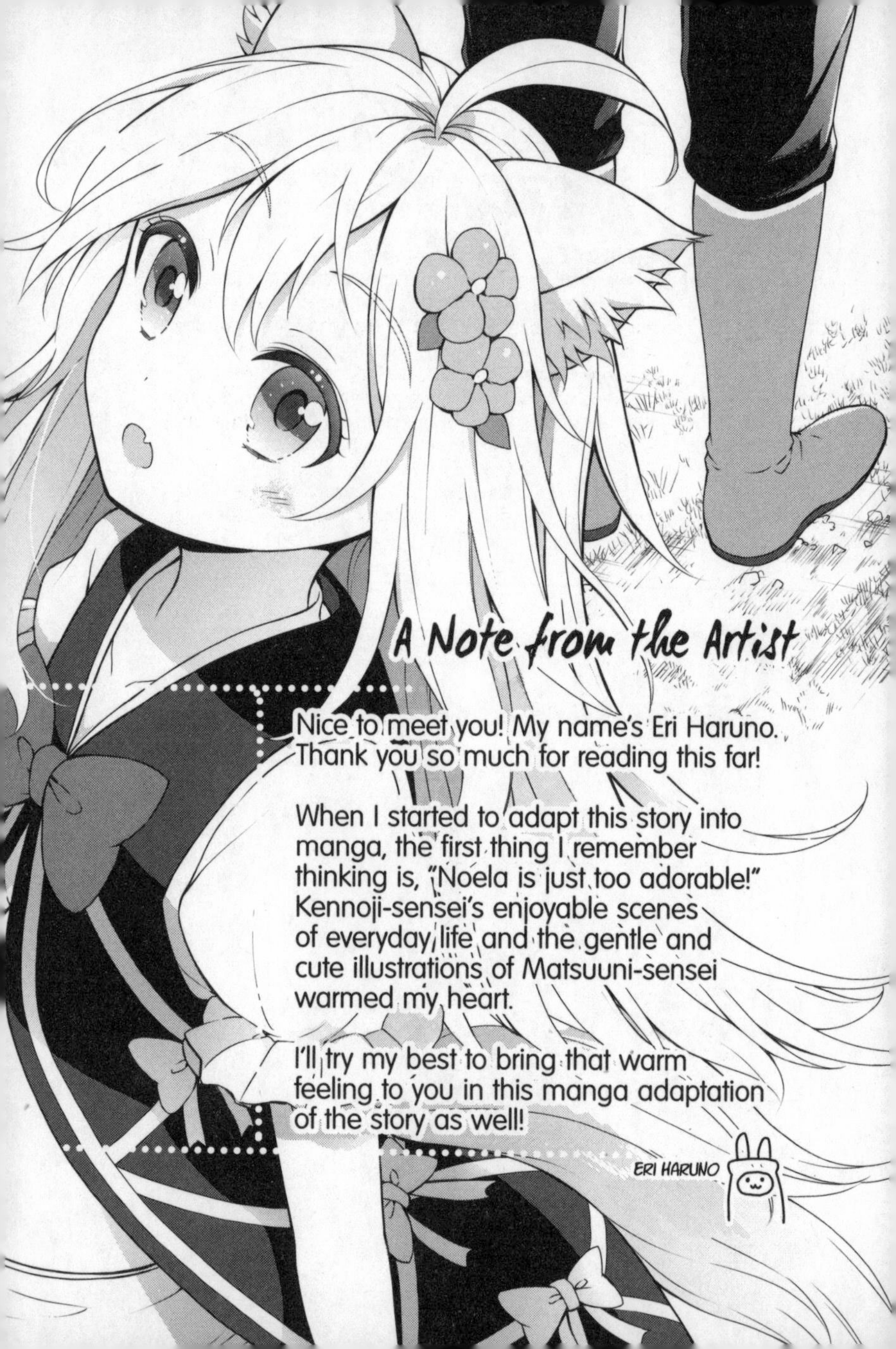

A Note from the Artist

Nice to meet you! My name's Eri Haruno. Thank you so much for reading this far!

When I started to adapt this story into manga, the first thing I remember thinking is, "Noela is just too adorable!" Kennoji-sensei's enjoyable scenes of everyday life and the gentle and cute illustrations of Matsuuni-sensei warmed my heart.

I'll try my best to bring that warm feeling to you in this manga adaptation of the story as well!

ERI HARUNO

KENNOJI

This is Kennoji, author of the original novel this manga is based on. Noela's expressions and mannerisms are so cute that I was always laughing to myself while reading the drafts they sent me. Even though I'd created the character myself, every time I read a new chapter I thought, "Wow! She's so cute!" In fact, her cuteness seems to be spiraling out of control. There are times when her expressions are funny in surprising ways. I truly am captivated by this manga adaptation.

The story of Reiji and Noela's slow life together is going to continue in the next volume, and I'd be very grateful for your continued support there, too!

CONGRATULATIONS ON YOUR FIRST VOLUME!! WE'RE SO HAPPY! NOELA IS OFF THE CUTENESS SCALE IN THIS MANGA EDITION!!

SEVEN SEAS ENTERTAINMENT PRESENTS

DRUGSTORE in Another World

The Slow Life of a Cheat Pharmacist

VOLUME 1

story by **KENNOJI**   art by **ERI HARUNO**   character design by **MATSUUNI**

TRANSLATION
Ben Trethewey

ADAPTATION
David Lumsdon

LETTERING
Kris Aubin

COVER DESIGN
Hanase Qi

LOGO DESIGN
George Panella

PROOFREADER
Cae Hawksmoor

COPY EDITOR
Dawn Davis

EDITOR
Peter Adrian Behravesh

PREPRESS TECHNICIAN
Rhiannon Rasmussen-Silverstein

PRODUCTION ASSISTANT
Christa Miesner

PRODUCTION MANAGER
Lissa Pattillo

MANAGING EDITOR
Julie Davis

ASSOCIATE PUBLISHER
Adam Arnold

PUBLISHER
Jason DeAngelis

CHEAT KUSUSHI NO SLOW LIFE Volume 1
© 2019 KENNOJI / ERI HARUNO
Originally published in Japan in 2019 by TAKESHOBO Co. LTD., Tokyo.
English translation rights arranged with TAKESHOBO Co. LTD., Tokyo,
through TOHAN CORPORATION, Tokyo.

Seven Seas press and purchase enquiries can be sent to Marketing Manager Lianne
Sentar at press@gomanga.com. Information regarding the distribution and purchase of
digital editions is available from Digital Manager CK Russell at digital@gomanga.com.

Seven Seas and the Seven Seas logo are trademarks of
Seven Seas Entertainment. All rights reserved.

ISBN: 978-1-64827-070-3
Printed in Canada
First Printing: March 2021
10 9 8 7 6 5 4 3 2 1

///// READING DIRECTIONS /////

This book reads from *right to left*,
Japanese style. If this is your first time
reading manga, you start reading from
the top right panel on each page and
take it from there. If you get lost, just
follow the numbered diagram here.
It may seem backwards at first,
but you'll get the hang of it! Have fun!!

Follow us online: www.SevenSeasEntertainment.com